CHOOSING TO LIVE

CHOOSING TO LIVE

Stories of Those Who Stepped Away from Suicide

By

CLIFF WILLIAMS

Department of Philosophy
Wheaton College
Wheaton, IL

With a Foreword by David T. George, M.D.

CHARLES C THOMAS • PUBLISHER, LTD.
Springfield • Illinois • U.S.A.

Published and Distributed Throughout the World by

CHARLES C THOMAS • PUBLISHER, LTD.
2600 South First Street
Springfield, Illinois 62704

© 2017 by CHARLES C THOMAS • PUBLISHER, LTD.

ISBN 978-0-398-09171-2 (paper)
ISBN 978-0-398-09172-9 (ebook)

With THOMAS BOOKS *careful attention is given to all details of manufacturing
and design. It is the Publisher's desire to present books that are satisfactory as to their
physical qualities and artistic possibilities and appropriate for their particular use.*
THOMAS BOOKS *will be true to those laws of quality that assure a good name
and good will.*

Printed in the United States of America
MM-C-1

Library of Congress Cataloging-in-Publication Data

Names: Williams, Clifford, 1943- author.
Title: Choosing to live : stories of those who stepped away from suicide /
  by Cliff Williams, Department of Philosophy, Wheaton College,
  Wheaton, IL ; with a Foreword by David T. George, M.D.
Description: Springfield, Illinois : Charles C Thomas, Publisher, Ltd.,
  [2017] | Includes bibliographical references.
Identifiers: LCCN 2017013862 (print) | LCCN 2017020861 (ebook) | ISBN
  9780398091729 (ebook) | ISBN 9780398091712 (paper)
Subjects: LCSH: Suicide--Prevention. | Suicidal behavior.
Classification: LCC HV6545 (ebook) | LCC HV6545 .W55 2017 (print) |
  DDC 362.28092/2--dc23
LC record available at https://lccn.loc.gov/201701386-2009020443

"I want to speak my truth, because it is so healing to do so."
—Penny

"Staying alive is so worth it. It is so worth it."
—Robyn

FOREWORD

I am a psychiatrist and am extremely honored to have the opportunity to share my thoughts on *Choosing to Live*. It is definitely a must-read for all individuals who have ever struggled with suicidal feelings, and for their friends and relatives who have vicariously suffered with them. Caregivers will undoubtedly gain new insights into the mental anguish that taunts individuals who struggle with the inner turmoil of facing each new day.

My experience is that patients with medical illnesses such as cancer are typically overwhelmed with emotions, i.e., anger at their situation, and ask "why me?" They are fearful, out of control, and overwhelmed by the future. They call their family. The family rushes to their side and cries with them. Their best friend is devastated and is at the house in an hour to provide support. The neighbors give them a list of names of people who have volunteered to bring meals.

Suicidal individuals are also overwhelmed with emotions, i.e., anger at their situation, and ask "why me?" They are fearful, out of control, and overwhelmed by the future. But who do they call? Given the biology associated with depression, the suicidal individual feels isolated and alone; they perceive that they are living in a room with no doors or windows. All too often they may think about reaching out for help, but without hope, why bother?

Choosing to Live offers people who are struggling with suicidal thoughts the opportunity to meet other people who have been in their shoes. Some were caught in the whirlwind of family dysfunction and felt unwanted or unloved. Some were bullied and made to feel that they were insignificant. Some were sexually abused and saw themselves as damaged or disgusting. But all struggled with similar feelings of hopelessness, emotional pain, and darkness. Each person's story serves as a source of encouragement and speaks with a loud voice to all people who struggle with suicide that they are not alone! Many of the people in the book tried to talk about their emotional pain, but all too often felt that no one understood. Sexual abuse got shoved under the rug, and the victim was left with the idea that somehow they caused it. Some turned to alcohol, drugs, and sex to help them feel better.

Many seemed to live a dual life; on the outside no one would know that anything was wrong, but on the inside the world looked black—no future. Worst of all, when things hit rock bottom, many expressed the feeling that no one seemed to care. That was the time when they cut themselves and even overdosed—it was the only thing that made them feel in control.

Most importantly, readers will be encouraged by the reality that although the people they will meet in the book struggled, each one managed to dig their way out of despair. Some realized that the problem was not so much that they wanted to die as it was that they didn't know how to live. Initially they viewed talking as a waste of time—what good could it do? But according to the peoples' accounts, therapy helped them find new roads that they never knew were there. Some stopped running from the past and gradually cut the chains that were tied to self-doubt and the hurts of rejection stemming from failed relationships. Some needed a safe place to regroup and were hospitalized. Some found medications to be a lifesaver. But I think it is fair to say that, in spite of all the pain and challenges, everyone was glad to be alive. They realized that suicide is a long-term solution to a short-term problem. Having a vision for CHOOSING to live provided the switch to turn on the light at the end of a dark tunnel.

DAVID T. GEORGE, M.D.

David T. George, M.D., is a practicing psychiatrist in the Washington, D.C., area. He is Clinical Professor of Psychiatry at George Washington School of Medicine, Senior Clinical Investigator at the National Institute on Alcohol Abuse and Alcoholism (a division of the National Institutes of Health), and author of *Untangling the Mind: Why We Behave the Way We Do* (HarperOne, 2013). His M.D. is from the Duke University School of Medicine.

INTRODUCTION

A little over thirty years ago, a student came to my office wanting an extension on an assignment because that morning she had been to the hospital to have her stomach pumped. She had tried to kill herself with an overdose of pills. I gave her the extension, of course, but had no idea what to say. So I asked a doctor friend what I could say to someone who had just tried to kill herself. He said, "Listen."

When the student came back, I listened. She told me about her family troubles. She told me she hated herself. When I arrived at my office one morning two months later, there was a note from her, slid underneath my office door the night before. She was going to kill herself that morning. "Remember me as a rotten person. I deserve it," she added in a P.S. Fortunately, she didn't succeed.

Weeks later she charged into my office and announced that she was going to kill herself no matter what and that there was nothing I could say to prevent her. I said, "Yes there is." She retorted, "What!?" I replied, "I care about you." She sank into the chair and said tearfully in a broken voice, "I guess that's the only thing that is keeping me alive." Subsequently, through counseling and medical intervention, she was able to become stable, and now she is happy and well.

This moving experience made me realize that people crave to tell the story of their lives, even if it involves wanting to die–especially if it involves wanting to die. I learned that listening conveys understanding and care, and that it can keep people alive. When a suicidal person tells an attentive and gracious listener their innermost thoughts and feelings, they are more likely to want to keep living. As Penny, whose story appears in this book, declared, "I want to speak my truth, because it is so healing to do so."

This book of stories of people who tried to kill themselves, told in their own words, is based on my interviews with them. I changed their names and identifying details to preserve their anonymity. In addition to these stories, the chapter, "From Despair to Hope," contains short answers to questions I asked in the online notice for the book: "What did it feel like when you were struggling with despair and hopelessness?" "What do you like most about living now?" plus others. The last chapter contains answers to my question, "What would you have liked for someone to say to you when you were suicidal?" For each story I have provided a short introduction to give its setting and a commentary at the end to highlight the turning point in the author's life.

The age range of people I interviewed is eighteen to sixty-one. Some of those in their twenties, thirties, and forties were teenagers when they first tried to kill themselves, and some were much older. Most had attempted suicide more than once. Several were homeless for a while. Many had been diagnosed with a mental illness, such as depression or bipolar disorder. One person had been in hospice care, one had served in the Iraq war, some had a very difficult home life when they were young, and some had been bullied.

None of the people I interviewed were in the throes of suicidal despair when I talked to them–all were reflecting on experiences that had taken place earlier, often many years earlier. All of them, though, were feeling effects from the distress they had gone through. At the same time, nearly all of them knew what their lives were about because of their earlier experiences. They had found something to keep them alive.

I asked the people I talked to two questions–"What led up to your suicide attempt?" and "What keeps you alive now?"

Each person recounted their life story, often starting with early childhood. Many of them relived the pain of wanting to die. A few sniffed or cried as they described the emotional distress and overwhelming hopelessness they once felt. A few told me that they had never told anyone about their suicide attempt.

Each person also told me the details of their attempt. I have included most of these details, not to pander to the human proclivity for this kind of drama, but to depict the trauma each person went through. These details are embedded in a larger narrative of each person's search for hope and meaning, and they make the answer to my second question, "What keeps you alive now?" more compelling.

Often those I talked to found little things to keep them going. Ethan said, "I try to look people in the eye and smile, and I occasionally greet others with a hug or an embrace. Before my attempt, I had completely stopped doing what was clearly a lovely thing to do." Rachel wrote, "What I love best in life, and what keeps me alive now, is surprises–the good kind, like when you unexpectedly run into a friend you haven't seen for a long time or when you first hear about a movie you know you're going to want to see." Margarita said, "I like to watch things. I like to hear stories."

Sometimes the people I interviewed found a vocation they believed in, such as Orlando, who became a therapist specializing in working with victims of bullying. "I have an energy that pushes me to treat patients who are going through the same things I went through," he said.

A few found meaning in religion: "Love keeps me alive—God's love," Penny said. And, she added, "My husband's love. Plus my therapist's unconditional love."

Several were still searching. Anne said, "I'm not sure what keeps me alive now. Maybe there's a hunger deep inside of me to know that I'm loved. That's a constant search for me. I haven't left any stone unturned in that quest. I want to believe that I have inherent worth."

According to the Centers for Disease Control, suicide was the tenth leading cause of death in the United States in 2013, and it was the second leading cause of death in both the fifteen to twenty-four and the twenty-five to thirty-four age brackets, behind unintentional injuries. The Centers estimate that there are about twenty-five attempts for every actual suicide, but in the fifteen to twenty-four age bracket they estimate that there are 100-200 attempts for every suicide.

According to the World Health Organization, almost one million people worldwide die from suicide every year. In the last forty-five years, it reports, the suicide rate has increased by 60 percent. Attempted suicides occur up to twenty times more often than completed suicides, the World Health Organization estimates, which means that up to twenty million people in the world attempt suicide every year.

From time to time, well-known celebrities kill themselves. Their suicides become prominent news and prompt people to wonder why they killed themselves.

These facts show that suicide is a major health concern, both in the United States and in other countries. They also show that understanding suicide is important. This can be done from an objective, professional perspective and also from the perspective of those who have actually been suicidal. Both perspectives are needed, I believe, to understand suicide. Professionals analyze the phenomenon from medical, psychological, and sociological perspectives, and those who have been suicidal describe what it feels like. This firsthand perspective is given in this book—accounts of what people felt and did as they dealt with mental illness, mistreatment, stress, and strong feelings.

I have grouped these accounts according to a prominent theme in them so that readers can have a central concept to guide them as they read. However, in every case, there are more factors involved. In many of the persons these factors include diagnosed mental disorders and medical conditions, as reported by the individuals.

I hope the stories in this book will help reduce the stigma against talking about suicide. I hope that those who wonder why anyone would want to kill themselves will now understand why. And I hope that those who have attempted suicide, thought of doing so, or are depressed will find themselves in these stories so that they can be encouraged to stay alive.

This book is for both the living and the dead. It gives voice to those who have succeeded in their attempts to kill themselves–Janine's mother, who could not live with herself; Marshall's father, for whom the stress of living became too overwhelming; and Ilene's husband, who could not endure the memory of having had to kill innocent villagers in Vietnam or himself be shot by superiors. (I have changed these people's names.)

This book is also for the living. It is for parents who have a child who is depressed, mentally ill, or suicidal. It is for teenagers who have been bullied or treated badly by their classmates, or who have been dumped by a special friend. It is for therapists who want their patients to know about others with similar feelings. It is for psychology students and professors who want a first-person account of a subject they may know only theoretically. It is for children of abusive parents, for adults who are in desperate circumstances, for those who are afraid to talk about suicide with their suicidal friends, for the tens of millions who have attempted suicide, for those who think about the meaning of life. Last, this book is for those who are now thinking of killing themselves so that they can know they are not alone and that there is hope.

ACKNOWLEDGMENTS

I want to thank Gretchen Marie Alarcon, for her expert transcribing, Jesse Flanagan for interpreting my conversation with Orlando, Ann Eberhardt, Claire Gerus, Richard Heckler, Matt Heller, and Dennis Humphrey for their input, and Linda Williams for her tireless copyediting and listening. I also thank everyone who contributed to the book. It took great courage and emotional energy for many of them to recount the trauma they experienced.

With regret, and gratitude for their lives, I acknowledge the two who succumbed to suicide after my contact with them–Hannah, whose story appears on page 29, and Alistair, whose contributions appear in the last two chapters.

CONTENTS

CHOOSING TO LIVE

1 REJECTION

If you are constantly criticized by people whom you desperately want to love you, you are likely to feel badly hurt. If you do not have emotional support, you may feel worthless or even hate yourself so much that you want to kill yourself.

HARMONY: "I AM A MISTAKE"

Harmony did not identify the feeling of severe rejection as the source of her desire to die until more than twenty years after her first suicide attempt. She felt rejected because her mother constantly criticized her. Her mother had been criticized by her own mother, which prompted her suicide at forty-two. Harmony began healing from her scars in her late thirties, which motivated her to want to keep living beyond forty-two. She was forty-one when we talked.

My first suicide attempt occurred when I was sixteen. I was dating a boy whom I liked very much. One night he called me looking for someone to talk to. I could tell that he was upset, but I said, "I'm really busy right now, trying to catch up with homework," which was true. When I called him back a couple of days later, I was informed that he had hanged himself. That was a huge triggering event for me. I felt rejected and defective. I found some pills of my mother's and took them, wanting to die. I ended up being rushed to the hospital and having my stomach pumped.

That year was the height of shaming from my mother. I had become mildly overweight—140 pounds at 5′8″. But my mother was very focused on appearances and wanted me to be thinner. She said things like, "No one will ever love you because you're fat." If something bad happened to me, it was my fault because I should have known how to avoid it. Whenever I was having fun or being happy, my mother criticized me, because she couldn't allow me to be happy when she wasn't.

At one point I fought back. When my mother said that I was unlovable because I was fat, I retorted, "That's not right. You're wrong, Mom. People aren't mean like that." But I just got more criticism for saying that.

I was a cheerleader for high school basketball, and once at half-time, when we were saying the names of us cheerleaders during the cheers, I got booed when we got to my name. That was just a bunch of young boys being dumb, but it validated what my mother was telling me. Nobody was going to love me, because I was fat.

When I was twenty-one, my mother committed suicide. She was forty-two, one year older than I am now.

Her mother did to her what she did to me, but much worse. It took the form of wanting my mother to conform to societal expectations and norms. Any deviation from that was shamed or punished. When my mom was little, she started to write naturally with her left hand, and her mother told her absolutely not: "You must learn to write with your right hand." They had a constant, knock-down, dragged-out, battle of wills as long as my grandmother was alive.

What my mom experienced, and what she passed on to me, was that if the world doesn't approve, then you are embarrassing to your family and they can save face only by rejecting you. My very existence was humiliating to my family. My mother used to say to me, "You are an extension of me. And, hence, if you look bad, I look bad." I learned that I am a mistake—not that I had made a mistake, but that I was a mistake.

After my mother committed suicide, I started playing poker and going to casinos. I ended up gambling away my entire college fund. It was easier to care about winning money and playing games in a casino than it was to care about the nightmare my life had become outside a casino. I looked for someone to love me even though I was fat. When I had sex with someone on the first date and the person never called me after that, I saw that as validation that no one would ever love me.

Two years after my mother committed suicide, I tried to kill myself again, when I was twenty-three. The rejection and shame played a part, but the lack of money played a bigger part. I couldn't pay for someone to help me, and I couldn't even drive a car to get help, because that cost money. I took a bunch of pills, whatever I could find. At the hospital, I had to drink charcoal.

Between then and several years ago, about fifteen years, I mostly disengaged from human contact. I had plenty of relationships, but they were all superficial and non-intimate. I kept people at a distance so that I could feel safe.

Three years ago, when I was thirty-eight, I got into a relationship with a man who wanted to get farther into my thoughts and feelings than I was willing to let him. He was trying to know me and love me and be intimate with me, but I was frightened of that and rejected it and pushed back. I finally realized, because of the way he connected to me, that the toxic shame I had gotten from my mother had made me believe that my whole self was fundamentally flawed. This had caused me to reject myself and had made me be in constant fear of having my flawed nature revealed. And this meant that I had to hide what I felt about myself in all my interactions with others. Otherwise, I would be re-inviting pain. So it was more than I could handle when this man wanted to see into me. We fought, and I ran from him.

He, however, reacted with love and understanding, unlike my mother, who had shamed me further when I was upset or needy. With him, I could come out of the shadows and get validation that I was okay.

It was a terrible thing to believe that I was a mistake and that everyone allowed me to exist out of the goodness of their hearts. I constantly apologized for my very presence. I always assumed that I was at fault. I assumed that if someone was unhappy about something, it was more than likely due to something I had done.

To be happy, I had to look to others for validation, since I was so defective. Getting that validation was the only way I knew how to earn my right to exist. I became a perfectionist and an overachiever for the same reason—to show that I was not a mistake. My biggest fear was to be blamed–blamed for what I said or did, blamed for my whole existence.

As a result, I became hypersensitive to facial expressions and afraid to use people's names and look them in the eye. I kept up an incessant vigilance to determine whether the world was safe. My default assumption was that the world was unsafe and that everybody was unhappy with me. I continually looked for clues in other people's faces that the world was okay.

Up until three years ago, I felt that there was nothing that could be done about my being flawed. I was incurable. But now that I am a year away from the age at which my mother committed suicide, I have a big motivation to find healing. I want to break the cycle from my grandmother to my mother to me. And getting into a relationship with the loving and accepting man three years ago made me realize that a different life was possible. I felt myself healing.

The biggest part of the healing has come from understanding what was going on. It has enabled me to acknowledge that I had shame. It gave me power over the shame. It gave me hope that things would get better. And it gave me relief, overwhelming relief, at being freed from the prison that shame had created for me.

I am still in the relationship, and still slowly healing.

Sometimes it takes decades to discover how childhood experiences have affected one's life. For Harmony the discovery came when a new acquaintance accepted her simply and without reservation. As a result, she became aware of how she had been hurt as a child. And with that awareness she realized that she did not have to remain in the prison of self-rejection. She developed new patterns of thinking about herself. She did not constantly search others' faces to feel that she was safe. Because her wounds were deep, her healing was slow, but it was, nevertheless, real.

2

OVERWHELMING STRESS

Sometimes stresses pile up so much that one gets frazzled and undone. When the stresses are severe, one can feel like not wanting to live. This happened to the three people in this chapter.

ALEEMA: RAPED, SICK, FIRED

Aleema left home when she was fifteen because of the trauma there. She returned when she was eighteen, but soon had to leave again. She fell into prostitution for a time, found a job as a singer for a band, and for several decades presented herself as good and whole despite the painful memories of her youth. At fifty-nine, when we talked, she finally had begun working on unfettering herself from those painful memories.

The home I was raised in had so many conflicting messages. We were supposed to be a deeply religious family, but my father was not religious and he cheated on my mother. We weren't supposed to smoke or drink. My father smoked cigarettes and he drank. We weren't supposed to eat meat, especially pork. But my father brought pork into the house. I was confused a great deal because of all that.

I adored my father and wanted to be accepted by him. But I didn't get the messages that a father is supposed to give his daughter, like, "You're beautiful. You're special. Here's how a man is supposed to treat a woman. Here's what I won't tolerate from your boyfriend." I wanted him to be my protector and provider and all the things a little girl looks for in her father. He was absent from our home a lot, and that also hurt me deeply.

Sometimes my father came home in a drunken stupor, and I found him passed out in the middle of the living room floor when I came home from school. I never brought friends home. There were days when my mother packed us kids into the car and went looking for my father. Often she had a knife with her, to cut her way through whatever she found, I guess. We dragged him back home.

Once when I was twelve, a girl who went to the same school I went to invited me for a sleepover at her house. I wanted a friend, so I agreed to go. My idea of a sleepover was that a bunch of girls got together and ate pizza and stayed up all night, then fell asleep in the living room or in her room. That wasn't what it was. They put me in a bedroom downstairs, away from the rest of the family. I was alone. That night my friend's older brother came down and raped me.

I wanted to talk with my mother about it, but I didn't feel safe talking to her about anything. She reacted negatively whenever I tried to open up to her. One day when I was coming home from school, a bunch of kids jumped me, and my glasses got broken. I was more afraid to go home because my glasses were broken than I was upset that I had been attacked. I knew my mother was going to beat me for breaking my glasses. When I got home, sure enough, she beat me. I was never able to tell her what had happened. So I started running away if I had a serious problem or got into trouble at school. One time I spent the night in a park.

What I needed from my mother was to be able to tell her all the things I was going through. Instead, she took me to some kind of place where there were other kids, and I was put into a room by myself. I started crying and screaming, "I want my mom! I want my mom!" They wanted me to be quiet, but I kept screaming and crying. Two big men took me out into a big, open room. One of the women sprinkled rice all over the floor. They took away my clothes and made me kneel on the rice.

That was really painful. I had to kneel there for what seemed like hours. Everything went black. When my mother came to get me, she was furious with me. She said, "You're not coming home. You're going someplace else." She took me to the city police station, and the police took me to an adult prison and put me into a cell. I don't know why they were allowed to do that when I had done nothing wrong.

Everything was green in the cell, the bed, the walls, an ugly institutional green. The bed was made of iron with little round holes in it. There was no mattress and no blanket. They took my clothes.

All I could do was lie on the bed, day after day. There was one little window, and outside the window there was a church with a clock that chimed the time. I lay there listening to the clock. They brought me horrible food and laughed at me because I had no clothes. It was male guards who saw that I was exposed.

I don't know how long I was there, but it was a long time. Eventually my mother came and took me home. She never talked about it. I was never able to tell her what I went through. And I never told her about the rape, or anyone else, either. This is the first time, almost fifty years later. The rape changed me. I couldn't focus. I withdrew into myself.

When I was thirteen, I got a job. I had no use for my pay and was saving it. My father was not home during this time, but he decided he wanted to come home. My mother found out that I was saving my money, so she asked to borrow it to get my father home. They promised to pay me back. I thought, "Wow, if I could use my money to bring dad home, life will be great." He came home, but they kept fighting and abusing me. I never got my money back.

One thing I can say about my father is that he never put his hands on me. He molested my older sister, though. My mother was ashamed of her because she accused my father of molesting her and because she announced she was gay. At one point I saw a bloody shirt in our bathtub and heard that my father had been stabbed because of the molestation. I never found out whether it was my sister or my mother who had stabbed him.

At some point when I was around thirteen years old, I took a bunch of pills. I don't know how my mom found out, because I didn't leave a note. I think my sister thought something was wrong with me and told her. My mother got mad and made me drink a lot of warm water until I threw up.

When I was fifteen I started dating an older guy. I told him I was seventeen, about to turn eighteen. He paid attention to me and I felt that he was a father figure who could also be a boyfriend.

One morning, early, I heard horrible screaming coming from the kitchen. I got out of bed and headed down the stairs to investigate. My father was coming up, running from my mother, who was throwing scalding hot water on him. I called the guy I was dating and said, "Will you come get me? I need to leave." I just walked out of the house. I didn't say anything to anyone. I met my boyfriend at the end of the street, and we drove to a city in another state.

We stayed in the basement of some friends of his, an older couple. The basement was full of cockroaches, and the man beat his wife every night. I didn't like the rotting bed in the dirty basement, and I didn't like the violence, because I had just left a house full of violence, so I left.

I found a little place down the street but couldn't afford to get the utilities turned on. I got a job working nights at a pizza place and slept during the day so that I didn't have to worry about rats coming out at night. This was in the ghetto.

After a year I contacted my older sister, who had moved away from home. She said, "Where are you? Mother's been looking for you." I said, "I can't go home. I'm never going back. I just wanted to hear your voice." She said, "Well, why don't you come live with me? I'll send you a ticket and you can come and live here with me." So I did. My sister lived in the Southwest. I enrolled myself back into high school and found a band I could sing with. I sang at night, worked in a bar as a waitress, and went to school. I told the people at the bar that I was twenty-one. After a while, though, I decided to get a place of my own.

I had a kitten that got sick and had to be kept at the vet's. One day I was at the bus stop, waiting for a bus to visit my kitten. I was dressed in a pair of jeans and a man's button-down shirt. Two Mexican guys came along and forced me into their car. We drove around for a while. They took me to their house. I had to stay in the car while they were in the house. They came back to the car and we drove around some more. Eventually they took me to a big field, where they raped me at gunpoint. Afterwards they drove me back into town and let me out of the car.

I went to my sister's house and told her and her partner what had happened. They took me to the hospital and the police. The police didn't do anything. Back at that time, rape was something that was always the girl's fault. I was a black girl in a Mexican town, and the police didn't care.

The two Mexican guys must have lived in my neighborhood, because I saw them driving around. When they saw me, they slowed down and laughed at me and said things in Spanish. I was frightened. One day I saw a police officer and said, "Those are the guys right there who raped me." The officer didn't do anything. I knew then that nothing was ever going to be done about it.

I became afraid to be alone. I couldn't get on an elevator with anybody. I couldn't go to school. I ended up having to leave that town because I was afraid to be there.

I went back to my mother's house. By this time I had turned eighteen, so I figured my mother could no longer be cruel to me. My mother had told me that things had changed, but they hadn't. At some point, something happened that made me leave the house again. I don't remember what it was, but I ended up walking the streets.

A guy approached me—he called himself Macaroni—and he turned out to be a pimp. He introduced me to a life of prostitution. I lived that life for a while until one day I got arrested and ended up in jail. It was in all the newspapers, which was embarrassing. My mother helped me get out of jail and took me before the judge. Because I had no prior record and had not quite graduated from high school, he said, "If you go back and graduate from high school, I'll close your record and we'll forget about this." So that's what I did. I finished high school, got my diploma, and the judge closed my record.

But while I was finishing high school, I got sick. I went to a free women's clinic, because I had no money. They told me I needed to go to an emergency room right away. So I went to the emergency room. I don't remember anything after that; I just remember everything going black. When I half woke up, I heard voices around me, people crying and praying. I wanted to say, "Why are you crying around my bed? What's going on?" Then I finally woke up, and I saw that there were tubes in me and that people were all around me. They told me I had developed a serious infection in my uterus. I don't know whether it came from the rape or the prostitution or someplace else, but somehow my body had become poisoned. The tubes were in me to pump out all the poison. They told me I had almost died.

Later I had to go to the hospital again because I was passing out. I was told that I had not healed successfully from the illness and that I had to have a hysterectomy. I let them do the hysterectomy, which I went through alone. I thought, "Who is going to want to marry me?" I felt a lot of rejection. On top of that, two high school teachers molested me. First one did, then he must have told the other one. I was nineteen.

I stuffed everything away inside of myself–my mother, my father, the rape when I was twelve, and all the other trauma. On the outside, I had everything going for me. I was attractive. I had a nice apartment. I had a job singing at a nightclub, which I got after I graduated from high school. On the inside, though, I was shattered.

I took a job singing with a traveling band. That took me out of the depression and anxiety I had. I was doing something that I really loved, and I was getting paid well for it. Plus, I was getting to travel, which I had always dreamed of doing. One night I got sick again, and I couldn't stand up to sing. We were in the South at the time, back in the early seventies. There was still a lot of hatred of blacks then, and I was the only black person in the band. We often lost jobs when people found out the band was traveling with a black girl. I had my car bashed in at one town, I think it was Boston. At one club, a man burned me with a cigarette. So when I got sick, the doctors weren't that willing to help me. I had a high fever. I couldn't get out of bed. And I couldn't sing. So I got fired.

My sister came and drove me back to the Southwest. By the time I got to the hospital there, I was all swollen. They told me I had contracted hepatitis. I stayed in the hospital for a time and then stayed with my sister. That's when I really started to spiral downward.

One night I was home alone and everything came in on me. I heard voices. The room moved, as if I was hallucinating. I thought, "I can't do this anymore." So I took a lot of pills.

I woke up in the hospital, having my stomach pumped. They observed me, but no one was interested in what had happened to me. When I went home, I tried to live a normal life again–went out, had fun, found a band to sing with. But it wasn't working. I made another attempt. I drank all the liquor I could find in addition to taking all the pills I could find. I left the house so no one would find me, and I started walking in the middle of the street. A police officer stopped me, and as I was talking to him I passed out in his arms. I woke up in the hospital again. This was when I was twenty-two or twenty-three.

I kept on living, but I wasn't getting anywhere. Nobody knew I was a mess. I couldn't talk to anyone, though I attended a group for rape survivors for a time.

I went to the West Coast and tried to start over there. I joined a church and sang in it. I did all the church things. Then I moved back to the Midwest and eventually got married. It was to a guy I had been friends with there and had gone to church with. He accepted my inability to have children. He had been married before and had two children from that marriage. We adopted two boys.

I started feeling healed for the first time in a church I later went to in the Midwest. They did a lot of wonderful things for me, and I felt that I had finally found a family that loved me. While I was there, I got a phone call one day from my mother. She was calling to tell me that she was sorry for everything she had done to me. I had waited so long for that call. I had thought, "When that day comes, I'm going to let her know just what a bitch she was. I am really going to tell her." But when she called to apologize, all of that anger disappeared, just fell away, and I couldn't retort the way I had thought I would. I said, "Mom, it's okay." I just wanted her to acknowledge what she had done to me through the years. Her apology told me that she knew. So I forgave her.

And I forgave my father. He flew out to the Midwest—my parents had divorced years earlier—and he asked me to forgive him. I did. Shortly after that, he died. I was devastated, because I didn't get to have the relationship with him that I wanted. But I did have my mom for a few years before she started losing her mind to dementia. I moved her in with me and my husband and kids, and we took care of her until she had to go to a nursing home.

Despite these good things, I have had a rocky road the past several decades. When I was thirty-six, I started smoking crack and cocaine. That messed up my religious life. Everyone at church found out about it. I confessed my drug addiction to the church, then went into recovery and stayed clean for twenty-some years, until just recently. I don't know whether that means I'm on a path to another attempt to kill myself.

Eight years ago I left my husband because he started becoming abusive to me and the kids. I had a stroke, which left me crippled on one side. The two women I lived with for a while mistreated me. My younger sister treated me badly. My older sister died. My car got repossessed because I couldn't work anymore. I got a part-time job, though, and later was promoted to a full-time manager. But I injured the ulnar nerve in my right arm and hand while working. Surgery did not fix the problem, so now I can't work. I have constant pain. Plus, I am diabetic.

The depression is pressing in on me again. Sometimes it feels as though I've got dark, heavy clouds of blackness over me. That's when I think it would be such a relief to be done with everything.

People think they know me, but they don't really. I can sit down and have a conversation and no one knows that I struggle with stopping myself from committing suicide. I can go to work and teach people and be happy and greet customers and all the things that people expect me to do, but when I get home, the heaviness comes over me. I am living a double life.

I don't have anything to live for. My singing is not the same. I don't have the confidence I used to have. I found a band to sing in recently, and I am trying to make that work, but it's superficial. My younger sister doesn't want to talk to me anymore, and I grieve that daily. She's my only living relative. It feels as if that is the last thing to be taken from me, the last thing that is keeping me alive. So I think, "Who would miss me if I died?"

This is the same feeling I had thirty years ago when I was living on the West Coast. One day I went to the ocean. I looked at all the happy families on the beach—mothers and fathers with their children, playing and splashing and making sandcastles. I almost made an attempt then. I wanted to drive my car off a cliff or walk into the ocean. Who would notice if I did?

Recently I told an acquaintance about what I have gone through and afterwards I fell into a deep sleep and had a vivid dream of an old car I used to have. Everything I owned was in the car. I was driving, but I don't know where to. I parked and went inside of what I think was a hotel, then decided to drive someplace to find something to eat. When I arrived at the place to eat, I noticed that everything in the car was gone. The strange thing was that the car was clean and neat. And the windshield was gone—no rough edges to indicate someone had broken into the car that way, just an empty rectangle where the window used to be. The entire car was spotless and fresh looking.

I was confused by that in my dream. I had a phone with me, so I called someone. I think it was my current boyfriend, because it was a male voice. I explained to him that all of my things were gone, except for one pair of earrings that I loved because I had taken them with me when I went into the hotel. He tried to comfort me.

About that time I heard my real phone ringing, and it was my current boyfriend. His voice drew me back to reality. I told him about the dream. He said, "That represents a loss—and that will be $50 please." We laughed. He doesn't know about my suicidal tendencies. I thought to myself, "Your comment is more profound than you know."

I think the dream might represent a cleansing. The fact that the car was completely clean and neat represents the fact that my life can now be free of the ugliness and pain of the past. The window, which allowed protection from my past pain, was broken because I no longer need to hide behind it. I don't need it to shield myself from anything anymore.

And I don't need to hold on to the horrible things in my past: The beatings and ugly names my mother called me. The abuse from people I thought cared about me. Feelings of unworthiness. Not being a whole woman because of being barren. The rapes, the molestation, the prostitution. All the pain. All the shame. I can let it all go. I have no more secrets.

Now I can work on forgiving myself. I'm not sure I'm there yet. I have a long way to go. I've lost so much of myself that I don't know who I really am. Perhaps I can finally shed the extra weight I put on to keep the world away. Perhaps I can finally sing a new song.

One way of dealing with severe emotional pain is to try to hide it from oneself. Aleema did this for several decades. The pain, however, did not disappear, but bubbled up and tormented her. When, finally, she was able to acknowledge her distress, she could stop living a double life and work on letting the pain go. This letting go involved giving up the resentment and bitterness that had dogged her for so long. After she gave these up, she felt as though she had been cleaned from ugly, unwanted clutter.

DRAKE: ALONE IN THE WOODS

Drake spent twenty years being homeless—ten on the streets in various cities and ten in the woods near a large city. He was fifty-four when we talked.

My father was in the army when I was growing up, and we traveled everywhere. By the time I dropped out of school in the eleventh grade, I had been to eleven different schools. I drank a lot and used drugs in high school. I had no direction. When I turned seventeen, I left home.

I couldn't find a steady job, so I ended up living on the streets. I drifted from city to city, from the east coast to the west coast, north and south, all over the country, doing little jobs—dishwashing, picking fruit at a farm in Colorado. I stayed at rescue missions and any other place I could find. After I made some money, I moved on. I had no concept of the future beyond a few days.

Soon after I became homeless, I was abducted and raped by a homosexual man in Kansas City. I thought the guy was going to kill me. That set off my depression, and I was messed up for a long time. I withdrew from the world. Even among homeless people, I was kind of an oddball because I was so withdrawn.

When I was thirty or so, the depression caught up with me. I bought a .22 caliber revolver off the black market and was going to shoot myself in the head. I put the gun to my head. But I got to shaking so badly, and a million thoughts went racing through my mind, that I couldn't pull the trigger. I put the gun down, got a hacksaw, cut the gun up into small pieces, and dumped them into a lake.

I ended up in a mental hospital in California and was diagnosed with major depression. Because of side effects, I couldn't take the medications they gave me. I couldn't function, period. So I got off the medicine and went on as I had been.

Then I discovered that if I lived in the woods I did a lot better. I didn't have all the hassles from the streets. I had my own little shack that I built. I found tools, an old hammer, nails, and other stuff, all from dumpsters. It was actually a pretty nice place. I put a lot of work into it. This was in Florida, so I could stay there all year round.

I lived pretty good. You can find a lot of good stuff dumpster diving. I found batteries to power radios and lots of other things. But the years went by and I found myself sinking. I looked at the trees and thought, "I could hang myself from these trees and end all this." So I got a rope and put it on a tree and around my neck. I was going to see how it feels first. It hurt. It really hurt. I'm not much for a lot of pain. So I gave up that idea.

When I was out dumpster diving I found some polonium that was embedded in an anti-static brush. It was like sand material that was glued onto a little strip. It wasn't much, but I scraped the polonium off the aluminum, or whatever it was glued to, and I ate the stuff, hoping to induce cancer and die that way. That hasn't worked yet, though.

I worked for labor pools from time to time, but I got so depressed that I couldn't do that. So I picked up aluminum cans and other scrap metal from around the neighborhood to sell at a recycling center. I left about nine in the morning and was back to my shack by two in the afternoon.

One day when I was out picking up aluminum cans on my bicycle, I was hit by a pickup truck and got a pretty bad head injury. My forehead was scraped back to the skull. The surgeon was able to make my forehead look right, but I still have a horrible scar. I had some contact with my family then, but nobody offered to help. So I stayed out in the woods until I healed up. That took eight months.

When you're homeless, people try to hurt you. I've had bricks thrown at me and drivers who slowed down and threw drinks at me. Once two teenagers spotted me on the street at night. I had come out to get a Diet Coke at a convenience store, and they started chasing me. They were serious about hurting me, so I took off to the woods. I knew they wouldn't come down there.

Then somebody bought the land I was living on and I was told I had to leave. I actually had three camps back in the woods, so I gave up the one camp and went to another one. But it was a constant, "Who knows who might come and boot me out of this one?" The isolation of being homeless contributed to worse and worse depression.

I saw no light at the end of the tunnel living in the woods. "If this is as good as it gets," I thought, "I'm in trouble." It got to the point where I wanted to die again. I knew that if I was to keep on as I was, I wasn't going to come out of the woods alive.

I got a job at the recycling center that I had sold my scrap metal to and saved $3000. I decided I would travel to Salt Lake City and start a new life. I would need a bicycle when I got there, and I wanted to save money, so I figured I would ride my bicycle from central Florida to Salt Lake City. I had been on the bicycle long enough to know that I could handle it. To save money I would only drink water and eat dry dog food. I set out.

Ten days later I arrived in a town on the Gulf Coast where I knew some people. I called them and said, "When I get to the west side of the Mississippi River I'm not coming back, and I'd like to see you to say goodbye." We got together and they said, "Why don't you stay here and try to get a job?"

I stayed at a motel and got a job changing oil in cars. Then I got a job at a factory. I talked to a friend about career choices, because I needed a stable career in which work was plentiful and I wouldn't have to be faced with lay-offs. Becoming a nursing assistant was the best thing I could decide on. There is plenty of work doing that. You can go to just about any small town with a nursing home and usually find work caring for people.

I got a grant to go to a community college. When you become a nursing assistant, you have to have a clean police record. I didn't have a police record, though there were plenty of opportunities to get into trouble as a homeless person. So I went to school for several months, qualified for nursing assistant, and got a job at a nursing home right away. I've been at it for almost a year.

It's brutal work. I'm trying to take a man's underwear off him and he's fighting. I'm trying to hold him up and wipe his butt at the same time, then dress him. Yesterday I had thirteen guys and old men I had to care for. I had to give six of them baths, and then I had to work in the cafeteria feeding people. When they go to doctor's appointments, I have to get them out of bed, dress them, and get them ready for the appointment. People die on you.

I've thought about quitting. And I've thought about suicide a lot lately. Right now I'm running on a basic animal instinct to survive. I have a gun. One day I thought, "I'll pick up a gun and have it around just in case things get too unbearable and I totally lose it." Things have been so hopeless that I sometimes think that that's the only way out. But I keep telling myself I've come too far to give up now. I'm hanging on, holding on the best I can.

When Drake realized that he would not get out of the woods alive if he kept staying there, he thought to himself, "I have to do something—or else." That's when he took charge of his situation in order to start a new life. Though he had done that before when he built the shacks in the woods, this time was different. He planned, he traveled, he studied, then got a job. The job did not cure all of his depression, to be sure, but it did give him a different platform from which he could deal with his depression.

GARRETT: COLLEGE PRESSURE, GENDER IDENTITY

A number of circumstances prompted Garrett to want to kill himself, including bipolar disorder, stress in college, and a gender change from female to male when he was twenty, which his parents did not accept. The combination led to deep depression. Garrett was twenty-four when we talked.

My parents divorced when I was in fourth grade. My mom had me first, but she was not easy to live with because she was abusive, and she had been diagnosed with borderline personality disorder. My dad got me by the time I was in ninth grade.

In high school, I had been a straight A student, but during my freshman year in college I started skipping classes, because I became depressed. I felt so bad by the end of each day that I contemplated jumping out the window of my dorm room, which was on the tenth floor.

During that year I started getting racing thoughts. I couldn't quiet my mind. Imagine that someone is flipping through television channels, but imagine that all the sounds in those channels are playing at once and that there's static over it. That is what it was like in my mind. The "noise" in it was so loud that I couldn't ignore it, and I couldn't stop it, either. I felt anxious and depressed at the same time.

During the summer after my freshman year in college, I got more symptoms for what would eventually be diagnosed as something on the bipolar spectrum. I was living on my own then, and sometimes I thought about hanging myself. I even made a practice noose.

After my sophomore year I decided to change my gender from female to male. When I was a kid, I struggled with my gender identity. When I discovered that changing gender was an option, it was as if floodgates were opened. I had a reason to look forward to living. I anticipated getting on hormones and feeling more comfortable in my body.

However, my parents' perception of my gender change was not the best, to say the least. My mom thought my friends had convinced me I was transgender, or something like that. I will always be her little girl. My dad was more concerned with how a gender change would affect my social acceptance and my ability to get a job. He thought that people aren't accepting even though they say they are. He also thought I would regret the change. My friends, however, were accepting, so that helped a lot.

I didn't fully transition then, because I couldn't afford it. I still can't. Hormone treatment and surgery, plus dealing with the legal issues, are all very expensive. The most I could do was change my name, which I did. It's Garrett. People refer to me as that and use male pronouns. My parents don't call me that, though. They call me by my birth name. My new name is not on their register.

Knowing that I could not afford the change was frustrating. It made me feel more hopeless about life in general. And when I learned about society's attitude toward transpeople, I felt even less hopeful about changing things. This just added to the overall stress I was feeling in college.

By the time I was in my junior year, being depressed had become a norm. I did, though, get support from my best friend at the time, who was also depressed. We made a promise to each other that if we ever decided to kill ourselves, we would contact the other person before doing so. That gave me something to hold on to, because no matter what, I always thought of him when I was tempted to kill myself.

I had been accepted into the teaching program, but I had trouble adjusting during my senior year. Some days I was so overwhelmed that I didn't go to the class observations required in the program. My professors noticed that. So I told them, "Hey, I'm really depressed. I've got issues I'm trying to work through with a campus therapist. But it's pretty difficult, and I need some assistance and understanding from you."

Luckily, I did not get kicked out of the program. But it became another stressful thing for me to have to worry about–people watching over me and making sure I wasn't messing up. Also, I was feeling that teaching English wasn't really my thing. Originally, I had wanted to be an art teacher. So I talked to my dad about possibly changing schools or changing degrees. But he pressured me into continuing with English because he felt that I would have an easier time getting a job as an English teacher.

My dad is my guiding light. So when he said, "No, you need to keep doing what you are doing," I felt numb. He had good intentions, I know. But I don't think he fully understood where I was coming from. He certainly didn't know I was as depressed as I was.

When you are depressed, it changes your whole view of everything. A normal person can look at a flower and see it as wonderful. But if you're deeply depressed, you're not going to see it in the same way. You're only going to see the negative. That's not a willful choice. It's just how you see things. Simple things, such as getting out of bed or brushing your teeth or taking care of yourself, seem pointless. You can't get yourself to do them. There's a hopelessness about the world.

When you get too overwhelmed, your mind and your body shut down. You stop feeling. You stop caring. You don't even think about your family or friends. That's the state of mind I was in. I didn't have any fears about killing myself. I didn't have any worries about what my family or friends would think. Killing myself seemed like the thing to do.

I made a noose. I made a will. I wrote a note. Then I put the noose around my neck. I put a chair into my closet, and hung the other end of the noose from a bar in the closet. I leaned forward to hang myself. I don't know what stopped me. I think ultimately it was being aware of the finality of death. I'm an atheist, so I think it was this ceasing of consciousness, the ending of everything, that stopped me in my tracks. I wasn't thinking of the promise I had made to my friend. I told him what I had almost done, and he told me how glad he was that I had not actually done it.

When my boyfriend saw what I had done, he made me throw out the rope. He had known that I had suicidal feelings, so what I did was not surprising to him. Still, he was distressed by it, and he stayed with me that night.

The semester after I graduated I got into an even deeper depression. I wanted to silence all the noise in my head. Things got so bad that I spent each night sitting by railroad tracks with my laptop, seeing if I could lie down in front of a passing train. I updated my will and final letters to everyone.

I was planning to go to a convention with some friends. I told myself, "I'm going to see how this convention goes. If I still feel horrible afterward, I'm going to kill myself." So I went to it and was miserable the entire time. I separated myself from my friends a lot while I was there because it was stressful to be around people. I wandered the city the convention was in, thinking of jumping off bridges and wanting to find a train to jump in front of.

When I got back from the convention, I decided to go through with suicide. I told the boyfriend of my best friend that I was feeling suicidal. He and I had talked about suicide before, because he himself had attempted it. I knew he wasn't going to call a crisis center, and I knew he might want to help me do it.

We decided to sit down by the railroad tracks across the street from the restaurant where my best friend works. A couple of nights after getting back from the convention, the boyfriend—I'll call him "Dean"—and I went to the tracks. I was ready to jump in front of one of the trains or lay my head on one of the tracks. The trains go by there around thirty-five or forty miles an hour.

The first time a train went by we were sitting about ten feet from the tracks. When you're that close to a train it's very loud. The sheer size of the train roaring by is frightening. I asked Dean if he could hold my hand, because I was terrified.

As each train went by I mentally prepared myself. I imagined laying my head on one of the tracks. I got ready to jump. I could tell ahead of time when the train was coming because of the nearby dinger. The engineer would not have seen me, because Dean and I were by some bushes.

Just before a train went by, Dean crossed the street and went inside the restaurant to say hi to my best friend, who was working right at that time. Dean said, "I don't want him to think I pushed you." So whenever each train went by, I was alone. I couldn't budge.

We decided to do the same thing the next night. I brought ear plugs to stifle some of the noise. And I sat closer. We did this several more nights. I got up to about five feet away from the tracks, hiding behind a bush and mentally preparing myself.

The last night we were at the tracks Dean told me he had brought some alcohol. We both knew that alcohol lowers your inhibitions. I said, "Give me some." I was not a drinker, because I had chosen to abstain. Within two drinks I was definitely drunk.

Dean told me a story that he said was about himself. I had heard it some-place else, so I knew he was lying. That snapped me out of my depression for a second. And my drunkenness helped my mood some. I wasn't as fully focused on killing myself as I was on the fact that I was tipsy and that he was lying to me. Also, I got suspicious of his motivation. Earlier, I had become attracted to my best friend, his boyfriend, and we had a short fling. It occurred to me that Dean probably didn't have a problem with seeing me dead, because he had been upset with me for that fling.

I decided to go inside the restaurant to say hi to my best friend. He, of course, noticed that I was drunk. He asked, "Since when do you drink?" I said, "Since now." Then I told him what was going on.

He was not happy about it, especially about the fact that his boyfriend was helping me kill myself. He told me how distraught he would be living in a world without me. I broke down and cried, realizing how close I had come to hurting him. I was five feet from those tracks, and it was just a matter of willing myself to jump onto them.

A couple of months later he and I talked about our relationship. He had been thinking about breaking up with his boyfriend, but could not bring himself to do it. I told him he was a coward, and that made him decide he would not be my best friend anymore. I had destroyed his trust, he said, because we had decided years earlier that we would not judge each other.

His decision jolted me. I felt I had lost something incredibly huge. And it was all my fault. The one support system I could always rely on was gone. I felt that I didn't have anything left.

"Okay this is it," I said to myself. "I'm just going to do it. I'm not going to bother writing a note." I didn't think of my future. I didn't think of my talents. I didn't think of my family. I tied a rope around my neck and then onto the bar in my closet. It's not high enough to hang from, so I leaned forward. The rope tightened and I felt my heartbeat racing and pressure building up in my head. My goal was to knock myself unconscious and let the rest of it do its thing. But that didn't happen. I tried two more times but ultimately got overwhelmed by the pounding in my head and the dizziness that came with it.

I realized I needed to get out of my house in order to keep from killing myself. I called a couple of friends and asked to stay with them. I called work and told them I couldn't go in.

That was two years ago. Several things have kept me alive since then. One is that I have a little scrap of hope that maybe I can make a difference in the world. Sometimes, though, that little scrap leaves me because I haven't done much. When that happens, I think of what my suicide would do to my friends and family.

My best friend and I patched things up. He realized he was just being angry. Our closeness has been reestablished. So there's that.

The big thing is the finality of suicide, knowing that there is no going back. I like to imagine that killing myself is like going to sleep and then waking up and everything being okay. But that's not how it is. I would never get to listen to my favorite music, never get to enjoy my favorite food, never get to draw again. I would never be able to cuddle with my best friend again or see other people I love. That's what scares me.

Garrett declared, "I didn't want to die. I just wanted the pain to end." Eventually, he dealt with his pain by finding several things worth living for—making a difference in other people's lives, not wanting to hurt people to whom he was close, and wanting to continue a number of activities he loved, including having a close friend. If he were to die, he realized, all of these would be lost. In choosing to keep living, he chose hope over despair—hope that he could continue engaging in what gave his life meaning in spite of the pain he had endured.

3 | BULLIED

Some people are bullied so badly that they feel worthless and shamed. If the emotional scars from the mistreatment don't heal, they fester and may lead to a desire to die. Here are several accounts of people who felt intense emotional wounds from being violated.

ORLANDO: RAPED BY CLASSMATES

Orlando, who lives in Mexico, was twenty-five when we talked, which was done through an interpreter.

When I was four years old, I was a victim of bullying. That continued through first grade and elementary school. On one occasion I was playing with my friends, and some older kids came over. I was seven years old. They were thirteen or fourteen. One of them pulled out a knife and told me to lower my pants. He started to touch me. I felt defenseless because he had a sharp knife at my back and said he would stab me if I didn't let him rape me. The next day at school he told my classmates what he had done. Everyone made fun of me and called me a homosexual, along with many other insults. My grades went down after that.

At first my parents didn't know what happened. I don't think it was even important to them. They were only worried about economic problems and problems that were going on in their relationship. Later, they found out what happened and turned against me. They made me feel I had accepted the sexual abuse that had come my way. My father hit me until my nose bled. I felt alone and abandoned. We had to leave the city we lived in because it was a big shame for my parents.

When I was eight years old, I had my first thoughts of disappearing. I ran to the top of a large hill and sat thinking. I stayed there for about four hours. My feelings of anxiety were extremely strong. But there was a part of me that said I should continue on.

23

I lived alone for ten months when I was eleven. It was in a large house that belonged to my grandparents. There was a large kitchen and ten bedrooms. My grandparents didn't stay at that house–they came by only to drop off money. I went to school from seven to noon, and I worked from three to eight.

While I lived there, I met a friend who spoke really good things into my life. He was several years older than me and, like me, had been abused by his father. He was very wise about life. We shared our experiences and were very close, but he died five months after we met. I grieved. He had been my only support.

Four months after my friend died, my parents came and asked if I was okay. I said nothing was okay. I wanted to leave that city and go to a different city. I told my parents that if we didn't leave, I was going to kill myself. That was how I told them I needed to leave. We moved to a different part of Mexico. At that new place, I played sports. I felt a little bit of happiness, and the thoughts I had about suicide went away.

When I was seventeen, I started to have romantic relationships. I could not live without being with someone, without being in their arms. I had strong feelings for the persons I loved. They were always older than I was. But all of my relationships were failures.

I began to like men. I met a person who made my life impossible. There was infinite suffering, sexual abuse, and physical violence from him. After that relationship I made my first attempt at suicide. I took some pills and slept for nearly twenty-four hours.

When I woke up, I felt worse. I was a coward and a failure. Even my attempt at suicide had failed. I had to do it again. I bought some aspirin at a pharmacy and took it. But there was a part of me that said I should not have done it. I drank a gallon of milk, which made me vomit. I was eighteen then.

During those days, I didn't have anyone. All I wanted was to disappear. My back became injured and I couldn't play sports anymore. I felt that everything in life was against me. Everything was made to make me suffer.

I started to drink alcohol and use drugs, especially Ecstasy. The drugs blocked out my bad feelings. I had all kinds of sexual relations, especially with gays. Even though these felt good at the time, I felt as low as I ever had been. I felt insignificant.

It was about six in the morning when I decided to go to a nearby beach. I was in a bad state, sad and drugged. I wanted to die. Everything was telling me I should drown myself. I walked into the ocean. In one of the waves, I went under water. I saw all my suffering pass before my eyes. A voice told me it would all stop and everything would change. I felt weak and tired, and I closed my eyes. I entered a trance state.

A fisherman came and pulled me from the water. He hugged me. It was the first time someone listened to me and gave me the advice that I should press on. He told me that life has highs and lows and that when it gets dark, it's because the sun will rise soon. He told me that he had a son who drowned near where I was trying to drown myself, that he would give anything to have his son back, that he couldn't stand seeing me do this to myself. That made me reflect. I decided to start over. This was when I was nineteen.

I went to a different state in Mexico to study psychology. I lived in a house with other boys my age, and I saw that they had lots of problems. I wanted to solve all those problems. I wanted to answer all the questions I had since I was a young child. That's when I started therapy, which gave me a lot of relief. But I still felt pain. I felt a darkness in my chest, as if nothing mattered. Nothing made me happy that had made me happy before.

When I did my university residencies, I treated patients with depression. I am still doing that, but am attending only to those who have been victims of bullying. I am treating the aggressors, too, modifying their behavior to be less aggressive. My thesis for the bachelor's degree was on modifying attitudes of aggressive adolescents.

I have always had the fear of God. My family was strongly Catholic. I am not Catholic now, but when I was fourteen or fifteen I was afraid that if I committed suicide, I would be punished–I would go to hell. I asked God why I had to go through certain sufferings. I don't know whether he responded or whether he will respond. But I do know that when I was underwater in that wave and that fisherman stopped me from killing myself, it was God.

We all have a purpose in life, and we all have certain things we have to do. We all have to save people. The fisherman saved me.

Something in me says that I should continue onward, that everything will be okay, that everything will balance out in the end. I see it as an energy that pushes me forward to do the things I have to do, treating patients who are going through the same things I went through.

Still, suicide is something I think about from time to time. "What if I wasn't here? What if I didn't exist? What if I disappeared?" It is not something I am finished with. I am still fighting.

Orlando was deeply affected by the kindness of a stranger, who pulled him from the waves just as he was about to lose consciousness. Instead of shrugging off that kindness and returning to the ocean, he chose to become a therapist so that he could help others who were victims of harassment, plus those who themselves had bullying impulses. Even though he still fights suicidal thoughts, the energy that was awakened that day at the ocean keeps him pressing on.

LUKE: TAUNTED AND EVERYTHING ELSE

Luke was frequently taunted at school. He also had to deal with epilepsy, bipolar disorder, learning difficulties, and stammering. He lives in Malta, an island in the Mediterranean Sea south of Italy. He was twenty-four when we talked.

I was bullied heavily in primary school, throughout secondary school, and even in postsecondary school—verbally, physically, and on some occasions by pranksters. In physical education classes, the others pulled down my pants and give me a kick here and there and sometimes tripped me up. It always happened when the teachers weren't present. When I reported that I was being bullied, the headmaster did very little about it. I was even bullied by some of the teachers.

I didn't do very well in school because I had a learning difficulty. It was due to epilepsy, which wasn't diagnosed until I got out of secondary school. I didn't get grand mal seizures until then, but I did get a lot of minor, absentee seizures, one after the other. The common assumption of people who aren't familiar with absentee seizures is that the person is either daydreaming or couldn't be bothered with what they are supposed to be doing. Most of the teachers assumed that I was daydreaming and that I didn't care about school.

Because I wasn't being treated for my condition, I had appetite problems and felt very fatigued. I also had apathy problems. These added to the stress and anxiety of the bullying. There were days when I was so anxious that I could not eat at all.

During the last two years of secondary school I was afraid to go to school. Some of the teachers expressed their contempt at my poor performance and said to me in front of a whole class that I was wasting their time. But some teachers did suspect that I had learning difficulties. They tried to help me the best they could.

I am a very introverted person, so I was easy to pick on. I also had a very serious speech impediment and used to stammer a lot. For a time I was having nightmares about demons and devils. My psychiatrist prescribed antidepressants.

I was able to start postsecondary education in electrical engineering. Because of my poor performance and the way some of the teachers treated me in primary and secondary school, I found it difficult to summon up the motivation to do well in postsecondary school. I was bullied again by students, this time most of it physical. On one occasion it got so bad that I lost my cool and hit back, though it is not in my nature to be aggressive.

I began to have doubts about the religious beliefs I grew up with. Roman Catholicism is the state religion in Malta, so it had to be taught. I had gone to a church school, where they were fierce about religion, and my family was very religious. I was always taught that to have doubt was a temptation of Satan, so I became convinced that I was possessed. My psychiatrist referred me to an exorcist. When I went to him, he said, "You need to pray more." I left his office more scared than ever, which affected my sleeping cycle. This occurred when I was seventeen.

As part of the postsecondary course I was taking, we had to do a minimum amount of work to apply the electronics we were learning. I was not able to get a job in electronics, but I managed to get a part-time job as a waiter. The hours were long and late, which added to my stress. I lost that job, though, when I had an absentee seizure during a wedding reception. I was holding a tray full of champagne glasses and cocktails, and the whole tray fell to the floor. So they told me I had to leave or accept the job of a kitchen porter, which consisted of washing dishes. That didn't exactly help my morale.

At the same time, I was doing volunteer work with an organization to promote awareness of epilepsy. I also worked with another volunteer group called the Thursday Club that helped people in psychiatric institutions to become integrated back into everyday life. I made friends with a few of the others in these groups, and for the first time my confidence boosted a bit. At the same time, I became very afraid, because I didn't know whether my two conditions, bipolar disorder and epilepsy, would get better or worse. I didn't want to end up in the same situation these people were in.

About this time I was going to a youth fellowship program where teenagers gather and make friends. On one occasion when I went out with them—it was for a New Year's Eve party—they behaved as if I wasn't there. Picture a van full of teenagers, all talking and laughing and having a good time with their girlfriends and boyfriends. I am in my own seat, covering up my eyes because I don't want anyone to see me cry.

> *"My life was pretty much ups and downs—mood swings, taunting, and everything else. I decided I had had enough."*

One afternoon there was a misunderstanding between me and another guy who had feelings for a certain girl. We got into an argument. Imagine being ganged up on by ten people in the middle of a street. They are giving out to you about not being appropriate and staying out of other people's business. I am trying to explain to them that I was concerned about the girl, but they are not taking me seriously.

That night after supper I took twenty to thirty tablets of my epilepsy pills and about twenty of the antidepressant pills I had been taking. The epilepsy pills were quite a high dosage. After I swallowed them, I downed a full glass of Scotch to celebrate. That was something I had never done. Then I went to lie down on my bed and wait for the moment to come.

Suddenly I was calm. That felt strange, because I had been so traumatized when I was surrounded by those ten people in the middle of the street.

After a while I started getting very nauseous. I was able to get out of bed and go to the bathroom, where I vomited. I also got a headache and felt very dizzy and had severe spasms across my body. I fell asleep, and when I woke up the next morning, I had the most aggressive, full convulsive seizures I had ever had. Saliva came out of my mouth, and my lips were shaking.

My little brother found me and went to my mom. She rushed into the room. I had not wanted to burden her with my attempted suicide the night before. She told me to stay in bed and see how I was. The next day she took me to our physician, who told me I should go to the hospital. I did, and two days later I was discharged. There must have been an aftershock effect, because I became reluctant to do volunteer work anymore and my motivation to do well in school hit rock bottom.

Later in the year I went to Ireland to study. By this time, when I was eighteen, my stammering had gone, and I found the course I took interesting. However, I was still struggling to control my emotions. I felt culture shock and was homesick. It was my first time living and studying abroad, far away from my family, and I didn't know anyone in Ireland.

I began to be bullied by some of the people in that course. At first it was a lot of taunting. But then it got worse, because two of the girls in the course accused me of being sexist. I was learning to be assertive, but I wasn't very good at it. There was a girl whom I had feelings for, but I didn't know how to approach her, so I wrote her a six-page letter. Later she made fun of me in front of several others. Then she accused me of calling her a whore and said I had made a remark about her being dressed up in a cheap fashion. I said, "I do not recall saying such things." She gave me a slap on the face and everyone except my best friend walked out of the pub we were in.

The next day I was called to the office of the facilitators of the course I was taking, and the girl made the allegation that I had banged on the front door of the house she was living in and that I had stolen things from her house. It was embarrassing. The school said, "You are going to have to take the year off." So I went back to Malta.

When I returned to Ireland a year later, I was subjected to racial abuse. Some of the others in the house I was living in taunted me as a foreigner. They threw eggs against my bedroom window. They kicked and punched my bedroom door and shouted all sorts of hurtful things.

One night at half past three in the morning, two years later and in a different place, I woke to the sound of glass bottles being thrown at my room from the hallway. People were screaming, shouting, and jeering. For them it was a sport. The good thing was that my bedroom window was at the back of the building. I was so scared that I crawled out the window and went to security and asked them to bring a guard.

I thought about suicide again, but I didn't attempt it because I looked back at what I had been through and how far I had come. I said, "Luke, you have been through much worse. You've been through bullying before." Also, I had started to make friends, and I had a very good friend with whom I shared my experience.

What has kept me alive for the past few years is that I have had a change of heart and career. I have become more interested in journalism and have watched all sorts of debates about philosophy, politics, and religion. I love to read. I have become involved with the Humanist Association. I meet people on the Internet, and I stay in touch with the few friends I can trust and rely on to help me.

Another thing that has kept me alive is that my little brother has also been diagnosed with epilepsy as well as attention deficit disorder. So I feel responsible for setting a good example. I want my brother to be independent and not let the discrimination I faced do him in. I want him to live life to the full.

Studies show that people who have attempted suicide more than once are at higher risk for a repeated attempt.[1] Such people need to find reasons to keep living or else they may be strongly tempted to try again. Luke found reasons to keep going, despite repeated taunting and bullying after he tried to kill himself. No doubt the indignity of the further mistreatment hurt him significantly. But he had enough friends and interests, plus concern for his younger brother, that he was able to avoid succumbing to another attempt.

HANNAH: TEASED AND BEAT UP

No one likes to be made fun of or called names or ridiculed or criticized unfairly, even if they are strong and stable. It hurts, especially when it is repeated. Sometimes it is repeated so often and hurts so badly that the recipient wants to escape it by dying.

---

1. Will My Patient Attempt Suicide Again? by Elizabeth L. Jeglic, PhD. *Current Psychiatry,* Volume 7 (November 2008), 19–31.

A nationwide study of young people in the Archives of Pediatrics and Adolescent Medicine *reported that being bullied, attacked, physically threatened, or otherwise victimized by peers more than doubled the likelihood of a child's having suicidal thoughts. The study also showed that experiencing any type of sexual assault more than tripled the likelihood.*[2]

Adults, too, are ridiculed and made fun of. But children and teenagers are usually less capable of dealing with the hurt that ridicule causes. This fact makes it imperative for children and teenagers to be treated both fairly and gently.

Hannah was twenty-four when she wrote this account of being teased and assaulted.

I have been bullied since I was ten. When I was attending grade school, the other kids teased me because I was taller than they were. I also got teased and laughed at for accidents I had because of an illness I suffered from. Middle school was the worst time of my life. I got jumped by a group of girls who hated me for no reason. I was known as retard and as a slut, but I had no idea why. My mom pulled me out of middle school and sent me to a new one, which I liked.

In high school I didn't have many friends, and girls laughed at me. After a while I started cutting my wrists. No one knew it. At night I cried myself to sleep.

One day my mom found me passed out in the bathroom. I had overdosed on her meds. At the emergency room the doctor discovered the cuts on my wrists, and I was admitted to a mental institution, where I stayed for a year. Two months after I got out I overdosed again. And I cut myself several times a week.

As I got older I gradually forgot about being bullied, and I focused on work. I opened a Facebook account when I was twenty. I had friends and family, and I was popular. One day I met a guy on Facebook who told me he was single and wanted to get to know me. We exchanged numbers and texted each other.

After a month he and I arranged to meet at a movie theater for a date. When I met him there, I discovered that he had a girlfriend, who was with him, and that they were old classmates of mine who had bullied me a lot in high school. I stood there in shock as he, his girlfriend, and her friends surrounded me. Before I could say anything they beat me up.

I drove home and was hurting so badly that I drank some bleach with a bottle of vodka. I woke up in the emergency room again. My mom was crying. Later the police got a statement from me and witnesses at the theater about how I had gotten assaulted. The next day I learned that those girls and that guy got booked for assault and battery charges and went to jail.

---

2. http://www.cnn.com/2012/10/23/health/bullying-suicidal-thoughts/index.html

I don't know why my attempts to commit suicide failed, but there must be a reason for it.

The old saying, "Sticks and stones may break my bones, but words will never hurt me," is definitely not true. Words have the power to discourage and agitate. They also have the power to encourage and soothe. The right words uttered in the right way at the right time can help people deal with the hard business of living.

Although time healed Hannah of the painful memories of being bullied as a child, the attack on her at twenty hurt her again badly. She survived for six more years before overdosing again, this time ending her life. Her mother was devastated.

The pain of bullying is real, and it is sometimes fatal.

4 NOT GOOD ENOUGH

Unless a person feels that they are valued, they may shrivel up and want to die. Here are stories of two people to whom this happened.

CARA: LOST IDENTITY

Cara Anna requested that her real name be used. She works as a journalist in New York City and has lived and worked in a number of countries, including China and Pakistan. In this account, she tells of what led to the feeling that she had no identity. Her thoughts on talking about suicide follow her story. She was in her late thirties when we talked.

It started when I was about eight. I was outside washing the car with my dad, and my mother came out, looking distressed and sad. She gave me a big hug and kiss, then went back into the house. The next thing that happened was that my father and a friend of his were beating down the bedroom door, beating down the bathroom door inside the bedroom, taking my mother out, then taking her to the hospital.

That was the only suicide attempt my mother ever made, though there were times when she was very sad and withdrew into her room, curled up with the shades drawn. It struck me, "Oh, my gosh, this could happen to me. This could become a major theme in my life when I get into my mid to late thirties. So I need to do what I can never to have this happen."

I was determined to work hard and not show any sign of what I felt was laziness or sloppiness. "I'm going to be very disciplined. I'm going to work harder than others. I will not let what affected my mother catch up with me. If I just keep myself together, things like that will never happen."

My first suicide attempt occurred early in my senior year of high school. I felt very close to a good friend of mine, and sometimes there would be flirtation, but I could tell that we weren't going to be boyfriend and girlfriend. We were talking on the phone one evening and he had to go, and it felt dismissive. I thought, "He doesn't like me, and I'm going to end this. I'm going to put dramatic music on in my car, and I'm going to drive it into something, and he's going to feel very bad."

At the last second I must have turned away, so it wasn't a head-on collision. I banged up the car, but I didn't hurt myself. Someone drove up and asked, "Are you okay?" I said, "Yes, I'm fine," and I drove myself to the hospital just in case. My best friend's mother was working in the emergency room, and she didn't admit me. She just took me aside and said, "Hey! How are you?" She talked with me until my mom could come.

When I think of it now, this episode seems strange and shockingly impulsive. What on earth was I doing? But I put it aside and moved on with life. I went to college, joined the Peace Corps, got a newspaper job, went to China, came back, got another newspaper job, went to China again, traveled to India, Pakistan, and other places, and then got the job I have now.

All seemed pretty well. I was working hard, and at the core of myself I had confidence in the work I knew I could do. That was reflected in the positive things my editors said to me. They entrusted me with interesting stories. I was hustling and doing extra work and writing as well as I could. I was thrilled that I was promoted to work in New York City and thrilled that they were going to send me to China in time for the 2008 Olympics. It was going to be an exciting year. I thought, "Wow. I've done it." I was living my dreams.

But China is difficult for a journalist. They don't want you reporting on sensitive topics like human rights. They listen in on your phone conversations. My apartment was bugged. When I tried to cover certain events, police or other officials told me to go away. More than once they physically made me leave the scene.

I was not used to people not wanting me places, angry at me, picking me up and carrying me away, or shoving me into a car. It was really startling. I thought, "I'm not doing my job well." My Chinese was not good. I felt bad that I had to rely on a translator at times, and I felt bad when I didn't understand exactly what somebody was saying to me. And when I was unable to get to a story because of a police roadblock or some authority being in the way, I felt I had failed.

The most difficult thing was that, on top of the language difficulties and the pushback from authorities and the isolation I felt, for the first time in my life my editor was not friendly or encouraging. It wasn't, "Yes, you're great, go do this, go do that." He got angry. Sometimes he sent a harsh message or e-mail, and sometimes he shouted at me. It was always hard to gauge what would come from him. I asked myself, "Why? What am I doing? Am I that bad?" "I must be terrible," I thought. No one had ever talked to me like this before.

I had just hit thirty-five, and I thought, "Oh, my gosh. It's starting to happen. I don't have a good foundation, and now suicide stuff is starting to emerge." It was bad enough to feel that I was a failure, and it was worse to think that the only thing that held me together was confidence in my work. If I didn't have that, I didn't have anything.

I didn't have anyone to talk to. I tried going to a counselor. She very quickly said, "You have to deal with depression. You need to take medication." I didn't want to hear those things. I never wanted to have to deal with depression. I had worked very hard not to have it, and what she said upset me.

Eventually, about ten or eleven months after I arrived in China, I abruptly shut down. I faked an illness so I could stay in my apartment and not work. I changed the lock on my apartment. I did a lot of research on how to kill myself. I was annoyed by the fact that there was no clear advice and that everything was sketchy.

There was a shooting range in downtown Shanghai. I went there late one night thinking I could get into a booth by myself and get it done. But they wouldn't allow that. They said, "No, no, we have to be in there with you." So I thought, "Well, that's not going to work."

I took taxis to different hospitals, trying to collect barbiturates. One emergency room doctor said, "Oh, no, we don't give these out in large amounts because people will use them to kill themselves." I feigned innocence, and said, "Oh, really. I had no idea." I said to myself, "This isn't working. I just want it all to be over."

I lived on something like the thirty-second floor of an apartment building. A couple of times a day, I opened one of the windows and looked out and thought, "I am terrified of heights. This is going to be the last option." I thought of the people below. "What if I fell on them? What if people see it?" It was constant thinking: "This must be done. I have to do something to get over this shameful experience that is my life. I have to save face and get this done. But how?"

I ended up buying a razor to cut my throat. I cleared some space in my apartment and paced back and forth and checked and checked and checked my pulse for the best place to cut. I sat down and took a deep breath and said, "Okay." I sliced twice. Blood trickled down onto my stomach. I thought, "I didn't cut it deep enough." Then I thought, "I don't want to keep doing all this. It is exhausting. Why can't there just be a way to do it safely, to be able to announce, 'I'm done. Please give me a way to leave with a measure of respect'? Why do I have to be alone and desperate and ignorant and flailing around?"

So I stopped. I contacted the editor who scared me and said, "I need to come talk to you," and to his credit he said, "Okay, come on up." He met with me, and I told him what had happened. I showed him my journal and let him read what I had written the past few days. He was very concerned, and he handled things well. The editor spoke with his boss, and they sent me back to New York. I was very embarrassed. I thought, "Okay, nobody should know this. Let's keep this as quiet as possible." So I didn't tell my family that I was back in New York.

I saw a therapist, I got medication, I kept working. After a few months, my therapist reported to my employer that I was well enough to go back to China. So I did. I thought, "Okay, the problem has been addressed. For the first time in my life I have actually spoken to a couple of fellow journalists about the situation and have gotten encouragement and understanding, and now I know how to work on this and everything is going to be fine." I worked hard, I was enthusiastic, and things seemed to be okay. But then it slowly started again.

This time I was incredibly angry and frustrated at my editor. I was thinking, "This person I had confided in and had told something very personal to is still being harsh to me and saying things like, 'You're being manipulative. You're passive-aggressive.'" I got people's advice. They said, "You need to fight back." But when I tried, he said, "I don't like your attitude." I thought, "This is not fair. Why is this happening?" I could not get over it.

I understood that there were difficult bosses in the world, but he could not allow himself to be relaxed or friends or at least detached and professional with his staffers. I know this sounds as if I am blaming him for my suicidal feelings. But I had done everything I could to address the situation and it was still happening. Besides, there was the stress of being in China and the authorities pushing back.

At some point I said, "That's it. I have to get out one way or another." In Beijing, they have a rental system where you pay rent three months in advance. To me, that sounded overwhelming. I couldn't commit to three months. So about six months after arriving in Beijing, I left my apartment. I moved the few bags I had into the office, and for the next five and a half months I lived secretly in the office.

> **"I didn't know what to do."**

It had a kitchen, and there was a bed in the corner of the kitchen, behind a big pillar. I used the public showers, and I took my laundry out to a local laundry place. I was careful to stay outside the building until I knew the last person had left, and then I slept until a little after six, when the cleaning lady came in. She never asked me why I was in the office that early. This went on for some time, until finally somebody put two and two together and asked me very calmly, "Are you living in the office?" I moved to a proper apartment.

At that point, I was constantly adding things up, like math. "I'm not liked, my editor has decided I'm no good, which means I have no potential, which means I have no career, which means I have no identity, which means I have no life, which means I have no future, which means, 'Why I am hanging around?'"

I thought, "Nobody's talking to me, nobody's being social with me, I'm not being invited to things, I'm just terrible. If my editor doesn't like me, it's because nobody likes me, and there's something fundamentally broken about me. So who cares?"

At the same time, I was going to work, writing stories, and, strangely, running, a lot of running. I ran every day, maybe six miles, maybe ten miles, maybe twelve. I flew back to New York and ran in the marathon there, my first ever. That was an oasis of happiness. It was like, "I'm going to do it, I'm doing it, and I've done it. This is all me. There's nobody standing aside and saying, 'I don't think you can do it' or 'You're not doing it very well' or 'You didn't do it very well.'" It was exhilarating.

I came back to Beijing and put my marathon number on the wall of my cubicle. I mentioned to another editor in passing, "If you ever see this number gone, you should worry about me." He had had a sense that sometimes I could be sad, and he was very nice and was sort of looking out for me.

But the day came when I said, "I don't care." I pulled the number off my cubicle wall and put it through the shredder. I thought, "Nothing matters. This doesn't matter, either." The other editor didn't notice. And, of course, why would he? Nobody notices other people very closely. It was such a small sign that he was not going to pick up on it. That was a final action for me. I knew another attempt was going to be coming pretty soon.

It happened rather quickly. I was feeling bad one day at work, and my editor wrote to me, "I would have given this story to you, but why should I reward your lack of enthusiasm?" I thought, "I'm done. At the end of the day, I'm done." So I waited. I was the last person in the office. I wrote resignation letters. I took down everything I had, removed the passport photos of myself, and sent goodbye e-mails. I left my key, went to my apartment, cleaned it up and told the landlord I was moving out early in the morning. I gave almost everything I had to one of the maids in the apartment building. It was just me and my backpack.

I went to the airport and looked and looked at the departures board and finally I said, "There's no place I want to go anymore." I love to travel, but this was just it. So I roamed around Beijing. "What should I do?" I thought. "It's cold, it's winter. Perhaps I should throw myself into the canal and die that way." Then, "Are you going to do it or are you going to chicken out?" And, "If you don't do it, then what will happen?"

I finally went to a hospital that caters to the expat community. I saw a doctor and pretended I had trouble sleeping. I got a package of sleeping pills. I thought, "I know this is not going to be enough. But it's cold enough that if I knock myself out with these and I sleep outdoors in the cold I'll die of exposure."

There was an abandoned village outside of Beijing I had found while hiking. I hired a taxi, got close to the village, hiked up to it and spent a long afternoon and evening, pacing and preparing. I had everything. I had the sleeping pills, I had the bottle of wine, I had the anti-throw up medicine, I had food to settle my stomach.

There were pockets of snow on the ground. I debated, "Should I lie down on the snow, or is it so cold that I won't be able to get to sleep? Should I lie down next to the snow? Should I put the tarp down?"

It was all logistics, no longer the grand questions of life and death. It was very mechanical, one step and the next. I had long passed the question of, "What am I doing?" It was now just, "How do I get it done?" I decided I would lie down next to a patch of snow and hope I would roll over onto it once I was asleep. I decided I would knock myself out before the sun went down so I wouldn't become scared in the dark.

"Okay, all right." I had medication, I had wine, and finally I thought, "I don't know what I'm waiting for." So I took the pills, had a sip of wine, and went to sleep. The next thing I knew I was thinking, "Oh, it's morning and I'm cold." It was dawn and I was shivering. I opened my eyes and got up. I felt dizzy, and I thought, "It didn't work. I'll have to go back to the doctor and get something stronger."

I went over to one of the abandoned huts, where it was a little warmer, and curled up on the bed. Within an hour or two a truck pulled up, because in China there seems to be somebody everywhere. I walked out and said, "Can you drop me off at the nearest bus stop?" I got on the bus, went back to Beijing, and checked back into the youth hostel where I had been staying.

After getting lunch, I went to an internet cafe to check my e-mail, which I hadn't done since I quit work, because I didn't want any distractions and didn't want any feedback. I was alarmed at the responses, because I had assumed no one had any idea what I was doing. I had hoped people would think I had resigned and gone off to travel. However, on my way to the abandoned village, I had left my journal, containing a final note, at my therapist's office. The secretary assured me he wouldn't be in for a few days, so I thought that gave me plenty of time. But it turned out he shared the office with another therapist, who, amazingly, saw the journal, opened it, and started reading. He called my therapist, who called my editor.

My editor had told my brother, and my brother had written, "Please, please contact me. I love you." The editor above my editor had written, "Don't quit, we don't want you to quit. Please check in with me right now." Not only were they concerned, they hadn't accepted my resignation and wanted to talk with me. So I said, "Okay. I'm going to turn myself in." I e-mailed my therapist. He wrote back, "I will wait for you at the hospital." So I showed up at the hospital and he took me to the room where I stayed for the next week. There I was, almost, in a strange way, giddy. "I've done it, I gave it what I thought was my best shot, it didn't work. Now what?"

My editor came to visit a few times while I was in the hospital. Eventually we talked and joked, almost as friends. I thought, "Okay, if this is the last time we talk to each other, this works for me. He has a human side. But if I have to get to this point in my life to see the human side of him, I don't think it's worth it, and I'm not going to work for him anymore."

In the United States, people are so careful when talking about suicide. Everything is hushed, everything is calm and tentative. "Oh, are you okay? Is everything all right?" But my ex-husband, who is Chinese, called. He was blunt and practical. The first thing he said to me was, "Honey, are you stupid? What were you doing?" I had to laugh. I thought, "Thank you for talking to me like that. Thank you for cutting through all the crap that surrounds this topic."

I came back to the United States. My employer let me go on medical leave for a while. I considered quitting, but in the end thought, "No, I'm going to keep working." The international editor met with me and mentioned the idea of going back to China. I said, "No. I'm not going back there." Whatever things are over there, they set me off. I needed to find a different life in New York.

There was a period of anger. I didn't like having to work on myself again when I knew what was wrong. I did the therapy thing, the medication thing, and slowly transitioned out of anger. I stopped taking medication this past winter.

The work I am doing now is not too challenging. I'm told I can do it well. I'm in a good apartment. I have good colleagues. I have good roommates. Everything seems fine.

I decided not to keep my suicide attempt a secret. The key people already knew—my editors, my brother, my ex-husband. I decided to tell my mother. She was wonderfully supportive and understanding. I even told my father.

What keeps me alive now is being out of that environment and finding another world to explore. I like exploring new things, and in a strange way my suicide attempt is keeping me moving forward. I am trying to find people who have attempted suicide and who are willing to come out. I would love for several thousand other people to stand up and say, "Yes, this is my name and this is what I tried and this is where I am now in life." It feels such a relief to me when I come across someone else. Every time it happens, I think, "That's one less step back from crazy for me. It's one less step back from being alone."

It may seem too easy or irresponsible to blame others for one's suicidal feelings. Still, the events one is subject to and the way in which one is treated by others can have a significant impact, for good or for ill, as it did for Cara. Her mother's suicide attempt, Cara's rejection in high school, and an insensitive work superior all left their marks on her. When she moved to a new environment, her sense of identity returned and with it a desire to keep living.

Talking About Suicide

In the United States, many people whose relatives or friends have killed themselves feel shame when they admit that fact to others, and many people who are wrestling with suicidal feelings are afraid to say so.

The fundamental premise of therapy is that talking about an issue helps one to deal with it. In talking to a gracious and accepting listener, one feels understood. And feeling understood helps one to bear one's problems even though they seem insurmountable. Talking also helps one to explore alternative ways of dealing with a problem.

After Cara's last suicide attempt, she decided to see what she could do to change the stigma against talking about suicide. Her recovery involved creating a Web site, "Talking About Suicide: Because It's Not a Taboo," at http://talkingaboutsuicide.com/.

Why don't more people talk about suicide? Why are we so scared? Wouldn't it be more helpful to people who are caught up in suicidal thoughts if they knew the environment was more open to them? What if they knew that they could talk to people without the fear of that person shrieking and running away or snubbing them or locking them up? Wouldn't there be fewer suicides? Wouldn't there be fewer people in desperate isolation?

I decided I wanted to find other people who have come out, so to speak, who have been through a suicide attempt and acknowledged it and put a name to it and have gone on with their lives. I think people don't know much about suicide except that people do it, and it's sudden and it's scary and there was no warning and they're gone, and there's the question "Why?" People also see things on television or in movies or in books or in media reporting in which there's dramatic music and people crying or even romance. It's something that's not exactly real.

Even the people who work with suicide prevention groups or at crisis hotlines are too careful about what they say. I wish there was a group or a movement or an environment in which people could just say, "Yeah, sometimes you feel awful, sometimes you feel driven to want to kill yourself. It's dreadful, but it happens. Let's talk about it without everybody panicking, because the panic only makes it worse."

I wish people would relax and not worry about setting people off by talking about suicide –"This could trigger somebody. This could cause a contagion. It could provoke someone to kill themselves." You have to open up and talk reasonably about suicide without the hush or swell of music.

Cara is right. People often don't know what to say to someone who has tried to kill themselves. And she is right to ask, "Wouldn't there be fewer people in desperate isolation if there weren't such a stigma against talking about suicide?" Yes, asking someone about a suicide attempt is scary. One might be embarrassed or say the wrong thing. However, displaying a willingness to listen, via words, facial expression, or body language, can create an atmosphere in which people in trouble feel welcomed. And this in turn can open up life-saving conversations.

DAKOTA: WORKING ON SELF-ESTEEM

Being in the hospital after a person has just attempted suicide can be very unsettling, even frightful. At the same time, it can make a big difference. Dakota describes both of these aspects of her hospital stay. Anger, depression, and low self-esteem were large parts of her life, which she worked on while in the hospital and also afterward. We talked when she was twenty.

When I was little, I threw tantrums and hit my head on the floor because I was so angry. Then when I got to eighth grade I started cutting as a way of releasing anger without showing it to people. I wanted my parents to think I was okay, because they had other things to worry about. I thought, "I'm not going to cause any stress for anyone. I need to be secretive about this." But after a while I said to myself, "Screw this. I'm not going to hide my cutting anymore. I'm not going to make myself wear long sleeve shirts in the summer. If anyone is going to say anything, then they are." But no one did.

I went to my mom and told her about my cutting and she flipped out. She said, "Show me your arms. I have to see them right now!" I showed her, but we didn't talk about it until later. I stopped cutting for a while, but did it again on and off until my freshman year of college, when it got really bad. I cut several times a day then.

To me cutting was comforting. When I got angry at myself or sad, I expressed it through cutting. It was a control thing, too. I thought, "Oh, I can harm myself. I can stop it or I can do it more. It's my call." I needed cutting to calm myself down. Once I had it in my mind that I was going to cut, I had to do it. It wouldn't go out of my head until I did, almost like a compulsion.

My suicide attempt occurred about three months ago, when I was sophomore in college. I was at work from nine in the morning to four in the afternoon. I had forgotten to take my medicine that morning, so I asked my girlfriend to drop it by the store where I work. She seemed a little off when she came to the store. I asked her if I had upset her, and she said, "We'll talk about it after work." I said, "No, you need to tell me what's wrong now." She replied, "No, we'll talk about it after work."

That bugged me. When I went on lunch break I went to a pharmacy and bought razors. I left the razors in my car because I was going to use them after I got off work. Then I went back to work. I was really upset.

After work I waited in my car in the back parking lot of the store I worked at until everyone left. I started to cut myself. Then I drove to my girlfriend's dorm at the university where we are students, stopping on the way to cut myself again. When I got to her dorm, I called her to tell her I was there. She said, "Okay," but she didn't come right away. I had a whole bottle of mood stabilizers and a whole bottle of antidepressants with me. I took all of the antidepressants.

When my girlfriend finally came to the car and saw me, she freaked out. I took all of the mood stabilizers, which she couldn't prevent because I had locked the car. She called 911 and my parents. I started feeling really sick.

The fire fighters came first. They asked me questions and I threw up a few times. I got into the ambulance, and they kept saying, "Okay, Dakota, stay with us." I was in and out of consciousness—it was really hard to stay awake. I was taken to the emergency section of the hospital, where a bunch of people were holding me down because I kept lifting myself up. I was throwing up everywhere. At one point my mom ran up to me.

I was acting strangely, so they kept me in the hospital for three days. A nurse had to be with me at all times. I wasn't even allowed to take a shower unless someone was in the bathroom with me. At the end of three days, they told me I needed to go to a psychiatric hospital. I went home to grab some stuff, ate dinner with my family, and then my parents took me to the hospital. I thought, "Okay. This is going to get me better."

I was put on "red band," which was top security. They put me into a room with a camera and went through all my stuff. They took away a whole bunch of it. They even took the shoelaces off my shoes. I couldn't have certain types of bottles. It felt as if they had taken away my rights.

I wanted to be with my family, but I couldn't go to them. My best friends didn't try to see if I was okay. The camera was always on in my room. I was treated like a kid, and I felt trapped. I don't like being trapped or anything that's restraining. I thought, "I'm dead and I'm going to be here forever." It felt as if I deserved to be there because I had done something so selfish.

There were a lot of older people in the hospital, but there was another girl who was only a year older than me. We bonded some, and she stuck with me the whole time. I didn't like her that much, but she was all I had in there. People from outside were allowed to call me. The hospital staff left little sticky notes when they did, and I called them back during certain hours. I called my parents and my girlfriend every day because I was scared.

We were on a set schedule every day. We had a certain time we had to wake up and get breakfast. We met with an individual therapist twenty minutes a day maybe, but mostly we did group therapy. At first I said to myself, "I don't want to be in this group." I was stubborn and wouldn't contribute to the talks. But after a while, I thought, "These people want to help me." So I started participating in the group talk, and it helped a lot. I became comfortable talking to people and listening to their stories. It opened my eyes to listen to other people's views on things.

A year before, a therapist had diagnosed me with bipolar disorder, and in the hospital I was also diagnosed with borderline personality disorder. That involves a lot of self-destructive behavior, which I do a lot. I also get upset at simple things most people ignore. Little things irritate me. I treat them as if they are the end of the world. Another thing I have is black-and-white thinking—something is either all bad or all good. There is nothing in between. And I do a lot of unhealthy mind reading—"Oh, that person is thinking this about me," when I don't know for sure.

I have done a lot better because of the therapy. I learned to think, "Okay, I'm acting like this. I need to stop." My parents came to get me on a Saturday, and I was put into partial hospitalization. I kept on with the group therapy and art therapy once or twice a week. I really liked doing those.

When I was in the hospital, I explained to the group therapy leader that two of my best friends weren't trying to understand what was going on with me. She said, "You just need to hang out with them and let what you did come up naturally." After I got out of the hospital, I texted them and one of them texted back, saying, "Because of what you did, we are re-evaluating our friendship with you. We don't want you to contact us. If we want to talk to you, we'll contact you." I was really upset by that, but my mom and my girlfriend helped calm me down. That was three months ago.

About two weeks ago, one of those two friends told my girlfriend that he wanted to talk to me. At first I thought, "No, not at all." I sat down and thought about it. Then I said to myself, "You know what? It's not going to hurt anything." And my girlfriend said, "He seemed to be genuine, and it sounded as if he was changing. Before, he was cynical and a jerk all the time."

I met with him and he said he was sorry and that what he had said was immature and stupid. He realized this, he said, because he had made new friends at the LGBTQ community at our school. They were good people, he saw, and he made friends with some of them and talked to them about what I had done. He explained to me that he and my other best friend thought I had attempted suicide just for attention and that I was being selfish. He said, "I understand now that that is not what it was at all. You had some issues, and you had to handle stuff." Now he and I talk. He has opened up to me, and I've done the same to him.

He told me, "I want you to hang out with me and my friends." There is a place on campus where people go between classes. My self-esteem is so bad, though, that I don't think anybody there is going to like me. Every time someone walks past me, I think they are thinking, "That girl is ugly and fat. And she is stupid. Why would she . . . blah, blah, blah." But that is completely ridiculous because it's probably not what they are thinking at all. They are probably not even registering any of that. So the big thing I am working on now is self-esteem.

My family showed me a lot of support after my suicide attempt, even my extended family, plus my girlfriend and people who are not close friends. Everybody supported me. That made me appreciate how many people care about me. I don't want to die anymore. I haven't self-harmed since my attempt, and I don't want to. I want to get better, and I want to have a good life.

Often there is no one thing that contributes to a person's getting better. For Dakota, healing came through being in the hospital, supportive parents, a loyal girlfriend, and an acquaintance who was willing to apologize and welcome her. There was, in addition, Dakota's willingness to accept the caring of these people. This willingness may, in fact, have been the decisive element in her renewal, for without it the support of others would have been of little help to her.

5 PAINFUL MEMORIES

When something dreadful happens to someone, the thought of it is often repressed. Being constantly conscious of it is too painful. But the memory does not disappear, and it often makes its way back into consciousness years later. Then it may hurt even more and cause the person to have traumatic emotions. This can happen to soldiers. It can also happen to children who are abused. Here are three accounts of wanting to die because of painful memories.

NOLAN: HAUNTED BY THE DEATH OF A CHILD IN WAR

Nolan served in Operation Iraqi Freedom 2. He was forty-two at the time the event he describes occurred. The picture of the girl was taken by Nolan as the convoy he was in passed her.

It happened on May 28, 2004. I had volunteered for Operation Iraqi Freedom to try to get my life back. Prior to deployment, I had gone through a long, painful process in which my faith in God was tested, and I did not feel I had passed the test. My quest was to reconnect myself to my faith. I wanted back my core values and character, which had provided me with joy and peace.

I had different jobs in Iraq, but the one nearest my heart was to take care of my troops, making sure they had the supplies necessary to keep them safe. Sometimes I spent a morning purchasing goods from local vendors, the afternoon volunteering for a convoy, whether official for the Army or unofficial for a vendor. Or I waited at the airport at one a.m. to welcome a soldier back to the combat zone. That may not sound like a place to be welcomed back to, but seeing a friendly face might help one remember that they weren't ever alone, even at war. It didn't matter to me whether the soldier was a private or a general, because their safety and comfort were my personal missions.

I was not stationed with the soldiers I deployed with, so I had a great deal of alone time. I found solace in listening to the praise and worship songs I grew up with and reading the stories of those who lived in biblical times, such as Joshua, Moses, and especially Paul.

On that day in May, I was on a simple mission to escort fifty trucks into a holding area just south of Baghdad. The day was beautiful—sunny, but not too hot. The camel herds seemed to be enjoying the sun. The watering holes were plentiful. The drop-off was successful, and we headed back to camp.

When you drive through villages in Iraq, you pass people standing at the edges of the roads, usually children and older women. Most often they are hoping to collect an MRE—a meal ready to eat—or some other food or trinket that we would toss to them. On this particular day the "parade spectators" were there as usual—an old woman chasing a youngster away from the middle of the road, a group of boys sitting on a sand pile smiling at the heavy equipment and cool trucks driving by, and a little girl standing at the edge of the road with the cutest smile I had seen in a long time (see Figure 5.1).

Just as the truck I was in passed the girl, there was a loud explosion. I was startled. I didn't know what it was at first, whether a tire had exploded or a round had gone off in one of the trucks. I turned to look at the road behind us and saw a cloud of dust. As it settled to the ground, what I saw stunned me. The girl was gone. She wasn't missing; she was gone. A roadside bomb

Figure 5.1.

hidden in the sand had detonated. Destruction that was meant for me had taken an innocent child.

There was no paperwork or report of the incident, as the trip was an unofficial escort mission delivering supplies for a vendor. The Army, in typical move-forward mentality, gave me Prozac for twenty days. And then it was back to normal duty—no talking, no counseling, no therapy, just burying it, sucking it up, and moving on.

Several weeks after the mission, I walked to the edge of the base camp, alone. I had my weapon with me, but it was not for defense. I carved "No Return" into a piece of scrap wood, my hands becoming bloody from the knife and the sharp edges of the wood. I wanted to put the image of the girl's broken body behind me, but I wasn't able to pull the trigger.

Instead of getting back closer to my faith and finding what I had lost, I became more of a drinker than I had ever been. I and three of my friends—Jimmy, Johnny, and Jack—went to rooftop parties. And when I couldn't go to a party, I had my own in my private room. Within three months, the memory of the girl had received a proper Army burial, drowned in medication and illegal alcohol. Then, out of the blue, I suffered a heart attack and was sent home to the States.

Something changed after I got back, but I didn't know what it was. I often forgot why I went to a store. At Walmart once I sat at the base of some shelves and cried because I couldn't remember why I was there. I woke up startled in the night, unable to breathe. I got angry over nothing and sad over everything. My favorite activity became sitting outside in the woods, alone, watching the squirrels scamper about.

My family did not accept me. I wasn't invited to my parents' fiftieth wedding anniversary celebration. My mom wouldn't speak to me, and my dad stayed clear of me, too, because he knew that if he talked to me my mom would argue with him. My brother, who had always been my best friend growing up and the only one who hugged me before I went to Iraq, suddenly didn't want to take sides. Even my own kids didn't know how to relate to me anymore. They had not communicated with me while I was in Iraq—their mother had not allowed them to send one single letter or package to me.

It felt to me as if I had been given a life sentence of unhappiness, and I was unable to find anything to cling to. Once when I was out driving I let go of the steering wheel as I pointed the car at a tree. But a self-preservation instinct took over and I grabbed the wheel just before going off the shoulder of the road. Oftentimes I drank heavily and took pain killers.

On one of my birthdays, I took some time off from work so that I could spend an hour alone. I drove home and sat in my garage, agitated and confused. I loaded a bullet into the chamber of a handgun, pulled the hammer back and placed the gun under my chin. As tears rolled down my face, I waited to hear God say, in an audible voice, "It's okay. I'm ready for you to come home." But I did not hear that voice. Instead I imagined my family coming home and finding me dead, with an image they would never be able to forget.

I wondered what was wrong with me and how I had become this person who wanted to kill himself. And then one day as I was moving some things in a closet, I found a card from a digital camera. Curious, I loaded it into a computer. Pictures I had taken on that day in May, which I had successfully blacked out, were again in front of me—camels lolling in the desert, a woman chasing a child from the middle of the road, a group of boys watching the convoy pass, the little girl with the delighted smile, holding her hands in front of her, and then the one of a cloud of dust where she had just been standing.

I fell apart totally this time. Suddenly every reason I had to end my life became validated. The sleepless nights began again, the heavy drinking, and finding whatever pills I could to numb myself. I tried to speak with counselors, but it never did any good. I was on a one-way road to eternity, and now I had the justification to accomplish this one last mission.

Why have I not gone on this mission? The answer is that I still haven't heard the voice of God giving me permission. I still have my faith, although sometimes I wonder how strong it is or even where it is. When it's truly my time, God will tell me, and he will be there to help me through. But for now, he is here helping me survive each day.

One of the major concerns with soldiers who have returned from war zones in the Vietnam, Iraq, and Afghanistan wars is the high incidence of post-traumatic stress disorder (PTSD). PTSD is defined as "a mental health condition that is triggered by a terrifying event, either experiencing it or witnessing it. Symptoms may include flashbacks, nightmares, and severe anxiety, as well as uncontrollable thoughts about the event" (from Mayo Clinic Web Site). These symptoms, which Nolan had, may increase the risk of having suicidal thoughts. Although Nolan nearly killed himself several times, his instinct to live saved him, along with his belief that he needed permission from God in order to die.

PENNY: A SLOW DEATH

When she was in high school, Penny did not want anyone to know that she wanted to kill herself. So she ate less and less, hoping no one would suspect she was deliberately trying to die. Now in her early thirties, she is safely beyond wanting to die. Her thoughts about whether someone is responsible for trying to kill themselves when they are in a desperate situation follow her story.

I was sexually abused by a long-term babysitter when I was five or six years old. He came into my bedroom to put me to sleep and he molested me many times. I kept it secret because I was afraid I had done something wrong and would get into trouble for it. I was also afraid he would get into trouble for it, which I didn't want to happen, either. And I was afraid worse things would happen if he knew I was awake, so I pretended to be asleep. Even though what he was doing was so painful that I knew no one could possibly have slept through it, I held in the screams and poured all my willpower into being still.

When I was in junior high school, I started to think about what had happened. I felt dirty because of it, really disgusting. If people knew about it, I thought, they would hate me. I thought I was bad. At the same time, I started to read books on the subject because I was desperate for information on it. All the books suggested that the first step was to tell somebody. But that was terrifying–really, really terrifying.

I believe in God, and I got a strong sense that God wanted me to tell someone and get some help. At one point I did try to tell someone, but my throat closed up. I couldn't breathe. I couldn't speak. I started to shake uncontrollably.

I went to a church youth group retreat. The theme of the retreat was, "All things are possible through Christ Jesus," a verse from the Bible. That was huge for me, because I felt that God was telling me I would be able to talk about what had happened even though I didn't have the strength to do it. I was in fact able to tell a friend, and then later I was able to find a therapist.

The things you have to work through for sexual abuse are incredibly painful. During therapy I said to myself, "It's going to get darker before it gets lighter," a quote from the *Wizard of Oz* when the Tin Man, the Cowardly Lion, and Dorothy go into the forest.

That was what therapy seemed like–everything was getting darker and more painful the more I opened up all the deep feelings and thoughts I had. I knew that eventually once I did all the hard work I would come through on the other side and there would be healing. But so many times I couldn't see the other side. I tried to believe it was going to be there. But as I got further and further into therapy, I started to lose hope. I kept telling myself that there had to be light at the end of the tunnel, that other people had been through this tunnel before. But it felt as if I was locked in the dark and could not find my way out.

During this time, my relationship with my parents began to deteriorate. My father was in the military, and he was extremely controlling. Things got worse after he retired from the military and took an administrative job at the church we went to plus became a deacon at it. He sat the whole family down

> *"If you don't take a good hard look at the lies you believe, you can never find out what the truth is."*

and talked to us about how he would lose his job if he wasn't seen to be a father in good standing. So we had to make sure never to misbehave in any way. That was a huge amount of pressure, which I felt very strongly. If I had any problems, if anybody saw that I had problems, especially at church, my dad would lose his job and his position as deacon.

He was harsh with me, and he never forgave me for anything. Whenever I did something wrong, or whenever he thought I was doing something wrong, he responded with extreme anger and sometimes violence. He hit me on a few occasions, but I didn't have any marks or bruises, so I felt that I couldn't get any help. Sometimes I argued, sometimes I tried to explain myself, but I never really knew what it was I had done wrong or how to avoid the next screaming episode.

Once my dad backed me up into a wall and pinned me there. He leaned over me, his face inches from mine, and screamed about what a horrible, stupid, worthless thing I was. Spittle flew into my face, but I didn't flinch. I did not cry. I would have been in more trouble if I had done those things.

He slapped me on one occasion and sent my glasses flying across the room. When I failed to apologize for the comment that had earned the slap, I was forced to stand in place for several hours without moving as further punishment. Another time he grabbed me, shoved my face against the wall, and twisted my arm behind my back until I screamed in pain and told him what he wanted to know.

The worst of it wasn't the hitting; it was the emotions he provoked. I was so afraid of making him angry that I tried everything I could think of to placate him. But there wasn't anything I could do, because no matter how I acted, he always found something to be angry about.

My mother was very much a peacemaker, but unfortunately her way of peacemaking was to sacrifice herself to my father's rage. Whatever she thought she could do to make him stop being angry, she did. I was never able to sacrifice myself in that way, although I tried.

Before my father got home each day, my mom came and told me, "Your dad is on his way home, you have to be quiet. You have to make sure not to make him angry tonight." If he got angry, it didn't matter what I had done or said, whether I was wrong or not. She backed him up and never me. So I felt betrayed by my mother.

One of the ways I tried to avoid my father's anger was to make myself invisible. As much as possible, I didn't talk. If I said something, even something innocent, he could twist it the wrong way and make my words into something I never intended. I avoided going into rooms that he was in. If I had to be in the same room, I made myself as small and quiet as possible so that he wouldn't notice me. If he didn't notice me, then he couldn't find anything to be angry about.

One time the youth group in my church was planning to go on a short-term mission trip, and I very much wanted to go. I had to ask my father for permission, and he got very angry at me when I did. He said, "How dare you ask me to go on this mission trip. How dare you to think of yourself as a missionary. How are you going to teach others when you don't know how to behave yourself?" I was very hurt by his telling me I wasn't good enough to help others.

Another time he mentioned that he'd read some survey saying that the average person says a certain number of words every day. I was in my very quiet phase, so I thought, "Wow! That's a lot of words." Before I stopped myself, I said, "I don't think I say that many words every day," just thinking that I may be different from others. He got extremely angry and shouted at me for hours because I had back-talked to him. He took it that I was trying to argue with him, that I was saying that he was wrong, that people didn't talk that much, when all I was saying was that maybe I'm different from the average person.

After things like that happened I wanted to talk to my father even less. But this was the thing–I never knew what was going to cause him to snap and what wasn't, so I was always afraid. When I was younger I cried when he screamed at me, and that made him angrier. He yelled, "Stop crying! Why are you crying? I'll give you something to cry about," which made me cry more. I couldn't control it.

He wanted me to control everything. And he wanted to control everything about me. Once I had the hiccups that I couldn't stop. He said, "You need to stop that." I tried. I held my breath, I drank a glass of water, I hopped up and down, but none of it helped. He screamed at me because I was being disobedient.

Any attempt to explain myself or talk about the fact that what my dad was demanding was impossible was treated as insolence and back-talk and earned me more hours of getting screamed at. I wanted desperately to obey him, to be a good and acceptable daughter, and I worked so hard at it. But it was impossible. It couldn't be done. I felt that something was completely wrong with me for never being able to do what I was supposed to do, to honor my father and obey him. I cried myself to sleep at night because I couldn't make him happy, I couldn't ever do things right, and I didn't have any idea how to fix myself to make him like me.

My mom and my dad knew I was in therapy for sexual abuse. My therapist had to get my parents' permission, since I was a minor. So I had to tell them. They were very sad that the sexual abuse had happened, and they wanted me to get therapy, which I am very grateful for. But as the therapy went on, my dad because less supportive.

First of all, no one was paying for the therapy. I was fifteen and had no money. The therapist was a friend of mine, and she agreed to give me therapy even though she was a professional therapist and even though I could not pay for it. I didn't know whether my parents had the money for it. But they never offered to pay. I always felt guilty about that.

The other problem was that my therapist lived in a town that was some distance away, so I couldn't see her very often. I had to make long distance phone calls whenever I needed to talk, which at first my parents said was okay. But later they complained about it, and so I felt that my therapy was costing them too much money, even though they were paying only for the phone calls. My father always came up with different punishments for me, and sometimes it was that I couldn't call anyone on the phone. He knew that the only person I usually ever called was my therapist. So telling me I could not call anyone on the phone was telling me that I couldn't do therapy.

I spent all my free time during my last year of high school at home, alone, sleeping, lying on the floor, and crying. I had almost no friends. The only places I went were school and church. At church one of the women I was close to noticed that I was more and more depressed, and she asked me about it. She said, "I'm worried about you. You're showing signs of depression." I said, "Yes, that's true. I've been really depressed recently." She said, "Have you talked to your parents about it." I said, "No, no, I think that's not a good idea. I've talked to my therapist, but I can't talk to my parents about it." She said, "I think your parents need to know." I said, "Please don't tell them." But she insisted, and so went and told my parents.

The next day my mom and dad sat me down and said, "We've heard from someone that you are depressed. Is that true?" I said, "No. No. That's not true." My dad yelled at me for a long time for making him look bad at church, because if people think I'm depressed then he's obviously not doing his job, and he's not a good father, and it's really terrible for his reputation, and how could I do this to him?

The first time I wanted to die was when I was in junior high school. I imagined ways I could accidentally die—in a car accident or by being crushed by some heavy machinery that fell over. That way I could die without actually committing suicide. My junior high school had a new building under construction in the middle of the campus. I had to walk past it several times a day, and often I looked up at cranes carrying construction materials over my head and wished for some malfunction or accident that would result in my death, but wouldn't harm anybody else. I daydreamed so many ways to die—murder, car crash, anything I could imagine, painless or not, that would take me away.

During my senior year of high school, I started to be much more serious about wanting to die, not just dreaming, but thinking about how I could do something to die. I was still afraid of the reputation of my family, though, and I didn't want to hurt them. I knew that if I committed suicide it would destroy my family. I was very sensitive to the fact that my father was working in a ministry position and that he was a leader in the church. If his reputation was destroyed, people might lose their faith, might lose their belief in God, because they looked up to him so much. I didn't want to do anything that would destroy the ministry of the church.

I started to hurt myself through not eating. That was my slow suicide. It was my way to die without killing myself overtly, without anyone knowing that that was what I was doing. I became very anorexic. I ate as little as I could get away with. Before school I made sure to get out of the house before anyone else was up so they wouldn't know I wasn't eating breakfast. At school I claimed to have eaten a big breakfast, so I wouldn't eat lunch. And then when I got home I claimed I had a big lunch at school and wasn't that hungry for dinner.

One morning I decided to eat breakfast, as I was feeling very weak and was afraid I'd faint at school. (I'd fainted a few times but never at school.) I grabbed a clean bowl from the cabinet and poured myself a bowl of cereal. My dad came into the kitchen and saw I was using one of the large cereal bowls. He started screaming that I was a disgusting pig for using a large bowl. How could I be so inconsiderate to eat so much? I tried explaining that the other bowls were dirty; I tried explaining it was only half full; but it was no use. I left for school wiping away tears and vowing not to eat breakfast anymore, at all.

It was easy to lose weight. Nobody paid much attention to what I ate, and I became very thin. At some point I was about eighty-five pounds. I'm five feet six and a half inches, so that's very thin. My parents, as far as I know, never noticed. They never spoke to me about it. They never asked me why I wasn't eating or treated it as a problem. To this day, they don't know I was anorexic.

That was my way out. When I was depressed, I ate less, and when I was trying to pull through, I ate more. I was never hospitalized, but I did faint quite often. When I stood up I became lightheaded and got tunnel vision.

When that happened, I was afraid people would notice, so I ate something so that I wouldn't faint in front of anyone. I thought about dying all the time. That was what I was thinking about when I didn't eat.

There were also one or two times when I was so despairing that I wanted to do something that would be faster than not eating, but I couldn't bring myself to carry it out. I got some plastic bags and thought maybe I could put one over my head and lie down and go to sleep and see if I would suffocate. I put one on and tried to lie down, but I couldn't follow through. I was afraid of what would happen if someone found me like that and what it would do to my family and what people would think about me if I survived. I couldn't betray the people who had helped me. So I never followed through.

Also, I couldn't do it because I felt it would be a betrayal of what God had done in my life. He had been there through all of the pain and had given me help when I needed it. If I killed myself, I was saying that God wasn't strong enough to help me through. I couldn't believe that. So even though I was despairing and didn't want to live, I couldn't follow through with killing myself.

Unfortunately, anorexia has long-term effects which I didn't care about at the time, because I wanted to die so badly. I was convinced I wouldn't live for very long and it wouldn't matter what happened to me. Anorexia can cause damage to your internal organs, including your heart. Now I'm concerned that my heart may have been damaged. I often have heart palpitations, and every time I get a health exam the technician who runs my EKG is concerned about it.

Also, anorexia can damage your ability to bear children. The first few years I was married, my husband and I did not try to have kids. Now we're not trying to have kids, but we're not trying to prevent it either. It's been several years like that, and I haven't gotten pregnant. I don't know whether that's related to my anorexia. We have been married for nine years.

My therapist played a huge part in saving me. She was the one person whom I felt I could talk to, and she loved me unconditionally. Even though she knew all of my deepest, darkest secrets, the things I hated myself for, she loved me. Her love was so refreshing to me that I couldn't get enough of it. It was as if I was so thirsty when drinking from a cold spring of water that I couldn't get enough to drink. Her willingness to nurture me, to be my therapist and my friend, and her caring, saved me.

She taught me what was true and what was false. She taught me that the sexual abuse was completely not my fault, was completely out of my control, that I bore no responsibility and no guilt for it. That took me a very long time to believe. But when I finally got hold of it, it changed how I felt about myself.

Going to college was a big turning point for me with eating, because I finally got out of the oppressive environment in my house. Everything was new and everything was hopeful. I could breathe, I could speak without fear, I could live and choose things without being afraid of how it would be received. So I started to eat again.

However, I had difficult situations when I stopped eating for a while. But I started to build a network of people I could talk to, who encouraged me and watched out for me. If they noticed I wasn't eating, they talked to me about it and encouraged me.

The biggest healing came from my husband. When we started dating, I couldn't hurt myself anymore, because I could see how much it would hurt him. I couldn't do that to him. That was the end of my anorexia. I gained weight and haven't been in danger since.

I ended therapy in college, because the sexual abuse didn't have a lot of power over me anymore. But I went back into therapy about two years ago, this time to deal with some of my family relationships. I am beginning to admit that my father was abusive and am trying to heal from that.

I am trying to have a relationship with my mother again. She has been willing to dialogue with me about a lot of the issues from the past, and I'm grateful for that, because I know it is incredibly painful for her, as it is for me. Sometimes I don't want to eat because of that. That's been my response to emotional pain as long as I can remember. But I force myself to eat even though the thought of food makes me nauseous. I can't go back down that road again. I don't want to die. I want to live. I kept too many secrets for too long. Bringing those secrets out helps break their power.

> *"I want to speak my truth, because it is so healing to do so."*

Love keeps me alive. God's love. And my husband's love. All my friends care about me. My therapist is still the same woman I had at fifteen, and she still won't take my money, even though I'm an adult and have a job and am happy to pay her. I think she thinks of me as family, and I think of her in the same way.

My dad recently had a serious heart attack and needed bypass surgery. When I thought it was possible he might die, my first feeling was a flood of relief, a sense that there was a new freedom on my horizon that I'd never yet tasted. But then immediately I was filled with guilt over feeling that way. My internal emotional overload switch must have flipped then, because I went numb. I stayed that way for weeks, which made me feel guilty, too, because wasn't I supposed to be feeling sad? Here my dad was having heart surgery, and I felt nothing.

I asked myself whether there was anything I wanted to say to him before his surgery in case he didn't make it through, and I couldn't think of anything. I called him but we didn't talk about anything significant. After he went home to recover I was sad that he didn't have anything significant he wanted to say to me. I don't have hope for any sort of reconciliation with my father.

If he dies, I will have an opportunity to have a new kind of relationship with my mother. My mother betrayed me. But it was to protect herself and to protect us. Her heart was good. If she had taken us away from our father, that would have protected us, but she didn't feel able to do that, or didn't know how she could do it. Even though the things she did and said were hurtful and damaged me, I know she did them out of love. So I see a future and a hope that my mother and I can have a relationship.

But I have never felt that my father cared for me in any other way than as a prop for his ego. I was nothing to him except a way for him to have power over someone. That hasn't changed. So I don't see a way to have a relationship with him without him trying to put me under his control again. And I'm not willing to be under his control again.

Penny's story demonstrates the life-saving effect that divulging one's deepest feelings to another can have, in Penny's case, to her therapist. Studies show that "talk therapy" after a suicide attempt significantly reduces the number of repeat attempts.[1] Penny's story also demonstrates the powerful effect of knowing one is loved. She found that it was wonderfully healing to tell her story to someone who accepted her as she was.

How Responsible Are You for Trying to Kill Yourself When You Are in a Desperate Situation?

As I listened to each person recount their suicide attempt, several questions repeatedly came to mind: Are people responsible for trying to kill themselves when they are in a situation in which they can see no way out? Suppose I myself was in so much pain that I could not bear to live any longer. And suppose every alternative I could think of was at least as painful. Could I be justly blamed for wanting to die?

The best answer I can think of is, "Yes" and "No." A suicide attempt is indeed a person's own choice. And yet that choice is often made under extreme duress.

---

1. Suicide risk falls substantially after talk therapy, Johns Hopkins Bloomberg School of Public Health, November 24, 2014. http://www.jhsph.edu/news/news-releases/2014/suicide-risk-falls-substantially -after-talk-therapy.html

Penny reflects on her attempt to kill herself by not eating and gives something like this yes and no answer.

A woman I know convinced me to ask my parents to take me to a doctor to discuss my weight. I did that. I went to see the doctor with both hope and dread, hope that he'd see the eating disorder I had and find a way to help me, but dread that I'd be discovered, that he'd find out my secrets and I'd be sent to one of those places where they weigh you every morning and force feed you if you don't eat. Plus I was terrified that everyone would find out.

So I was torn in two. I wanted help and yet I was afraid of it. I remember sitting on the exam table as the doctor took my small white hands and turned them palm up, resting in his large black ones. He gently examined me for signs of bulimia and found none. He looked into my face and asked, "You're not doing this to yourself, are you?" "No," I said. "I'm not."

The doctor sent me to talk with a nutritionist about how to get my weight up, and she prescribed a nutritional supplement every night with dinner. There was no mention by anyone of eating disorders, and nobody paid attention to whether I drank the Ensure or not.

The obvious question is, "Why did I lie to the doctor?" Actually, I was lying in so many ways to so many people. I lied to my camp director when she asked me if I'd ever been sexually abused. I lied to my parents when they asked me if I was depressed. I lied with a smile on my face at church when I pretended that everything in my life was fine. I lied when people asked me how I could possibly be so thin and said things like, "Yes, it's so frustrating. I eat and eat and just don't gain any weight!"

Why did I, the goodest of goody two-shoes church girls, lie so much to so many people? I lied because I was so incredibly frightened of what would happen if I told the truth. I was so afraid of it that on occasion when I tried to tell some of those secrets, I started to shake and shake and was physically unable to speak. That's how strong that fear was.

Was I doing it all to myself? Yes, in a lot of ways, I did it to myself. Not eating was a choice I made. It was my slow suicide, killing myself quietly, trying to tiptoe out of the room without anyone noticing.

But in so many ways it was not a choice. Was being abused a choice? Absolutely not. There was no way for me to save myself from that or from the consequences of it (although for a long time I blamed myself for not being strong enough to resist, and even now I have to fight to remind myself that I was a child). Was the depression a choice? I hated that hopeless load I was sinking under. The depression, the anorexia, the suicidal feelings—all those things were related, tied together with the hopelessness and pain I felt as a direct result of the abuse and dysfunctionality of the family I was in. I don't want to get into the blame game, whose fault it was–his, hers, yours, mine. But I have to say, although, yes, I was doing it to myself, at the same time, really, no, I wasn't.

How, practically, can one accept both that each person bears responsibility for their life and that others can rightly be blamed for causing someone to harm them- selves? Perhaps one way is to say that suicidal people need encouragement to make good choices, because emotional pain makes it harder to take responsibility for one's life. With encouragement, people with emotional pain are more likely to take that responsibility.

How, then, can one encourage suicidal people to make good choices? One good way is to listen to them nonjudgmentally and with compassion, as Penny's therapist did. When a suicidal person experiences such listening, they are more likely to feel under- stood, and thereby feel more hopeful about their life, and then, thereby, to take more responsibility for pursuing good choices.

LOUISE: TRYING LIFE IN A DIFFERENT WAY

Louise thought that the molestation she experienced as a teenager was just a nor- mal way to be loved. Later, she felt a good deal of distress because of it, and after her suicide attempt, learned there was a different way she could live. She was fifty when we talked.

From the age of twelve until I was seventeen I was regularly molested by an uncle. There was overwhelming evidence that he behaved the same way toward a lot of young girls. I thought that if everyone knew what he was doing, then maybe that was the way it was supposed to be. Besides, my uncle said to me, "You know I love you. You know I do this because I love you." So my whole notion of what love was became twisted.

When I left home at seventeen, I dabbled in drugs, alcohol, and promis- cuous behavior so as to numb the sadness and isolation I felt. There was something hanging over me, something that had not been addressed, but I didn't know what it was and wasn't able to express what I was feeling. Everything had been shoved under a rug by my family.

I straightened myself up and got a good job. But I could not shake any of the painful emotions that plagued me. By my late twenties I had spiraled to a place of darkness. I had trouble concentrating. I missed work. I didn't socialize. I was in such emotional pain that I started thinking about killing myself. I didn't try right away, because I didn't want to hurt anyone else. In the end, though, easing my own pain became more important than not hurt- ing someone else.

I had moved to a not-so-good part of town, and a friend of mine who was a police officer loaned me a small revolver until I could change the locks on my doors. My first thought was, "This ought to do it."

I sat in my bathtub so that no one would have to clean up any mess I would make. It was the first time in my life that I felt at peace. It was an overwhelming peace, just overwhelming. I thought, "This is what I'm supposed to do." I was confident and grateful. And I cried, because I knew my pain would end.

I had never touched a gun before, and I didn't know that when I pulled the trigger the gun would jerk. The bullet grazed my scalp. But it knocked me out.

I lived in a duplex, and my neighbor heard the gunshot. I don't remember anything that happened next. My first recollection was of being so drugged in a hospital that I couldn't move. As my thoughts became clearer, I felt miserable because I had failed to kill myself. I still wanted to be dead.

After I got out of the hospital, I went to group support meetings. Some of the people in the group had also failed in their suicide attempts. It was ironic to listen to them, because they had little to say other than that they did not want to be alive and resented the intervention that had saved them.

As a result of the gunshot, I lost hearing in one ear and somehow lost feeling in my hands. When this physical damage started to subside, I thought, "Maybe other things will correct themselves." Some of my bad feelings began to go away. I felt myself healing bit by bit and discovering new ways to approach what was emotionally painful. I gradually found myself wanting to live.

My psychiatrist gave me great encouragement. He never told me that what I had done was wrong. He only asked if I wanted to try my life in a different way. I was skeptical at first. But I felt that if I wanted to try, he would help. Dr. B. and I sat and talked about nothing in particular. Then he threw out a question. I felt emotionally safe for the first time in my life. Before then, I didn't know what that was. I had never felt secure. I had never felt confident.

Dr. B. worked with me for almost four years, until I moved. I found that there is more than one way to look at your life, more than one way to solve a problem, and more than one way to love. There is more than one way to choose your own journey.

So I relearned a lot of things. Earlier I had said to my sister, "I love you," but I didn't understand what that meant. In love there is reciprocity and affection. That was something I never had as a child. And I certainly didn't have it with my uncle as an adolescent.

The love I feel for certain people helps keep me alive now. After two decades of relearning life, I have come to the place where I can say that I am glad I am still alive.

Louise learned about love the wrong way—by being used as an object of pleasure. When she discovered that real love is far different, she wanted it. That love, she found, is worth living for.

Struggling with Faith

Louise grew up Polish Roman Catholic. Here she reflects on the connection between her faith and feeling suicidal.

When I began to ponder taking my life, my first thought was, "That's a sin. Now what?" But I convinced myself that the sin was that I was living. The only way to absolve that sin was to take my life. I thought, "This is living hell, and I'm not strong enough to endure it."

Ironically, my faith in the years that followed my suicide attempt came back to me. But it came back in a very different way. I don't go to church, but I have a strong faith that there's something bigger than me that has some goodness in it. I am here to do something good, even if it's only to buy a box of candy for someone.

Suicidal thoughts afflict people of faith for the same reasons that they afflict those without faith. People of faith, though, have an added dimension they must deal with— how to connect their faith to their suicidal impulses. Sometimes doing so increases their trauma, and sometimes their faith becomes a resource which helps save them. Louise set aside her faith for a time, but regained it in a new way when she learned that she could live differently.

Talking About Suicide

Louise went through years of silence before she could trust anyone enough to talk about her emotional pain.

Those of us who have made the journey out of darkness have many things in common, the most important of which is silence. We learn to cloak our illness from others. Slowly, life becomes isolated the more we do not speak about what we feel. I know beyond a doubt that if these journeys were spoken, our culture would take the first important turn toward understanding suicidal people. If the silence could be lifted, others who have endured the darkness might find some light.

Here, in the words of a formerly suicidal person, is testimony to the truth, enunciated by therapists and psychologists, that talking about suicide with someone who is thinking about suicide does not make it more likely that they will kill themselves. In fact, it does just the opposite, Louise declares. Done with the right person in the right way, talking about one's suicidal impulses can be marvelously healing, as Louise discovered.

6 TEENAGE STRESSES

Teenage years are in many ways the most fragile. Teenagers are trying intensely hard, almost desperately, to be accepted by people outside their home. When they are bullied, treated badly, or dumped by a friend, they tend to take it as undermining their whole existence. Unless they have a secure sense of worth, a good family life, or people who love them, they may decide that they want to die.

In addition to the three teenagers whose stories are in this chapter, a dozen other people whose stories appear in this book attempted suicide when they were teenagers. One of them, Robyn (page 89), said this:

One of the things that makes me clench my fists in anger is when people dismiss the suicide attempts of adolescents simply as the result of emotional upheavals, thinking the adolescents say, "My boyfriend broke up with me and I wanted to get him back," or "It was just a silly mistake I made in one large emotional outburst." None of these were true for me. I wanted to die. I believed that there was nothing after I was dead, and I longed for that relief. I think that should be taken seriously and not just dismissed as if adolescents aren't whole people. They might not be mature adults, but their thoughts and feelings are real and valid.

A teenager's suicide attempt should be taken seriously, Robyn declares. It should not be construed simply as a passing phase or merely as a ploy to get attention. It can, however, be perceived as a genuine cry for help, in which case the proper response is to give the right kind of help. This help might involve medical or psychiatric intervention and will certainly involve strong, caring emotional support from classmates, teachers, and parents.

PIXIE: BLACK CLOUD OF THE FAMILY

Pixie and I talked when she was nineteen.

When I was about five, I was sexually assaulted by a family member. I didn't understand what was going on at the time and didn't know that it was wrong. It happened again later on, and ever since I have had a growing depression. Although I was generally happy, in the background there was always a tinge of not being completely happy.

When I got to middle school, my dad started working the eleven-to-seven shift at night. He wasn't getting enough sleep and his anger issues emerged, like the anger issues his own father had had. He took it out on us children. If we didn't do something right, he blew up. And sometimes he shook us, but not to the point that it would be physically damaging.

At the same time, the other kids at school made fun of me. They called me butterface behind my back and even to my face—not my friends, but the popular kids. The guys were catty too—cliquey and nasty. I didn't feel that I fit in, because I wasn't interested in things that the others were interested in.

In the seventh grade, it got too much for me and I started cutting. When I was a freshman in high school, I told three of my friends about it. The first one was very concerned and told me that she too had been cutting. We couldn't help each other, though, because we were both in the same situation. The second friend thought I was just asking for attention and didn't believe me. The third friend tried to force me to go to the school counselor and tell my parents. I said, "No, no, no, no."

My parents didn't know about my cutting until my sophomore year of high school. I went on a mission trip to China. The leader of the trip found out and told me that I needed to write to my mom and tell her what I had been doing. I wrote my mom from China and told her that I needed to talk to her when I got home. When I got home, I told her everything. She promised not to tell my dad, because he was the reason I cut. I kept cutting, though.

When I was sixteen, I dated a guy for three months. The day we broke up was a Saturday. I had never dated anyone before, and I didn't know how to deal with the breakup. I felt horrible, as if I was in a black hole. I was not nice to my parents that day, and my dad was upset with how I was acting. I tried to explain to my parents that it was because I had just broken up with someone. I think my dad got sick of my being sad because he screamed at me that I couldn't go to a friend's house, as I had been planning.

I started crying. I called my friend to tell her I couldn't see her. My dad was sitting right next to the phone, and when I hung up I accidentally leaned into it too much and it sounded as if I slammed the phone down. My dad jumped up with a red face and said, "That's it!" He screamed and screamed at me, and my mom cried and begged him to stop.

I said, "This is just like before." And he said, "Before what? Before you started cutting?" I completely stopped. I fell to the floor, and the time felt as if it was going super slow because I had no idea he knew. He told me that if I had problems with cutting he would send me to the psych ward. I went to my room. My mom came in, and as she was crying said, "Look me in the eyes and tell me you're not going to cut anymore." I had to do that. Then she reaffirmed what my dad had said about the psych ward.

They left to go to a baseball game, and I was home all alone. Actually, my brother was home, but he was in another room and didn't come to check on me. He had given me a knife for Christmas. I got it out and held it, ready to end everything. But I kept saying to myself, "I am not going to do it. I will not do it." Eventually I calmed down, and strangely felt completely okay.

My cutting increased after that. I started with my wrists and then did my legs. My legs couldn't feel as much, so I could make more lines there. I cried and cried and cried, but stopped crying when I cut. It calmed me down and made me feel better. It was something I had control over. I could do whatever I wanted to myself. Somehow that had power over what other people were doing to me.

I was fascinated with the scars. They were a visual reminder of what I had been through. I needed that reminder so that the memories could sink in. For some reason I thought that they were something I wanted to sink in.

I wrote a lot of poetry about how I felt, and it was very dark. My mom found it. As she was driving me to school one day, she called me the black cloud of our family and said that I was the source of all our problems. That was the last straw for me. I tried to overdose that night, but I didn't take enough pills and it just made me sick. Even worse, I felt that I wasn't able to do anything with myself.

> *"I was distraught and hated that I wasn't normal and that I was a problem for my family."*

I stopped cutting for a while in my senior year of high school. I was happier and felt that I was more attractive and didn't hate myself as much. I became homecoming queen. That was very unexpected, because I was the underdog candidate. It made me happy that people actually liked me.

Then I started dating the worst person I probably could ever have dated.

I thought, "You know what? I'm going to date this guy because he is so exciting." The first three months were great and I had a lot of fun. But after that he started calling me stupid and constantly put me down. He made me the butt of his jokes and treated me like I was the dirt of the earth. He stopped talking to me as much when I couldn't drive him to parties. We had gotten busted at one of the parties and my parents had taken away my car. That was pretty much all he needed me for, plus sexual favors. He forced sexual stuff on me. This happened every time we hung out. After we broke up he sexually assaulted me when I was asleep at a couple of parties. It was very degrading.

I had repressed my sexual abuse since I was a kid, but the sexual stuff with this guy brought it back. I cried every night. I thought, though, that I was just being emotional and that things couldn't be changed.

During my high school years, I had started experiencing cycles of ups and downs. I didn't notice them then, but looking back I can see them. I was sad one day and happy the next. I didn't know that this was something that was wrong with me, because the highs were so wonderful. I was energetic and did lots of things at once, thinking I was getting things done when I really wasn't. Then I got completely depressed. I couldn't get out of bed.

After high school the guy I'm dating now said, "Pixie, that stuff you're going through isn't normal. You shouldn't have to feel like that." He told me he couldn't date me because of my problems. That freaked me out. The next day I called about getting into therapy because I was so miserable I couldn't take it anymore. I drank a lot. I drove recklessly, not caring about anything. I cut like crazy. I was seeing five guys at the same time. I hurt many of my friends doing that.

I started seeing a therapist. She decided that I might be bipolar. I got medication from a psychiatrist and started feeling pretty okay. I was able to get up in the mornings. Then the psychiatrist switched my medication and things got bad. I got completely out of control. It felt as if I was on the worst of the highs and the worst of the lows combined into one. I couldn't sleep. I missed a lot of classes in college because I was so depressed.

My parents said that if I missed one more class they would take away my car. I accidentally missed one, and they took away the car. I felt trapped, because my car was my freedom. I hadn't cut in a long time. I hadn't done anything to myself. But after my car was taken away, I snapped. One night I cut myself like crazy. It was deep cutting, not normal, superficial cutting. I was aiming for suicide. It was the worst cutting I have ever done. My mom called me, but I didn't answer the phone. She kept calling and I kept not answering. She finally came home because she knew something was wrong.

She walked in on me as I was cutting and saw that I was serious about what I was doing. She called my psychiatrist, who told her to take me to the hospital. At the emergency room, they cleaned me up. I felt embarrassed. I had disappointed everyone I knew, and I felt completely worthless. My boyfriend was hurt, and almost angry, too.

I have a new therapist now, and a new psychiatrist who is much better. He balanced out my lows and highs with new medication. I miss the highs every now and then, but I would never stop taking my medication just to have them again. If I had succeeded in killing myself, I would have missed some of the best stuff of my life. I like learning new things and looking forward to the future. Having that future to look forward to keeps me going. And the relationship with my dad has gotten better.

It is especially difficult to cope with both mistreatment and bipolar disorder. However, if the bipolar disorder is treated, it becomes easier to survive mistreatment. This happened to Pixie. Receiving proper medication for her bipolar disorder enabled her to handle the circumstances she was in better, and it helped her to find reasons for staying alive.

NATHAN: "NO, YOU ARE NOT DEPRESSED!"

Nathan was diagnosed with major depression, panic disorder, and agoraphobia when he was a freshman in college. We talked when he was nineteen and a sophomore in college.

When I was nine and in the third grade, I was bullied by my classmates. Most of it took place during recess or in between classes or outside school. One time I was playing a game of chess in the back corner of the classroom during an indoor recess. I won the game. The person with whom I was playing, who claimed to be my friend, threw me to the floor and punched me in the jaw. Then some of his friends hit me as well.

The bullying produced a marked change in my personality. When I was eight, I was very affectionate. I ran around. I did drawings. I played outside. My favorite color was yellow. But when the bullying began, I became melancholic and morose and sad. I stayed inside more and didn't talk as much. The change worried my parents. They didn't know what was going on.

In middle school there wasn't so much overt bullying as there was isolation and ostracism. I didn't have any friends and didn't have anyone I could talk to. The depression got worse.

When I was in eighth grade I told my mom that I thought I was depressed. She replied, "No, you're not. You're only thirteen. You couldn't be depressed." That invalidated my experiences, and I didn't talk about them with my parents.

About this time psychotic features of the depression manifested themselves. I had hallucinations of demons or malicious entities. I don't know what exactly I was experiencing. But I must have wanted so much to live in a world different from the depressing one I had been living in for four or five years that my subconscious mind made up a different world. My first suicide attempt occurred when I was thirteen. I tried to slit my left wrist, but I did not know what I was doing and I missed the artery.

A little later, when I was in ninth grade and fourteen, I began to associate with an unhealthy group of friends who harmed me emotionally. One of them, a girl who was five years older than me, yelled to my face or on the phone that I was a terrible person and that she hated me–I was worthless, I was stupid, I was arrogant, I had no value. At the same time, she said that she cared about me, even that she loved me and that she was doing what was best for me. I believed her, because I didn't know any better. I stuck with her pretty consistently for about six months, an hour or two a day. Her boyfriend affirmed the negative things she said and hit me with his fist now and then. Once or twice he choked me. The two of them made me call them "Mom" and "Dad."

Eventually I told them to get out of my life. But I didn't address what had happened. I didn't think about what they had done to me. It simply boiled around inside of me. Then, in the fall of my junior year in high school, when I was sixteen, I talked about it with a friend. I described some of the things the two had done to me. That conversation was very intense and overwhelming. After it, I decided, "I'm done. This is it. It's over." I went to my room and in a flash of fury and confusion I tried to hang myself. I attached my belt to my neck and then tied it to the pull chain that you use to get into the attic. I choked for maybe thirty seconds or so, but the belt came undone from the chain.

I was angry, but I couldn't find any other place in the room I could make hanging work. I didn't want to cut my wrist with razors, because it would make a mess for my parents. I didn't have access to any weapons. I didn't know how many pills or drugs to take. It seemed that hanging was the only option. But I didn't have a way to do that. So I angrily paced around my room until I collapsed and fell asleep. When I awoke the next morning, I went to school. I didn't tell my parents what I had done, and I didn't tell anyone else, either. I thought about suicide frequently. And I didn't realize how depressed I was. I thought it was normal.

I graduated from high school and went to college. Near the end of my freshman year, eight months ago, I talked with an adult mentor who said I should go to therapy. So I met with a therapist. I told him exactly what was on my mind. I had been abused. I wanted to kill myself. This was the first time I admitted that I was abused, even to myself. I spent the next month trying to accept that fact. I had stifled what had happened to me for so long that it took a while for my mind to embrace the fact that it was abusive.

When I met with the therapist again, he took me to a hospital. I spent a week there in crisis. I called my parents, who live in a different state from the college I go to, and told them that I was in a hospital because I was contemplating suicide and had been contemplating it for several years. I think they were shocked. They didn't know about the things that had happened with that girl and her boyfriend or that I had been bullied in elementary school. They didn't know about my suicidal feelings. It took my mom three months to fully understand that I was in a struggle for my life. I left the hospital still being suicidal. It wasn't until several months later, about five months ago, that the suicidal thoughts began to diminish after switching to a new medication.

The thought of suicide comes up now once or twice a day, but I don't hold on to it. I simply let it go. Still, I am only two or three steps away from going back to the hospital. In the morning I say, "Let me try to find a reason to get out of bed." Sometimes I don't find one, and I stay in bed until two or three in the afternoon.

There isn't any one thing that keeps me alive. Sometimes it's a fear of what comes after death. Sometimes it's a desire to go to graduate school after college. Sometimes it's a fear of hurting my friends and family. I feel as though I am juggling a plethora of reasons that are just barely keeping me above water.

My feeling that what happened to me was definitely not okay has been validated by my therapist, my psychiatrist, and by my parents, too. They finally realized the extent of what I had gone through. But before I left for college several months ago for my sophomore year, they asked me please not to call them from the hospital again. They're terrified for me, they're afraid for me. They don't want to deal with that kind of terror.

Nathan's turnaround began when he acknowledged that what had happened to him earlier was abusive. It might have started earlier if he had felt that he could talk to his parents. His story, and Pixie's and Rose's, demonstrate the truth that although teenagers want to be independent, they still need parents who actively support them.

ROSE: AN INNER STRENGTH

Rose was eighteen when she wrote to me.

I had a pretty unstable life growing up. My parents divorced, we were very poor, there was constant fighting, the cops were called, my mother was abusive, my brother was always in trouble, I was bullied a lot—every type of dysfunction you can imagine.

As the years went by, I fell apart more and more, and I hit rock bottom when I was fifteen. Everything that was going on had built up way too much inside me, and I felt that I couldn't take it anymore. The only thing going through my mind was wanting all of the pain to stop, and one night I decided that I was done living.

I cried frantically and grabbed a shirt out of my closet. I lay on the floor of my bedroom, tied the shirt around my neck, and pulled tighter and tighter. I began vomiting and feeling my oxygen being cut off, and all I could think was that this was it, my life was over. Then at that moment, something in me told me not to end it. I had to make a decision fast. Do I allow myself to die right now or do I keep fighting? I listened to the message deep inside myself, untied the shirt from my neck, and lay on the floor crying. In a way I felt as if I had let myself down by giving up my suicide attempt, but at the same time I was relieved to have another opportunity to live.

Nothing changed, though, and during the next year and a half things got worse. Soon after I turned seventeen I told myself that if something didn't change, I would take my life, this time for sure. I decided I had to tell someone how much I was hurting. I told my parents, but they ignored me and criticized me because of the pain I was feeling. I told my boyfriend at the time, but we fought constantly for months and finally broke up. I told my best friends, but they started treating me differently and I lost some of them. They thought suicide was cowardly and weak and didn't understand the extreme pain I was in. They didn't get it that I had to exert a huge and painful effort just to make it through each day. They didn't know what to say to me.

One night about a week before my eighteenth birthday, I demanded that my mom take me to the emergency room. I wasn't sure what was going to happen. I was afraid people would think I was crazy. I feared where I would end up. But the hospital people acknowledged my need for inpatient help right away and sent me to a treatment center.

As I walked down the gloomy hospital hallways, surrounded by others with similar or worse problems, with nurses checking up on all of us throughout the day and night, I realized that I needed to be there. I knew my decision to keep pushing for help would take me to a better place.

I am eighteen now and I still struggle day to day with mood disorder, suicidal thoughts, anxiety attacks, cutting, and an eating disorder. I have been on several different medications, but none have worked.

I often wonder why I am still alive. What's keeping me fighting this constant battle? I don't know. But I do know one thing: there is an inner strength in me that wants to keep living. I have always had big dreams for the future that I want to fulfill. Although I am not anywhere near better yet, I am working on it a little every day.

Although Rose genuinely wanted to die, she also possessed an inner drive to keep living. This drive prompted her to demand help, even though she did not know what that help would involve. It caused her to fight for her life despite being treated badly by friends. It engendered in her a desire to keep working on her anxiety and cutting. It produced hope that she could fulfill her dreams.

7

UPS AND DOWNS

Everyone has good days and bad days. But for suicidal people, the down days may be extreme. On down days, they may not be able to get out of bed until the middle of the morning, or even later. When they finally drag themselves out of bed, everything feels just as dark and gloomy as when they lay in bed wondering why they kept on living. On good days, they may seem to others to be perfectly normal. But the threat of a good day turning bad looms over them, filling the good day with dread. Here are two accounts of people who experienced extreme ups and downs.

RANDY: CRASHING AGAIN AND AGAIN

Randy spent over three years in hospitals and more than three years being homeless in his late twenties and early thirties. His bipolar disorder led to numerous down times, during which he felt frightful hopelessness and worthlessness. It wasn't until he was given a support system after he was discharged from one of the hospitals that he could begin to live a productive life. Now he is active in the behavioral health field, telling his story to others who are recovering from trauma. He was fifty when we spoke.

I started hallucinating in kindergarten. I saw people and followed them around. Every other week it came for a couple of days, maybe two or three hours each day. In second or third grade, I started hearing things. I panicked and got frustrated and angry and had outbursts, but I couldn't understand enough to explain to others what was going on. Later in elementary school I wanted to disappear. I don't know whether I wanted to be dead. I just didn't want to be around anymore.

In high school my bipolar disorder started manifesting itself, though I was not diagnosed with it until I was thirty-eight. In the first couple of years I experienced primarily the highs. They went on for two, three, or four months. I had unshakable energy. I went a hundred miles an hour–not outwardly: I couldn't turn my mind off. Then I crashed into a depression and felt hopelessness and worthlessness–"I hate life, I don't want to be here." That's when I started thinking of suicide. In late high school an acquaintance

70

of mine hung himself. I thought, "I wonder what that would be like?" I wished I had the courage to do it. But I didn't.

In college it was the same thing. First the mania kicked in, then the depression. When I got out of college I left home in eastern Canada and moved to western Canada. I went into a serious depression there.

One day when I was twenty-five or twenty-six I said to myself, "I am going to put a plastic bag over my head, tape around my neck, pass out, and not wake up." I walked to the cabinet, grabbed a plastic bag, walked to the closet, got duct tape, went and lay in bed, put the bag over my head, put the duct tape around my neck, and fell asleep. A couple of hours later I woke up. I had unknowingly ripped open the bag. I was frustrated that it didn't work. I didn't know I could call a counselor or a hotline. I wasn't thinking like that at the time.

I moved down to Iowa shortly after that and had my first psychiatric hospitalization, because I had been planning on buying a gun and putting a bullet into my head. I was still not correctly diagnosed as bipolar, so all I got was an antidepressant, which sent me into a mania. I started feeling really good and then was discharged from the hospital. I went two or three months with uncontrolled energy and mania, and then crashed. This happened every two years for the next ten or twelve years. I got high, and then I crashed.

At the very bottom the feeling was emptiness—"I give up. There is absolutely no hope. I don't care. Just let me go. I don't want to struggle anymore." The psychic pain was so debilitating that I didn't want to deal with the agony of living—"I'm useless. I'm garbage. I'm pathetic. I'm no good. I don't want to live any longer." When I had these feelings, I felt that the easy way out was to end my life.

With bipolar disorder there is something called racing thoughts. I have hundreds of thoughts coming to me all at the same time. It's like a teacher in front of a class having things shouted to him on fifty or a hundred different subjects all at the same time. I had conversations with myself. I heard this and I heard that. It was so exhausting that I self-medicated. I didn't drink until I was totally drunk, but it wasn't just one or two drinks. It was seven, eight, or nine drinks to calm the voices, to slow down the constantly shifting thoughts.

I attempted suicide again when I was about thirty-three. I was homeless at the time and had been sleeping in a car I owned in a parking lot in the middle of a bad part of town. I took a pill and then a sip of coke, another pill and another sip of coke. I must have had 150 pills in my system. After taking the last pill, I passed out. Three kids found me, and I woke up five or six days later in intensive care, strapped down to a bed.

It was such a severe attempt that the physician at the hospital wanted me to get long-term care. I had no insurance, so I was sent to a state hospital, where I spent close to a year. While I was in the hospital, my car was repossessed, and when I was discharged, I was dropped off in the middle of town with basically nothing.

Once again I used medications to try to kill myself. I was at a hotel, feeling sick to my stomach as a result of taking pills. I didn't want to be sick. I wanted to be dead. I called 911 and told them what I had done. By the time they came, I had passed out. I don't remember the police knocking on the door. I don't remember getting thrown into the ambulance or being taken to the hospital. Once again I had gone into a coma, this time for two or three days.

> *"If you beat yourself up enough and you have that worthlessness, that hopelessness, that uselessness, and have no support; if you believe you are a burden to society and to your family–those are some of the things that precipitate suicide."*

I decided to move to Arizona, from Iowa, but again became really suicidal, really depressed, down and out, so I went into the hospital yet again. I still had no correct diagnosis. The doctors never asked about highs and lows. They just asked, "Are you suicidal? Are you depressed?" And the answer was "Yes, yes." So they always thought I had clinical depression or dysthymia, and I got depression medication, never the right medication for bipolar disorder, until after my last hospitalization.

Many of the doctors also asked me whether I had trouble sleeping. My response to them was, "No, I have never had trouble sleeping." In my mania, I went two or three days without sleep. If I had been asked, "Have you ever gone two or three days without sleep?" my answer would have been, "Yes, absolutely, at least once a month." When the doctors asked me whether I heard voices, I lied to them because I didn't want them to think I was crazy. I thought people who heard things and saw things got locked up, and I didn't want to be locked up.

After I got out of the hospital this time, the public mental health system gave me services. They helped me get back into housing, they helped me find a job again, they gave me a nurse and a case manager. I had been in two other states and in Canada, and nowhere did they wrap services around a hospital stay. It was always a three-day supply of medication and "Good luck, Mr. D."

I worked for several years and started feeling a little better. But then I thought, "It's hot in Arizona, I'm going to Florida." I am a survey engineer by profession and had been working as a surveyor in Florida. I called my old boss, "Hey, do you have an opening?" He said, "For you, come on over." Within a month of arriving there I started spiraling down again. And once again I attempted to end my life.

I was in my apartment, and I took all of the medications I had. I had anxiety medication, sleep medication, and two types of antidepressants. I took the anxiety medication and the antidepressant medications, then the sleeping pills, about a hundred pills altogether. I knocked myself out for about forty-eight hours.

It was a Friday. Someone came knocking on my door at noon on Monday, because I didn't show up for work. I had woken up a few hours earlier, but was totally out of it. I couldn't stand up. When I had taken the last pill on Friday, I had fallen onto the floor from the couch I was lying on. I had vomited and had lost body fluids. When I came to on Monday, I hallucinated. I saw spiders and scorpions and snakes and bugs and ants crawling all over the place.

On Wednesday I called a friend in Arizona and asked, "Will you help me get back there?" Within a few weeks of arriving in Arizona, I met with a new doctor and was finally diagnosed with bipolar disorder. With the correct medication and support, I was able to start moving forward in my recovery. Slowly I got into working in the behavioral health field. I told someone a little bit of my story. They said, "Can you share your story with my case manager? I think it might have some merit." I did, and then I started working as an advocate for people who are in recovery.

What keeps me going now is that I am able to use some of what I've been through to help others get their lives back. I talk to groups about what is important and how they can develop the attitude that life can get better and that they matter and that people care about them. I use my personal story, and I use the values we hold near and dear in recovery—hope, respect, meaningful activity, compassion, helping others, helping ourselves.

From time to time, the thought of killing myself still pops up. "Why is life so difficult? It would be so easy if I were gone." But then I think of the old axiom, "Suicide is a long-term solution to a temporary problem," and when I do, I get hope again and want to keep living.

If Randy had been correctly diagnosed and given support services, he may have been able to tackle his issues earlier. When he finally had the proper medication for his bipolar disorder, along with good support, he was able to function well. He was, in fact, able to thrive by helping others who were suicidal. He could live out the values of compassion and respect and could impart hope to others, which was nearly impossible to do when he was depressed.

Randy's story demonstrates the claim made by Penny earlier that succumbing to suicidal impulses is a product of the stresses one is subject to from one's environment and brain chemistry along with one's own choices. His story also demonstrates the truth that revitalizing one's life often needs both a lessening of the stresses one is subject to and a choice. Neither by itself has as much efficacy as both together.

EVA: IN AND OUT OF HOSPITALS

Eva attempted to kill herself several times. She has had cycles of being in a psychiatric ward, feeling better, then going back to the psychiatric ward. We talked when she was twenty-two.

When I was five or six, I got a lot of verbal abuse from my extended family. One aunt said things like, "You'll never be anything. You're useless. You're lazy." One time she got a medal for singing and I said, "Oh, I want a medal for something." She said, "You'll never get anything like this." Other people in my family were good at making smirky comments out of nowhere, like "Those are nice shoes. Did you get them at a gas station?" Everyone gets teased, I know, but I think I took it harder.

As I got older, I was ignored. At Christmas and other events, I sat in a corner quietly and my aunts and uncles didn't say anything to me. They did not even acknowledge that I was there. My parents didn't do that, but they were very busy and gone to work a lot. Often they didn't know what I was doing.

I got teased a lot. On the school bus we had assigned seats, and I had to sit next to a girl who said nasty things to me. She made fun of my drawings and my clothes and everything else. I came off the school bus crying. When I was in second grade, there was a new girl who was having a hard time. The teacher asked for a volunteer to show her around and be friends with her. I volunteered. But she ended up being mean. One day she took her backpack off and swung it at my face and broke my glasses. I bled. She did that kind of stuff all the time.

When I got to be eleven, I was overweight and didn't have many friends. One day I said to one I did have, "You know, I've been sad as long as I can remember. And these kids keep teasing me. I am going to go to the woods and shoot myself."

My dad had guns because he's a hunter, and he had a revolver. When I was out on a bicycle trail, I found a hidden entrance to a clearing in the woods. I thought that would be a nice place to shoot myself. That's what I wanted to do–go into that clearing and shoot myself.

The person I told this to went to the school counselor and told them what I had said. The counselor was mean to me, too. She said, in a punching tone of voice, "I don't want to hear this ever again." She told my parents that I needed therapy. That's when I was diagnosed with a kind of depression called dysthymia. It is not as severe as major depression, but it lasts for a long time. I got on medication and started therapy. I didn't have major suicidal thoughts after that, though I was still depressed.

I started cutting when I was in eighth grade. I cut my forearms and wrists, not very deep, just enough to make them bleed. When I got angry about my life, I took it out on myself. That felt as if I was doing something about my problems instead of just sitting there thinking, "Why is this happening?" I could cut and make everything better. After I made a cut, my arm tingled and it felt really good. I did this until I was seventeen, when I was a senior in high school.

For the two years prior to that, I had been struggling with a bad drinking problem. I took vodka to school in a water bottle, and when I went home I drank probably half a bottle of Jack Daniels.

One day, after I had gotten home from school, I was doing my homework. I had already been drinking for quite a while that day. My dad came into my room and said something about how I would never get a boyfriend with my legs all hairy. I had not been shaving my legs because I was in a feminist phase. That comment of my dad made me angry at myself. I felt worthless.

I went into the living room, where I slept. I had all my medications there–my antidepressants and headache pills. I started shoveling handfuls of them into my mouth. I just kept taking them and taking them. I was so upset that I wanted to die. I felt, "My dad doesn't approve of me. Nobody likes me at school. I'm useless. I have nothing. I have no reason to live anymore." I kept taking those pills.

Then I started vomiting. My dad heard me, and I don't know how he knew, because I had put the bottles away, but he said, "What did you take?" I couldn't say anything, so I showed him the bottles. He took me to the emergency room, where I had to eat charcoal so I would throw up.

I started hallucinating. And I kept holding my mouth open. I was told to close it, but I couldn't for more than a couple of seconds. They thought I was messing around with them, but, really, I was out of my mind. Then they wanted me to do a urine sample, but I couldn't do that either. Somehow they found out that my kidneys had failed. At one point, I went unconscious and stopped breathing. They had to put a tube down my throat so I could breathe.

I was flown by helicopter to a children's hospital. The charcoal started working, and I vomited everything up. When I recovered, I was sent to a psychiatric ward. They put the law on me there, and I had to stay. They watched me very closely. If I had tried to kill myself again, they would have hospitalized me for a long time.

I stayed in the hospital for about a week. I hated being there–I don't like being forced to do things. A judge and a lawyer came to the hospital and I signed some papers agreeing to supervision. I was released a few days after that to my parents. I was not allowed to drink or do drugs, I had to keep all my appointments with the therapist and psychiatrist, and I had to take all my medication.

There were only two weeks left until graduation. The school I went to understood what had happened. They said, "You don't have to go to class anymore. Just come back for your exams, and you can work on them at your own pace. Then you can graduate with everyone else because your grades are good."

Most of my teachers understood. They talked to me when they brought the exams to me because I was taking them in a room by myself. They said, "I hope you're feeling better. If you have trouble with anything on the test, just leave it alone and I'll grade what you have." So I finished all my exams, got some decent grades, and graduated with everybody.

I tried going to college, but I stayed there for only three months, because I wasn't going to classes. I slept all day. I did not feel good and I did not make friends. So I left because my depression was getting in the way of school.

After that I lived with a boyfriend for a while. When he broke up with me, I wanted to jump out one of the windows where we lived. It was the second story, so jumping would not have done much to me. But I was sad that he didn't want to be with me anymore, because he was very kind and it felt good to be with him.

When I was twenty, I lived with another boyfriend, and he was very abusive. He beat me up all the time. He tried to isolate me from my family and friends. I wasn't even allowed to go anywhere without him. I was expected to do the dishes and clean the apartment. If it wasn't sparkling when he got back, he would be pretty mad.

> **"I felt very alone."**

There were a couple of times when I got sick of living with him. But I could not leave because he wouldn't let me contact anyone.

One night I drank a lot of brandy and locked myself into the bathroom and took a bunch of sleeping pills, thinking they would kill me. Instead, I just blacked out. I don't remember going out into the hallway and biting one of the neighbors, but that's what the neighbor said I did. So I was taken to the hospital again, where they pumped my stomach.

When I was living with the second boyfriend, I called the cops four or five times and said I was suicidal, just to get away from him. He made me feel so bad that it was hard to get through the day. I thought I was worthless. That's part of why I felt I couldn't leave him. I felt I could not do any better: "This is what I deserve. This is the best person I can get. No one else is going to want me except him."

Once I tried to slit my throat with a big knife. My boyfriend and I were drinking in the apartment and got into a fight. I wanted to leave, but he sat on the floor right in front of the door. I couldn't move him because he is bigger than I am. And I couldn't get out of the apartment any other way. I thought, "My only way to get out of this is to kill myself." But before I could do that my boyfriend grabbed the blade of the knife to get it away from me. He cut his hand pretty badly. I was afraid to call 911 because I thought my boyfriend would say I was trying to hurt him on purpose. I had already been in jail because I was constantly calling the police for domestic abuse.

I left him on the floor and ran outside. He was bleeding a lot, but I did not care what happened to him. I hid in an alley behind the apartment building. Somebody called the cops, or maybe my boyfriend called them, I don't know. They found me and they found him. He actually told them the truth—that I had been trying to hurt myself, and he had grabbed the knife, and I had not intended to hurt him. So they took me to the hospital instead of to jail.

We both ended up back in the apartment. That's when I finally decided to leave him. I thought, "If I don't leave, we're going to kill each other." My parents came to pick me up. While they were on their way, I was putting everything into garbage bags. He kept ripping them open and flinging everything out. I thought, "He's not going to let me leave." So I called the police to make him behave while I was packing. They came and watched while I got everything ready.

My parents arrived and took me home. I was finally free. It felt really good to be out of there. Actually, it was hard because I didn't believe I was good enough even to leave him. I had to force myself to believe that I was good enough to leave him. And I felt pretty good for a while.

Last year, though, I made another serious attempt. I had gotten my first job, at McDonald's. I had never had a job before, but I needed money, so I thought, "I guess I'll try working." I wasn't sure it was going to work because I get stressed out easily. And when you have depression, you can't call in and say, "I need a day off" if you are having a bad day. But I thought, "Okay, I'll try."

I was very surprised when I got hired. I had done interviews before, but nobody ever called me back. So I was pretty excited that they wanted me at McDonald's. I thought, "I'm going to have a job! It's going to be cool!"

On my first day, I spent about six hours watching videos about how to do everything. Then at lunchtime they had me cook stuff at the grill. After about two hours there, I couldn't take it anymore. It was too stressful. They wanted everything done yesterday. And it kept going and going. There was no break because of the lunchtime rush. It was so crazy.

I started crying a little bit, but I kept on trying to work. I thought, "I can't. I can't do it." So I went to the back room. The boss came up to me and said, "Hey, what's going on?" I said, "This is very stressful. I don't know if I can do it. I'm really scared." He said, "You know what? You can go home today. Come in tomorrow and see how you do then. Give it another shot and we'll go from there." That was really nice.

The next day they started me on the grill right away. And, again, after about two hours there, I couldn't keep going. I couldn't fry all those foods. So I said to the boss, "I'm going to have to quit. I just can't work." And he said, "You know, that's okay. Thanks for trying." After I quit, I went home and started drinking the vodka I had at home. I thought, "Man, I'm such a failure. I can't even work at McDonald's. That's supposed to be easy, something anyone can do."

I told my parents I was going for a walk. I wasn't too sure, though, what I was going to do, and I wasn't thinking too well, because I had been drinking. I walked to a bridge that goes over a nearby river. There was a drought that summer, so the river was pretty low. I looked over the railing and thought, "Oh, I could jump off this bridge. I could die and I wouldn't have to worry about bills and not being able to work." So I sat on the railing with my back facing the river. I saw that the river was shallower on the other side of the bridge. So I went to that side of the bridge and sat on the railing, again with my back to the river and holding the railing.

By this point, my parents had gone out looking for me because they knew I was upset. My mom found me, parked on the bridge, and called my dad. She looked at me but was too shocked to move. She saw me let go and fall into the shallow water.

It felt as though I was falling for a very long time. I still remember the feeling in my stomach. I thought, "Oh, when am I going to stop falling?" The bridge is probably thirty-five feet above the water.

I hit the water, and my head hit rocks. That cut my head open. I became disoriented and couldn't move too well. A guy who was going for a jog saw me and went into the river and pulled me out to the shore. I was embarrassed, because my attempt didn't work. I was angry, too, and disappointed.

My dad arrived and both my parents ran to the riverbank where I had been pulled out. A bunch of other people had gone down there by then. And a funeral procession was passing. A kid had hung himself. I didn't know that then, but when I found out later, I felt really bad. Here I was, in the water, having tried to kill myself, and these people from a suicide funeral were driving by.

The emergency people got me strapped to a board. They wanted to make sure that my back wasn't broken. At the hospital, they did x-rays and CT scans and stitched up my head. A cop came into the room after I was done being taken care of. He said, "I'll give you a choice. You can either go willingly into a service program or I can make you go." I said, "I am not going anywhere. I'm going home. I don't want to go to your stupid service thing." But I ended up saying, "Fine, I'll go to this voluntary thing."

My parents drove me to the place. The next morning, though, I thought, "Hey, I'm here voluntarily, so, I can leave whenever I want." I wanted to leave right then. I called my parents to come pick me up. They wanted me to stay, but they didn't have a choice, because otherwise I would have been wandering the streets of the city I was in. So they came and picked me up.

A few days later, a social worker came to my house. He had read my file. After talking to me and to the police, he decided that I should go to a hospital to be medically cleared. The police took me to the hospital, where I was tested, and then I spent a week at a psych ward.

I have been trying to stay out of the hospital since then. Whenever I had gotten out of a hospital in the past, I felt confident and happy. At first I told myself, "Life is worth living. You are a great person. This is going to be great!" But then the despair started to set in again, and it got harder and harder to fight it every day. Eventually it got to the point where I wanted to make another attempt or I had a serious talk with my therapist and doctor about how bad I was feeling. I have been trying to stop this horrible cycle. Recently I finally quit drinking and am hoping this will help me curb my impulses to harm myself.

What keeps me alive now is that it is not worth it to try again and fail and then get laughed at. And sometimes, not all the time, I believe life is worth living. Right now I have dreams I want to fulfill. I want to finish college. I want to start a career. I want to get married.

Also, I can't let my parents find me dead. That would be terrible. I sometimes imagine what it would be like for them if that happened. I go hunting with my dad in the woods, and we get separated sometimes. I could easily shoot myself. But I don't, because my dad trusts me with his gun and this is our trip together, this is our time to bond. I don't want him to hear a gunshot and then come looking for me and find me with my head blown to pieces.

Most people don't have to fight to stay alive, but some people do. Though there were times when Eva kept going pretty easily, there were other times when she was in survival mode—it was a battle for her just to keep living. She finally decided that she didn't want to go through these cycles anymore. The desire to pursue her dreams now makes it easier for her keep going. And she doesn't want to hurt her parents.

8   A STRANGE IMPULSE

Sometimes people aren't too sure why they do things. An impulse comes, and they act. At twenty-five, Emilee still doesn't know why, as an eight-year old child, she wanted to die. Her account of cutting when she was a teenager follows the story of her near suicide.

EMILEE: EIGHT YEARS OLD

Looking back now, it feels so strange that I would try to kill myself when I was eight. I got along well with my parents, but their punishments could be too harsh, bordering on physical abuse. And I highly suspect that I was sexually molested as a child, because I have odd memories of a man in my extended family or among family friends who scared me. He always touched me and was too attentive to me, and he put me on his leg and tickled me, which made me feel uncomfortable. I hid in the bathroom whenever he came over. I don't have any actual memories of the sexual abuse, but it feels as if it actually happened.

One night when I was in second grade, I was in my room by myself. My parents thought I was asleep because they had put me to bed, and the door of my room was closed. For some reason, I became angry and upset, and I felt something like fear, something like rage, but I didn't know what I was fearful of or raging against. Suddenly I had the idea "I should jump out the window." It felt as if I was being controlled by something outside of me, or maybe some part of me.

I went to the window, opened it, and climbed up so that I was sitting on the window sill, with my legs hanging out the window. This was the fifth floor of an apartment building. I looked down, concentrating, about to jump. I was there for at least several seconds, maybe even half a minute. I didn't make any noise, but I pulled my hair or did something with my hands to my head, still angry and upset. Then all of a sudden I called to God–silently–and instantly the feeling of being controlled left. I realized what I had been about to do, and I panicked. "Oh, my gosh! What's going on? I don't want to do this. What am I doing?"

I panted hard as I climbed back down, and my heart beat super fast. I sank to the floor, crouching on it against the wall, still holding onto the window sill, and crying. I was afraid to look up. Then I closed the window and got away from it.

I can't remember anything that happened right before this event that might have triggered it. The only thing I remember is that around that time I sometimes got scared out of the blue, and I didn't know what I was scared of. One time I cried out my mom's name, "Mom! Mom! Help! Help!" She came to my room, and I told her I had heard a voice in my head. Actually, it was more like a buzzing sound, almost like flies. It was creepy, and I thought it was Satan or something. My mom got freaked out. I did not have any suicidal feelings before that night, but that night I definitely wanted to die.

Studies show that a certain percentage of suicide attempts occur within five minutes after a suicidal impulse occurs in someone.[1] The impulse, though, is almost always a product of some discoverable background condition that produces it, such as depression or stress. Though Emilee mentions a couple of things that could have produced her suicidal impulse, her case is strange because it is not clear what actually did produce the impulse. What saved her, though, is pretty clear— the fear of doing something that would be irretrievable. That scared her into crawling back inside.

Cutting

During the very first interview for this book, Marissa showed me the scars on her arms from cutting while telling me her story (which you can find on page 132). A number of other people whose stories are in this book also cut at some point.

For many who are suicidal, cutting is a way of keeping suicide at bay. Sometimes it is an expression of self-hate and a sense of worthlessness. Often it relieves inner pain. Cutting is almost always more than a one-time occurrence—a habit, sometimes an addiction that is hard to break unless the underlying emotional trauma is addressed. In what follows, Emilee explains what cutting meant to her when she engaged in it as a teenager.

When I was fifteen I got depressed after moving to the United States from another country. I was homesick and was bullied pretty much on a daily basis at school. I started cutting myself then, and after a while I got psy-

---

1. Characteristics of impulsive suicide attempts and attempters, by Thomas Simon and others. In *Suicide and Life-Threatening Behavior,* Volume 32 (2002), 49–59.

chologically addicted to it. At one point I couldn't go more than a day without doing it.

It made sense to me at the time to hurt myself, because it relieved inner pain. I also cut to relieve the urge to kill myself. I had a lot of self-hate, and cutting was a way of self-destructing without doing it completely.

I visualized killing myself. When I walked along the sidewalk, I imagined jumping into the road in front of a passing truck. I thought, "I should do this," and in my imagination I hoped I would die. That was almost a vicarious thing that replaced the actual trying. Cutting was, too.

At first I cut my arms. But people started commenting on it. So I hid the scars with bracelets and long sleeves and started cutting my legs and hips and other parts of my body. I didn't want my parents to see the scars, because they were worried about me.

My parents found out about my cutting when I went to a counselor at school. A classmate could tell that something was troubling me, and she had noticed the cuts. I talked to the counselor for several hours. The school had to call an ambulance to take me to the hospital because they were afraid I might kill myself. They called my mom, but they didn't let her drive me to the hospital.

The hospital wanted to commit me to the children's psychiatric ward, but my parents talked them out of it. The cuts weren't very deep, and they weren't bloody. So the doctor at the hospital just gave me a prescription for depression, which I ended up not taking because my parents and I were iffy about taking a medication after seeing only one person. But I kept cutting myself, and shortly before turning sixteen I went on a cutting binge. I cut down my entire shin. It was bad, and there was a lot of blood. My mom caught me, because my pajama pants had dried blood on them. She freaked out and called the doctor, so I was taken to the emergency room at the hospital again. This time I went to the psych ward. There was no getting out of it. I was there for about ten days.

After I got out I started seeing psychologists and took medication. I saw a lot of different professionals, but there was one who helped me the most. She showed that she cared about me, and she was also patient. Other therapists I had seemed to get impatient. One woman I went to cut short my visits because I didn't say anything for ten minutes or so. I gave her artificial, shallow answers. But the patient person waited and waited. It took three or four months for me to open up to her about my real problems. But when I did, my depression got better and my cutting went away. I saw her for about a year. That was when I was sixteen and a half.

There have been periods since then when I have cut myself. I did it a few times when I was eighteen and again when I was twenty. I haven't done it for several years now, which feels good. I still get urges to cut, though. Just last week I had an extremely strong urge to do it, and I almost did. The only thing that kept me from doing it was that I knew how much it would upset my husband.

People cut for the same reason that leads some people to the bottle. If someone hits rock bottom, they get drunk. In the same way, cutting is a means of dealing with things. It is not a good one, but it does help to relieve pressure. For me it relieved the pressure that had built up inside me and made me feel better. Though it caused physical pain, at the same time I kind of liked it.

When Emilee felt that someone cared about her, she could talk about her problems, and the need to cut disappeared, for a time at least. She was tempted to cut again when she got depressed. Her account demonstrates the truth that the best way to counteract a desire to harm oneself is not to try to fight that desire in a raw battle, but to foster positive emotions. In a battle, one could easily lose. But with positive emotions, the desire itself dissolves.

9 PARENTAL ABUSE

Perhaps the most heartrending provocation of suicide attempts is mistreatment at the hands of one's own parents, especially when one is a young child and cannot easily cope with it. "How can parents do something like that?" one asks in astonished reproach. Here are two stories that end well despite the deplorable abuse their tellers suffered.

ROBYN: LIKE A PACK OF HYENAS

How do you deal with a mother who tells you repeatedly that you are worthless? What if you asked to see a counselor for family problems and were told that they were all your fault and that you had to pay for counseling yourself? What if you lived in a family in which everyone turned on everyone else, like a pack of hyenas? Robyn lived through these, survived a suicide attempt, and is now a social worker. She was in her late twenties when we talked.

My mother is pretty significantly mentally ill. She has a borderline personality disorder, though she is high functioning. Maybe the best way to describe her is to say that she's bipolar but with the intensity turned up a thousand degrees. That means she has extreme highs and lows, so there were days and weeks when she did not leave the couch, did not bathe or shower or do anything else. At the other extreme, there were nights when she slept for just an hour or two. She stayed up and painted. Or she made clothes for me and my older sister.

She was a fun mom sometimes. She did all sorts of projects with us and played with us. But sometimes the mania was not fun. One time when I was twelve she got hysterical and put me and my two younger sisters into the car and drove us to a different state a thousand miles away. I don't think we told my dad that we had left. My mom was speeding, so I was worried we might drive off the road. The whole thing was scary.

Part of the struggle for the kids in my family was that we were asked to become the adults a lot of times and to take care of things we shouldn't have had to take care of. When my mom was not getting up off the couch, it was my job to figure out what we were going to eat for dinner and to make sure that my sisters had clean clothes. So when we were driving that thousand miles I was trying to figure out how we could have a safe place to sleep that night.

In our family the role of scapegoat swapped. Four people were on her good side and one was on her bad side. Most typically that was my dad: He didn't love her enough, he didn't take care of her enough, he didn't work hard enough. She repeated these over and over.

Sometimes I was the scapegoat. More than once she told me and my older sister that she would have to have two more kids because her first two had turned out so rotten and so poorly. Sometimes she said she was depressed because we didn't love her enough or because we weren't doing the right things. Whenever she said these things, it created a lot of anxiety in me, whether they were directed at me or someone else in the family.

When she was mad at my dad, I tried to be extra good because maybe I could perk her up and fix the tension. Or if I was the one who was bad, I tried to disappear into the wall so that I didn't have to hear anything.

Although the big things were upsetting, such as the time she drove us away, the little things that were repeated over and over hurt the most. When I made little mistakes, she said, "You always do that." When I didn't want to go play at my friend's house, she said, "You're always not going to your friend's house, you're such a bad friend."

All of these picked away at my sense of self-worth. They communicated to me that I wasn't good enough. My mother said, "I wouldn't be on the couch if you had eaten your vegetables last night, or if you hadn't said you didn't like what I made for dinner, or if you hadn't left your stuff all over the house." If someone were to say these things to me now, I would say, "That's the most ridiculous thing I've ever heard, that's craziness." But as a kid you don't know anything else. I was four, six, ten, and I thought, "She wouldn't be like this if I picked up my room more."

My sister who was born just after me is deaf, and my mom wanted her go to a school in another state, where she could learn to talk. One day my mom just disappeared and drove to that state with both of my younger sisters and enrolled the one who was deaf in the school and bought a house there. My dad and I were still at home, and my older sister was in college. My mom called and said, "If you and Dad want to come live with me, you can, or you two can just stay there. I don't really care, but this is what I mean to do with my child."

Looking back as an adult and trying to feel some of the emotions I must have felt then, I realize that the experience was devastating. I was fourteen, and even though my mom was unpredictable, I still wanted her around. The fact that she up and left hurt. I felt abandoned.

My dad lost his job sometime after that, and he sunk into a pretty serious depression. He became even more withdrawn than he normally was. It was never very safe to be snarky with my mom, but I could say mean things to my dad, like, "I hate you, you're a failure," or "I would have fired you, too." Nasty, nasty things. I was trying to get some sort of emotional response from him. If I could say something that made my dad angry, at least I got something. That would have made me feel less alone, I think.

The decision was made to move to where my mom was at so that the family could be together. But moving didn't keep us together. At times there were big explosions between my mom and my dad. Sometimes my dad was relegated to another portion of the house, and you weren't supposed to acknowledge that he was there, which was very confusing and awkward. And you never, ever had your friends over because how in the world were you going to explain this bizarre thing that was going on with your parents? Eventually they separated and my dad moved into an apartment right next door to our house, which again was awkward.

These were hard times for me and my sisters. It was difficult to listen to our parents shout and scream at each other. The way I typically felt was, "Thank God it's not me." If my dad was taking the heat, then that meant I wasn't taking the heat. I still tiptoed around, but I didn't have to worry about my mom lashing out at me, because she focused her energy elsewhere. Unfortunately, when my dad moved next door, my mom didn't get as much of her emotional needs met, so I ended up being the new scapegoat in the house.

Families with dysfunction are like a pack of hyenas. Everyone turns on everyone else, and you are as suspicious as you can be with everyone. It's kind of like kill or be killed.

Ever since I was very little my mom punished me by ignoring me. She said I just wanted attention, so the only way to break whatever habit I was doing was to ignore me completely. That hurt just as badly at five as at fifteen. No one spoke to me. I was in the house, I was in the room, people were laughing, doing an art project or watching TV or having dinner, and I was not acknowledged as being there.

This was one of the breaking points for me. My dad wasn't in the house anymore. No one in the house was talking to me. I felt disconnected from my friends from where we used to live. I had some new friends where we moved to, but I didn't let them get too close, because they might start asking about things that were going on in our house.

Then I got into a riff with a friend. Her boyfriend had made a comment that I was the funniest girl he knew, which probably just came out of his mouth without any thought. But any teenage girl knows that that is a recipe for complete catastrophe. My friend got very upset and started icing me out, and one of her friends sent me an angry e-mail letting me know that I was the worst.

That cut my last little thread of human interaction. I had my own phone line at the time, but my mom had taken it away, so I couldn't talk to any of my friends. I was crying in my room and my mom heard me and came in and asked, "What's wrong?" I told her what had happened, and she said, "Well, if you weren't always trying to be so funny and be Miss Popular, you wouldn't have issues like this."

It felt like nothing was ever going to get better. I couldn't control anything, and I was in a lot of pain. I had asked at several points, "Please can we go to counseling? Can we just go together? Please can we try to work this out?" My mom said, "You're the sick one. If you want to go to a counselor, you get a job and you pay for it."

> *"Depression means that you are despairing in the truest sense of what that means—you have no hope. You stay in bed because you cannot conceive of a reason to get out, because there's just no point."*

At some point earlier it had occurred to me that I could kill myself and that that was a very large, permanent solution to whatever was wrong. I don't think I ever really considered it very seriously. So I don't know whether a lot of thought went into what happened next. I remember standing in the bathroom, looking at myself in the mirror and thinking, "It would feel so good to get relief from all this." At the time I didn't believe in God, and I believed that if I died, that was the end and there wasn't anything afterwards. That sounded really nice.

There was a bottle of family-sized aspirin in the medicine cabinet that was about three-quarters full. I took all of it. Pretty calmly. I don't remember feeling panicked or trying to shove it down or making a rash decision. I took as many as I could without choking. For the first time I felt there was going to be some relief. That was very comforting to me. I walked back to my bedroom, closed the door, lay down, and went to sleep. I thought, "Okay, this is going to feel a lot better in just a little while."

I wasn't looking for attention. To attract attention in my family was not desirable. That wouldn't have done anything for me. On the contrary, I had been spending weeks, months, trying to blend into the furniture, trying not to make too much noise, not doing anything wrong, because I didn't want attention on me. The last thing I wanted was to wake up.

Although my mom had taken away my phone line, she had plugged in a phone upstairs with my number, and one of my friends wanted to talk to me. Because he was a teenage boy, when no one picked up, he called back, over and over and over. My mom got tired of listening to the phone ringing, so she picked it up and said, "Who is this?" She shouted to my bedroom on the lower level, telling me to come and get the phone.

My mom had to go downstairs and shake me to wake me up. I think I had slept for three or four hours. I went up upstairs. I was very groggy and started to feel sick to my stomach. Before I could get to the phone I had to make a beeline for the bathroom, and I started throwing up. What came up was very foamy and had a lot of blood in it because the pills had started to make my stomach bleed.

My mom gasped and asked, "What did you do?" So I told her. I wasn't angry. I wasn't trying to throw anything into anyone's face. I was ashamed that I had been caught. My mom said to my dad, "You better take her to the hospital." She went over to the phone and said, "Robyn can't talk right now. She got melodramatic and tried to kill herself." Then she hung up. My dad didn't say anything to me on the way to the hospital. But he cried silently, tears running down his face. I felt ashamed that I had made my dad cry.

In order to get me to throw up, the people at the hospital made me drink tar, which clung to what was in my stomach. It was horrible to get down, and when I threw up, it tasted awful. The nurse who was helping me drink it was being empathetic and rubbing my shoulder and telling me it was okay. I don't know whether it was too much for my dad or whether he had to do paperwork, but he wasn't in the room, and no one else in my family was there, either.

After an hour or two my mom and sisters came to the hospital. My mom was irritated with me. I'm sure she was brokenhearted and upset and helpless and overwhelmed, but the way that was manifested was in sarcasm. She made some sort of comment like, "Well, it is the attention you need."

At that time the law was that if you made a suicide attempt you had to spend three days under watch at the hospital, so they transferred me to a children's hospital. Hospital policy was that they had to put me into an ambulance to take me there, which elicited another snide remark from my mother: "How much is that going to cost us? Much less than a funeral, I suppose." I was ashamed and embarrassed.

I went alone in the ambulance. My mom had told me at the first hospital that she wasn't going to reward my negative behavior with positive attention. So they would see me when I got out of the children's hospital. I spent the next three days at the children's hospital alone. Those were the three worst days of my life. It was so horrific. It was so lonely. I don't know how to describe the way it feels when you're a teenager and you've tried to kill yourself and your family will not come see you.

The nurses checked on me from time to time. There was also a volunteer who came. I begged her in my mind to say something to me, to ask me whether I was okay, or just ask me anything. It didn't have to relate to what had happened, just say something to me. But she was young and probably had no idea what to say, so we just sat there. That was pretty awful, too.

My parents were required to meet with the hospital social worker and me. The social worker told me I could be charged for what I had tried to do. I had tried to kill someone, which was very serious, and technically I could go to jail. I think she was trying to get me to feel the seriousness of what I had done. It didn't feel serious to me. I didn't feel that I had done anything wrong. I just felt ashamed that I had brought so much attention to myself and my family. And I didn't feel relieved that I had been caught. Certainly spending those three days alone wasn't a relief to me.

Part of the role my mother played in our family was to define things that were going on around us. So the way the family chose to characterize what had happened was that I was looking for attention and that I had done something dramatic to try to get it. I was a teenager. I was very emotionally volatile and had done this dramatic thing on a teenaged emotional whim to get attention. This was my mother's way of dismissing what I had done. I absorbed that, and that is how I described it, too, not just to the people I had to explain it to, but to myself as well. That's the mantra I repeated.

My mother had made several suicide attempts herself. My attempt must have stirred up a lot for her. She couldn't come to see me in the hospital because she couldn't handle what that might have meant for herself. "This is your punishment," she told me. The legal requirement was that I would meet with a therapist after I was released from the hospital. I don't know how many times it was required. If anyone had any sense it would have been multiple times. I went once. I'm not sure how we got away with that.

My dad was supposed to take me to the appointment, which I was relieved about, because I was trying to avoid my mom. But she ended up taking me instead, and I was very anxious about that, because I didn't want to be alone with her. On the way to the therapist she coached me in what to say. She said things like, "We need to go to the counselor because it is required, but we don't really need to go, and you know you don't really need to go, right?" I said, "Yaaah." She said, "You know it was really an emotional explosion, that you were feeling down because of the mean thing your friend said to you, but now you are feeling much better and you are never going to do it again, right?"

The thing with my mother is that she knows how to talk to people. She has probably seen a dozen counselors in her life and has gotten a clean bill of health when she wanted one. She must have said what she thought they needed to hear. So she passed that knowledge on to me that day in the car.

I was alone with the counselor, and I said exactly what my mom and I had talked about. The counselor said, "I think you are a very intelligent, well-adjusted girl, and you are just having a hard time with the move to another state. The girl in your class was very mean to you, but you know that killing yourself isn't a solution." That was the last time I talked to a counselor while I lived at home. My mom started speaking to me again, but we never talked about my suicide attempt, and no one ever asked me what was going on or how I was feeling.

Working at a hotline for teenage suicide prevention was one of the first steps in my emotional healing. It gave me an understanding of suicide, and it gave me something to stand on when my mom said that she had tried to kill herself because I was such a terrible daughter. I could say back, "That's not true. That's not what suicide is about." Moving out of my mother's house was another step in healing, though I still struggled with depression and anxiety and constantly worried about what was coming next. And I constantly had a nauseous stomach, because I tensed up and was waiting for some bad thing to happen. That was when I was seventeen, a little more than ten years ago.

I don't know whether everyone who has made a suicide attempt feels the way I do, but I feel as if it is like malaria. Once it gets into your body, it stays there. During my later teens and early twenties, it came up on a weekly basis as a legitimate option when things were going wrong. The more intense things got, the shorter my list of possible solutions got. And the shorter the list became, the more danger I was in of making another suicide attempt.

When I was twenty or twenty-one, I was having a hard time finding a reason to continue getting up and taking a shower. I was very shut down emotionally and could not have told you what I was feeling. I was just blank. The only thing on my list of solutions was to kill myself. By this time I had developed a really important, very supportive relationship with my older sister. She came over and asked me, "Do you feel suicidal?" I said, "I've thought of it. I don't have a plan. But it's out there as an option."

She contracted with me, "Can you promise that you won't hurt yourself and that if you are going to hurt yourself you will call me?" For some reason that worked. I think it was because of the human connection. My to-do list got one step longer—call my sister, commit suicide. She also made me promise that I would make an appointment with a counselor.

The counselor helped me acknowledge that I was anxious, which enabled me to start picking apart why I was anxious. A lot of it had to do with repeating the patterns of my family. For example, I was dating someone at the time who was doing just what my parents had done. That felt very hurtful to me, but it was also very comfortable.

I also became a Christian when I was twenty, and that contributed to my healing. It gave me something to aspire to. It gave me something to hope for. I started having a picture of the type of parents God wanted me to have. And I started feeling that I had value. I think that was the first time I felt that. I was lucky enough to be in a church community in which people had healed from abuse or depression or mental illness themselves. So I was in a place in which I could finally verbalize some of the secrets I had been keeping. That was healing to me, too.

One thing that keeps me alive now is that counseling has given me hope that I can break some of the patterns I grew up with. Earlier I thought, "No, things can never get better. This is the way it has to be." I have been liberated from that. I can breathe again.

I also finished the college degree I was working on forever, a bachelors in social work, so now I am a real live social worker. I work with women who are in a really dark place. I know they can get out and that they're valuable and beautiful. I love going to work every day.

I had a client who tried to kill herself last weekend. I wanted to go visit her, but I was nervous because I didn't know what to say. When I got there all I could offer was to be with her and to tell her I was glad she was alive and glad she had not succeeded in taking her life. I don't think anyone else said that to her. It is what I wish someone would have said to me. Being able to speak that way to someone keeps me going. It gives me purpose and drive and satisfaction.

The thought of killing myself still occurs from time to time, and the old feelings of fear and anxiety get dredged up. But now I know I have the strength to move through them and that there is hope waiting for me on the other side. I find myself feeling liberated and skipping through the house. Staying alive is so worth it. It is so worth it.

Often there are a number of factors that enable one to step away from suicide. For Robyn there was working at a suicide hotline, becoming connected to her older sister, being in a supportive church community, good counseling, and becoming a social worker who was empathetically present with her clients. She learned that there is something about giving herself to others that keeps herself alive and well.

CATHERINE: LOOKING FOR A NORMAL LIFE

Catherine grew up thinking that the trauma she experienced was normal. The first time she sensed that something was wrong occurred when an outside agency investigated her family. Some years later she was diagnosed with dissociative identity disorder, and she had to cope with alternate personalities within her, one of which wanted to die. She was finally able to start college in her early twenties and live a normal life. Catherine's account of people who said to her, "Just get over it," and her account of losing friends as a result of her difficulties, follow her story. We talked when she was nearly twenty-four.

My father was in Operation Desert Storm in the first Gulf War. It was hard on him, and he had already descended into a bad state of mind by the time my older brother was born. He was physically abusive to both my brother and my mother.

I have gotten different stories about my birth–my mother says she wanted me but that my father didn't, and my father says he wanted me but that my mother didn't. I don't care who is right. All I remember is that my father molested me from the time I was very young. My mother knew about it, but she blamed me for it. She formed the attitude that I wasn't so much a victim as that I was stealing her husband from her. She was very possessive of him even though he was beating her and my brother. She was desperate to get him back from me.

My parents divorced when I was not quite four, and from then until I was fifteen I lived with my mom and older brother. My brother took his frustrations out on me. I was his punching bag. Sometimes he threatened me with a knife. That went on until I was thirteen, when I offhandedly told the school counselor that my arm was sore from when my brother had beat me up. She looked at me and said, "Can you tell me more about that?" So I told her what was going on at home, and she asked me to go to the nurse's office. My mom got called in. When she got to the school, she was in tears and said, "I'm sorry, I didn't know any of this was going on."

When it was just her and my brother and me at home, my mother was an entirely different person from who she was in public. I eventually came to distinguish them as the good mommy and mom. The good mommy was the one who pretended to be nice. And mom, or mother, as I referred to her, was the real person at home.

Child Protective Services got involved. This was the first time I felt injustice from a situation I was in, because Child Protective Services said, "This situation is not good for you. It is wrong that it is happening." Until then, as far as I knew, everything that was going on in my family was just how things were. I didn't have friends at school, and I was never socially accepted, so I didn't have anyone to talk to so that I could realize my family situation wasn't normal. Everything—the way my mom treated me, my brother's treatment of me—was just normal life to me.

Child Protective Services mandated that my brother and I could not be in the same house together by ourselves. What resulted from this ruling was that my brother was allowed to stay at home after school and I had to stay at the school library until my mother got out of work and could pick me up. But sometimes the library closed early, or sometimes my mom stayed out late. So after the library closed at nine, I had to wait outside the library for her. I knew deep down that the situation wasn't right. My brother had done something wrong and he got to be at home, while I had to be outside waiting.

What finally turned my thoughts around about my mom was when my brother and I started visiting my dad and his new wife on school breaks. Being there revealed to me how abnormal things were when I was living with my mom. The first time my brother and I stayed with my dad, we didn't shower for three days. My dad finally said, "Why don't you take showers?" My brother said, "You didn't tell us we could." That was how it was done at my mom's house. We weren't allowed to do anything unless we were told beforehand that we could. So the difference between my mother's house and my father's house was eye-opening. And it was enraging. I was angry that my mother never told me there was another kind of life than the one I had been living.

When I was about fourteen, my mother started to snap. There were times when she came home at 2:00 a.m. on a school night and threw open my bedroom door and screamed at me that I hadn't cleaned something. I got up and did it again. One time, though, I looked at her and said, "No, I have to get up in three hours." For the rest of the night, she sat outside my door and threw things at it. She shouted at me and cried. I put on my earphones and put on music and went back to sleep. When I woke up in the morning, she was gone.

About this time my mother started hiding all the food in the house and wouldn't buy perishables you could put into the fridge. She bought dry food and locked it in the closet in her bedroom. I lost a tremendous amount of weight, and the teachers at school thought I was anorexic. There was an investigation of that. My mother came to school and was in tears about how out of control I was and how I stayed out until all hours of the night. She was pretty sure I was doing drugs and drinking and having sex. I was listening to all this and felt totally defeated, because I knew there was no way I was going to be believed over her. None of those things were true. I had never even seen a joint, and I didn't have people who liked me enough to offer me drugs. I just sat there and felt as if I was dead.

A few nights later I eavesdropped on a conversation my mom had on the phone with some agency. They said they were going to put me into a program for out-of-control youth. I was so angry, I called my dad right when I heard my mom get off the phone and said, "I want to come live with you." So I moved in with my dad when I was fifteen.

For the first year or so that I lived there, things were great. People at the school I went to seemed to like me. Before, people had never talked to me unless they wanted something or were picking on me. I felt I was getting to live a life I had only heard about before.

That lasted about a year. Then things began to change. My dad or his wife said things like, "Can you go get something for me?" When I got it for them, they said, "Why did you get this for me? I didn't ask for that." This was infrequent at first, but it got more frequent. Eventually I was accused of lying and trying to traumatize them. I didn't understand what was going on. I thought maybe I was lying, or crazy, or imagining they were telling me to do those things.

Once I had two friends over to my house. We were in my room. I was angry about something and I punched the wall. My dad came up the stairs, came into my room, grabbed me by the hair, dragged me back down the stairs, and threw me into a chair in the kitchen. He screamed into my face.

I was so shocked that I started to scream back at him. But I got no more than three words out of my mouth when his hands were around my throat. He was choking me, strangling me. I immediately shut down. He said, "If you ever raise your voice again, I'll snap your effing neck. Do you understood?" I said, "Yes." He let me go. I fell to the floor. He told me to get up and get back onto the chair. So I did. While his hands were on my throat, I looked over at my stepmom. She was just sitting there, placidly watching. I began living in fear.

At school my group of friends ostracized me. Somehow it turned into the entire school hating me. I couldn't go to school without some kind of harassment, and it became too much for me. I don't consider what happened next a suicide attempt, but I overdosed on sleeping pills one morning before school. The night before, I had cut my arms severely. They were bleeding badly, and I had wrapped them in Ace bandages. I drove to school, got into the building, and walked part way to the guidance office before I lost consciousness.

I woke up in my physician's office with my father and my stepmom. The nurses were putting new bandages onto my arms. The doctor was recommending a bunch of stuff, and the decision was made to pull me out of school. This was also the recommendation of the principal and the administration of the school. They didn't feel it was safe for me to go to school anymore. The staff could see that other students were cruel toward me. My nose had been broken two or three times, and I had a deviated septum.

I needed only two classes to graduate, so I studied at home and graduated the following summer. That was when I had my first psychiatric hospitalization. It wasn't because I tried to commit suicide or was cutting myself that I was hospitalized. There was so much in my life that was wrong and I had no way to make it right. I was confused because everything was so convoluted in my head. I didn't understand what was going on—"Am I making all this up, am I a liar?" I thought everything was my fault.

I was eighteen when I left my dad's house. He wanted me to go to college straight out of high school, but I didn't have the mental capacity to go to college at that point. He said to me, "You either find a place to go or I'm going to make you a ward of the state." So I went.

For about eight months I stayed with random people, until finally out of desperation I called my mom. I hadn't spoken to her in several years. I told her I needed a place to go to and could I come back? I was nineteen when I moved in with her and her husband.

It was the same scenario I experienced with my dad—life was wonderful for about a year. Then the same things started happening. This time it was not that my mom hid food from me, but that I got in trouble for eating. If she came home and I had a sandwich or salad, she got angry at me. What bothered me most was the guilt she placed on me. Guilt can be so powerful when it is placed on you by someone you are supposed to look up to and love as a parent. She had people thinking I was a terrible daughter who was hard to live with. She said things like, "She did this, this, and this." There may have been some truth at their core, but they were so grossly exaggerated that if I had had a salad she would say I ate half of what was in the refrigerator. She said these things within my hearing, as if she didn't know I was standing there. I never tried to defend myself.

One Sunday morning when my mom was washing dishes, I decided to ask her what I had been doing wrong. I had never done that before. I went up to her in the kitchen and said, "What have I done? What have I done that you're so mad at me for?" She said I made her life hard and she was tired of me. Then she walked away from me.

I didn't know what I could do, but I knew I had to leave. I had a car by then, so when my mom and her husband left for church, I packed all I had into my car, left my mom a note, and drove away. For the next week I drove to places during the day and slept in my car at night. None of my friends who had previously offered to let me stay with them actually let me stay with them. But they were angry at me for sleeping in my car. "You shouldn't be doing that," they said.

By the following Sunday, my mind was gone. I didn't realize it then, but I wasn't functioning in reality anymore. People at the church I went to had an intervention for me. They told me they felt I needed to be psychiatrically hospitalized. At first I said, "No, no, I don't need that. I'm fine, I'm fine." I was obstinate. But they said, "We really think you need to." They spent three hours with me, and finally I said, "Okay, I'll be hospitalized. You can hospitalize me."

At the hospital I met Dr. M. He was the one who eventually gave me the first diagnosis I was able to work with. I had been in psychiatric care since I was eleven, and had had all sorts of diagnoses tossed my way. The main one was bipolar disorder. I was never able to be stabilized on any kind of medication. Dr. M. diagnosed me with DID, dissociative identity disorder. That's a modern term for multiple personality disorder. I was in the hospital for nineteen days. During the entire time, I was trying to accept the fact that Dr. M. could be right. He told me all the indicators, and I discovered that I had all of them. I never knew that I was abnormal. I thought everyone's mind worked the way mine did.

During the next year and a half I was hospitalized more than a dozen times. Two of the hospitalizations lasted a month, and both of those were after suicide attempts. I spent that year and a half figuring out what dissociation is, how it starts, what causes it, how to live with it, and how to recover from it.

Even though dissociative identity disorder sounds fantastical and unrealistic and is hard to fathom, it really is a case of having more than one person living inside of you. Those persons are called alters. I had alters that were angry. I had alters that were sad. I had alters that were happy and functioning. The problem was that each of these alters could function in only one emotion. You couldn't ask an angry alter to be happy or sad, because she didn't know how.

When an alter is created, her job is to deal with a certain kind of experience or to separate a particular memory from the rest of the alters so it doesn't affect them. Dissociation is a survival tool. I had alters that had secrets for many years, secrets of pain they couldn't share with any of the rest of us because they weren't allowed to. It was their job to keep the secret. So part of working with alters was to figure out who was hiding what and why and to help them get over their pain. My alters were all ultimately me, but their pains were separate from me.

When you try to recover from dissociative identity disorder, you try to integrate all the alters into one cohesive person. Dr. M. warned me that sometimes alters can separate themselves again if they need to after being integrated. I tried to help my alters who were hurting or in pain. If an alter was still very raw in their emotional trauma state, I didn't try to integrate them. Dr. M. helped me with the alters that were more volatile. I did the majority of integration by myself at home.

Once alters are given acknowledgment and validation, they take that and run with it. They say, "Oh, I'm allowed to exist now, so I'm going to exist." And then they get out of control for a while. My angry alters were excited that they were finally allowed to express that anger in other places besides just in my head. Some of my alters were just moody and bitter, but others were hateful and wrathful, with constant rage, and wanted to die.

I had an alter whose name was Hannah. She was probably the angriest alter I had. The difference between Hannah and another alter, Nadine, was that Nadine was pleasant and happy and great to be around. Hannah was moody and hateful. She was the one who attempted suicide the first time.

What caused her to do that was the memory of becoming pregnant by my father when I was a child. I couldn't verify some of the memories my alters had, but the pregnancy and the abortion I had could be, which made it painful for me to deal with. It wasn't something I remembered. It was something one of my alters was carrying for me. That's the purpose of alters. When something is so painful for the whole, for the rest of us, an alter can be created that is able to handle that kind of pain and keep it from the other alters.

I was on a lot of medications, and one of my alters had been stockpiling them. I didn't know she was doing that. The host alter is the alter that is supposed to handle the other alters—to be "out." I don't know who my host alter was at the time, but she didn't get to be out as much as we needed her to be, because she didn't realize we weren't taking our pills and that someone was stockpiling them. Whoever overdosed took about six full bottles of different medications and also cut my right wrist—cut the vein open in two places.

Whichever alter was functioning at the time wasn't able to stop the other alter from doing those things. But after the other alter did them, she regressed back inside and someone else came out and called 911. That alter unlocked the door and then passed out. When we woke up we were in the intensive care unit at the hospital. We were in the mental section of the hospital for thirty days, trying to cope with the agony. This was three years ago in March.

The second suicide attempt wasn't nearly as severe, and I didn't end up in the intensive care unit. I didn't pass out, because one of my alters had called a friend beforehand and said, "Hey, I think we are going to try to kill ourselves. Can you please come over and help us?" By the time my friend arrived, the alter had taken only one bottle of pills, and she hadn't cut at all. My friend drove us to the hospital, and we were in the psych ward for about a week. This was in May of that year.

> *"After my suicide attempts, one of my best friends accused me of doing them just for attention. That was a knife into my heart."*

My most severe attempt took place two weeks later, in June. I was at my friend's house, and as far as she knew, I was doing well. Once again, one of my alters had been collecting medications, including over-the-counter pills. She took at least seven or eight full bottles of medications. There were well over 200 pills. In the midst of taking pills, she cut our wrist in the same area again. It was still healing from the previous cuts, but she cut it again. My friend wasn't supposed to be home until around midnight, but she came home early and called 911.

I woke up in the intensive care unit again. I had been in a coma and was on a breathing machine. I was very disoriented and had no idea what was going on. All I knew was that my angry alters had rage because we were still alive. They had failed in committing suicide. I know it is strange to tell someone I survived trying to kill myself by calling 911. But there were literally two different personalities functioning in me, one that wanted to die and one that wanted to live.

The turnaround came because the alters that wanted to get better really did want to get better. All we wanted was to live independently and have a normal life. The people who used to pick on me said, "You'll never be normal." But being normal was my fantasy. I never fantasized about being rich or traveling. I just wanted a house and a job and a husband and kids someday. I wanted a quiet life. I didn't feel that I had any semblance of a life. I felt I was living in an extended purgatory in which I was waiting–waiting and waiting and waiting. But I didn't know what I was waiting for. I just knew that I was tired. I was exhausted. I couldn't sleep enough so that I wouldn't be exhausted. And I was angry. I hated everything, but I couldn't scream enough to make myself not be angry. I was sad. I was depressed. But I could not cry enough not to be sad anymore. I cried and screamed and slept. That's all I did, but it was never enough.

At one time I had a strong support group and people who were dedicated to me. But one by one over two years they said to me, "I can't handle what you're going through," and "Your suffering is making me suffer." I lost them all. I lost people I loved, people who said they would be there for me.

The people who stayed the longest were the ones who inflicted the most emotional damage on me. They said things like, "You never think about how hard it is to deal with you. You always think about how much pain you're in. You never think about the pain we're in from dealing with you." That was hurtful, because it wasn't true. I was painfully aware of how difficult I was to be with. I was difficult to be with myself. I couldn't stand being with myself. I could not take a break from myself. Others could leave if they wanted to, but I couldn't leave myself. All I had was pain, and there was no place to go to escape it. And I didn't have any hope that I could escape it.

My psychiatrist, Dr. M., was a very, very, very good man. I couldn't afford the co-payments when I first went to see him, so he waived them. If I needed to be in his office for three hours, he would let me be there for three hours. It wasn't a case of "Get medicated and go home." He had a lot of faith in me from day one that I had the ability to live the kind of life I dreamed of. My dream was to go to school, have a job, and live quietly. He had every confidence I could do that.

There were no more suicide attempts, though I did have suicidal ideation for a long time. The idea that death was the easier option was still very attractive to me. I didn't know what it was like not to be in pain, and I wasn't convinced that having a normal life was worth it.

With dissociative identity disorder, you're never alone, because there are always voices chatting away in your head, sometimes saying random things about nothing, sometimes saying curious things. It was never quiet. But as integration took place, it got quieter and quieter and quieter. It was actually unnerving at some points how quiet it was. I had to force myself to confront the fear of being in the quiet. When the noise in my head was gone, I had to have music playing or the television on just for background noise, because I could not stand how quiet it was in my head.

The transition of going from abusive, unhealthy, dysfunctional thinking into functional life was difficult, because I didn't know what functional life was like. Living normally was off-putting. I found myself looking for things that were wrong, and sometimes I saw things that weren't there. I had to teach myself what normal was and how to be okay with it.

It turns out that I am very good at fixing computers. I started by fixing one person's computer, then the computer of a friend of that person. I did not have any formal training, so I decided to go to school to try to make a career out of it. The very fact that I'm able even to consider going to college and that I've been independently planning my life is phenomenal to the people who know me. No one except Dr. M. thought I could get better. No one thought I was capable of living without government aid. I am still on some government aid, but my goal is to be off it within the next two years.

What I like about myself now is that I have been able to handle situations that could have caused me to regress. It has been a huge thing for me not to get overwhelmed by stressful situations. I learned coping mechanisms in the hospital–how to implement them and which ones work for which specific situations.

I haven't had the idea or even the desire to die in five months. It trailed off until it became non-existent. I learned how to acknowledge my pain in a healthy way. It still takes a lot of effort just to maintain my sanity. But with practice, it has gotten easier. It has gotten easier to learn how to live.

I have lived too much. I don't like that, because I missed out on a lot. It took me a long time to accept the fact that I don't have a childhood friend I will remember fondly. I have friends now, and I love them, and I know they love me. I am not causing them grief with constant emotional anguish. I love my life now. I have an apartment of my own. I have furniture. I have money that I've saved up. I have income from the computer business.

For those not acquainted with dissociative identity disorder, Catherine's story and her renewal are nothing short of amazing. Her determination, or the determination of one of her alters, plus expert guidance and loving care enabled her slowly and with much effort to find a normal life. She acquired plans for her future, became able to function well even in stress, and gained a love of being alive.

"Just Get Over It"

In Aleksandr Solzhenitsyn's One Day in the Life of Ivan Denisovich, *Ivan, who is in a Nazi concentration camp, asks, "How can a person who is warm understand someone who is cold?" Ivan is cold and hungry and brutalized by his captors. He wonders, with some bitterness, whether anyone outside the camp can understand what those inside the camp are going through.*

No doubt those who feel suicidal wonder whether anyone who has never been suicidal can truly understand them. That is a fair question. Without certain kinds of experiences, people may not be in a position to understand others' suffering.

At the same time, nearly everyone has had feelings of hopelessness and rejection, even if these are not as intense as suicidal people feel them. And nearly everyone has been in a situation in which it was difficult to find a way out, even if the situation was not as extreme as those in which suicidal people often find themselves. Based on these experiences, nearly everyone can imagine what it must feel like to want to kill oneself. Human imagination is extraordinarily creative. It can be harnessed to give the gift of understanding to suicidal people.

Still, suicidal people often feel pain at being misunderstood. In what follows, Catherine describes what it feels like to be misunderstood and gives an example of what people should not do when talking with someone who is having a hard time overcoming a difficulty.

I have found that a very common method that people think will help someone who is in the middle of emotional trauma is to try to relate themselves to the hurting person's situation. Then, based on their personal experience, they will give a brief summary of how they overcame a difficulty. The intended purpose is to instill hope. For example, it was hard for me to deal with the emotional pain of accepting the fact that I would never have parents with the kind of mother-daughter, father-daughter, relationships that I craved so intensely, and I cried quite a lot over it. A friend of mine reacted by repeatedly telling me that she had lost her father when she was a teenager and she had gotten over it, so obviously I could too.

The problem with being told that it was as simple as "getting over it," was that I was just beginning to deal with acknowledging the issue, so her words meant absolutely nothing to me. I wasn't yet capable of having hope that someday the pain would go away. My friend's constant telling me that I should just get over my pain because she had gotten over her pain, and her resulting frustration that saying this wasn't making me any better, pushed me too far at one point. I yelled at her that it was unfair of her to say that, because it was too easy for her to believe. She didn't take my anger well because she misinterpreted what I said as, "You don't know what it's like to suffer like I am right now." She yelled back at me about how selfish I was in thinking that I was the only person in the world who had ever been hurt.

I wasn't able to articulate this at the time, but what I actually meant was that it was easy for her to say, "Get over it. I know you can because I did," because she had about forty-five years to deal with the loss of her father, while I was in the very first stages of realizing that I never had a father or a mother, and that I never would. I wasn't trying to compare my pain to hers as more significant. I was trying to convey that she was forgetting how hard it was for her when she first had to confront her grief, and that if someone had told her back then just to "get over it," she probably would have reacted as I did.

It takes a long time to heal from a major sickness, whether physical or mental. Acquaintances may easily run out of patience and be tempted to regard the sick person as healing too slowly, especially if they have recovered from a similar condition. Catherine felt frustrated when a friend displayed impatience with how long it was taking for Catherine to overcome her pain.

Losing Friends

People who are suicidal need human contact. This came through strongly in Robyn's account of being in the hospital for three days without having anyone she knew visit her (page 94). In what follows, Catherine tells how her friends gradually abandoned her, which hurt her a great deal.

I had a large group of friends from my church at one point, but from the day I ran away from my mother's house, I was treated differently by them because I was constantly sad. They told me that I was too difficult to be around because I was always moping. They complained that the curfews at the homeless shelters I was at inconvenienced them.

One by one, my friends all had private talks with me, explaining in various words how they needed to put up boundaries and not be my friend anymore. They made efforts not even to make eye contact with me. Eventually, the pastors at the church asked me to stop attending church altogether because my demeanor was distracting to the other members of the congregation. All I had left of my support system was one person. And it wasn't easy for her to deal with me all by herself. She just got tired after a while, because I had no one else.

The suffering from people I loved who misunderstood me was greater than that from the ones who abused me. The phrase that always runs through my mind is, "Sticks and stones only break my bones, but words may likely kill me." Whenever I see a poster of the old "sticks and stones" adage, I want to tear it down and rip it apart. Cruel words always rumble around inside me, especially when coming from someone I love. If someone were to hate me and punch me in the face, my broken nose would have far less impact on my emotions than someone I love telling me I'm too sick for them to tolerate being my friend anymore.

I have come to understand that I was very difficult to handle at the time, especially for people whose lives were going well. Being around someone who is perpetually sad probably takes a lot of effort, and I have accepted that my former friends weren't able to exert that effort for me. I am grateful that I had one person who did, because I know many people don't even get that luxury.

I don't know whether my suicide attempts would have been prevented if my friends had stayed with me and said the right things to me at the right times. But I do think that if they had expressed more compassion and loyalty to one who had legitimate reasons to be hurting, I may have found it easier to maintain a greater desire to live.

It is difficult to judge cases in which someone decides that they no longer want to be a friend of a severely depressed person. On the one hand, it is exhausting to be around someone who is rarely cheerful or is constantly preoccupied with their suffering. On the other hand, such a person needs steady attention. Even though Catherine may have been hard to be with, she still needed that attention.

10 DEPRESSION AND ANXIETY

Depression is present in nearly every suicidal person. It can come from numerous sources—medical conditions, stress, mistreatment, parental indifference, plus all of the other sources described in the stories in this book. Sometimes the depression gets intense, while at other times it stays pretty level but is doggedly persistent. Anxiety, too, comes from a variety of sources. Here are two accounts in which depression and anxiety are prominent.

BRYAN: LONELY AND MISERABLE

Bryan spent years being depressed without realizing that he was, because he masked it in various ways. He was forty-seven when we talked.

I didn't realize I had been battling with depression from the time I was a teenager until my suicide attempt, when I was thirty. The job I had in my twenties—telecom construction—masked a lot of the loneliness and dread and low self-worth I had. When I found myself in a rut, I got busy moving to a different town, which I did every six to nine months. The excitement of a move kept me from thinking about myself much. But all that moving was not conducive to the well-being of my marriage, which had become pretty miserable, and I got divorced when I was twenty-nine. That's when I settled down in one place.

I was fine for a time after that. But the more settled in I got, the more depressed I got, because I didn't have any distractions. I started partying, casually at first, but the next thing I knew I was waking up on the bathroom floor more and more after having gone there to throw up.

Then I discovered that one of my friends was involved with cocaine. I started using it regularly. Several weeks later I had a wedding to go to. I took a shower to wash the mess off me, because I had been doing cocaine for several days. When I got out of the shower and looked in the mirror, I realized that the mess had not washed off. Cocaine had become part of my persona. I was wearing cocaine like a cheap suit. Right then and there, I decided I was done with it.

As long as you're high on cocaine, you're not depressed about anything. After it got out of my system, a few days later, the depression started coming in hard. I felt that nobody liked me. "Why do I have such a hard time making and keeping friends?" I kept asking myself. I wasn't able to connect with a woman, even though I had been on numerous dates.

Part of my upbringing was that the whole world can't be wrong. Sooner or later it's got to be you who is to blame for something: "It's you. It's you. It's you." I struggled through work each day, constantly hearing that. If I was busy enough on the job, that overcame what I had running around in my head. But I was losing that battle, and increasingly suicide became a better and better idea.

I started amassing pills. On my way home from work, when I was often half in tears, I stopped at the grocery store and bought as many sleeping pills as I thought I could get away with. That came to two boxes each time. For three weeks I sat in my bed after I got home and thought about taking the pills. Sometimes my roommate was home when I got home, and sometimes he got there a few hours later.

One morning on his way out the door, my roommate said, "I'll see you tonight." I thought, "Wow. I'm home alone for nine hours." Then I thought, "Today is the day." I dumped all of the sleeping pills into one of those red cups that college kids use to play beer pong, a sixteen-ounce cup. It was about three-quarters full by the time I finished popping the pills out of their blister packs.

I sat there and looked at all the blister packs and foil. "This is a mess," I thought. So I brushed it all up into a plastic grocery bag, walked down to the end of the block, and threw it into a dumpster at a restaurant there. Then I turned around, walked home, and made a nice cup of herbal tea. I sat down and took the pills until they were gone.

I was told later that the hospital people stopped counting the pills when they got to a hundred, because the other pile was still bigger. And in therapy later, I looked at my psychiatrist and asked, "Was that a half-hearted attempt?" "No," he said. "You were dead."

Some people say that coincidence happens. Other people want to thank God. I don't know which it was. On that particular day, my roommate decided at lunch time that he had had enough and came home. I had taken all the pills and laid down to go to bed. He found me on the front porch. I woke up in the hospital four days later. Actually, I had woken up numerous times. They kept sedating me because I was not happy about being awake and was very antagonistic to the nurses. They couldn't even take my vitals. As soon as I came to, they put me right back out because they couldn't deal with me.

I signed the discharge papers with the names of Walt Disney characters. Then the ambulance came and I was taken to a residential treatment center, where I spent the next five days. The antidepressants they gave me started to work, and eventually I settled down. I became less angry and less antagonistic. The hospital people said I had clinical depression.

Several things kept me going after I got out of the hospital. One was that I found my birth mother. I was adopted as a baby, but my adoptive parents died by the time I was nineteen. In the months after my attempt, I petitioned the court to release my adoption information. I got the entire file, including my birth certificate. It named my mother. I sent seven dollars to the state in which I was born and got a copy of her birth certificate. That named her mother, my grandmother. I found her, and she told me where I could find my mother.

I had a lot of questions to ask my mother. When we met she reached into her purse, then into her wallet, and pulled out an old black and white Polaroid picture of me. All of a sudden I had no more questions. That one simple gesture answered ten thousand questions. When I tried to kill myself, I had no mother. I didn't care enough about anything to stop a suicide attempt. Now I did. I also found someone I could marry a couple of years later. She had two kids, and we had a happy little family. I still had a lot of stressors, but they weren't debilitating me like they had done before.

To explain what else kept me going, I have to say that I had gotten someone pregnant back when I was twenty-two. She gave birth to a son. I didn't find out about him until he was two years old. My then fiancée, who became my first wife, spoke to the kid's mom and said, "If we ever hear from you again, there's going to be big trouble." Then she burned her telephone number. The incident wore heavily on me over the years. I don't want to say that it caused my suicide attempt, but it certainly was something I used to demean myself with.

When I married again, I was finally able to find my son. He was twelve. We connected right away, at first with telephone calls, then with a visit. Several years later, my second marriage fell apart. That meant that I could go live near my son, which I did. That was eleven years ago.

Between then and now, I can't think of how many times that boy has saved my life. He never knew he did. All I had to do was think of him, or call. "Hey, ____, how's it going? What are you up to? What did they teach you in school? What you got going on at work?" If I ever had the thought of killing myself, I would say to myself, "Bryan, what are you thinking!?"

Two and a half years ago he was killed in a car wreck. That devastated me. I thought at first that I wouldn't be able to keep going. But he still keeps me alive. I have a picture of him on my TV. And next to it sits his ashes.

When I sit down at night and watch TV, I look up and am reminded of how much it hurts a parent to have a child die. I think, "I can't kill myself. I can't do that to my mom."

Bryan discovered that his depression did not have to be debilitating. First with medication, then with finding his birth mother, marrying again, and locating his son, he overcame his despondency. The image of Bryan glancing at the picture of his son on top of his television is striking and moving.

AARON: DREADING EVERY LITTLE THING

Aaron became anxious about many things and felt himself to be the only person in the world. He lives in England and was twenty-one when we talked.

When I was about thirteen, I started noticing that I had anxiety about a lot of unusual things. I dreaded everything you can think of, such as whether I would have to buy something in a shop or eat a meal with someone or walk into a classroom where there were people or even ask the teacher a question. This built up over time and it made me become almost a hermit. I wanted to stay in my room all the time. I didn't want to go to school, and I didn't do things outside of school. I just came straight home from school after it let out each day.

The anxiety got progressively worse to the point where I thought I was being watched by people who were driving past me as I walked along the sidewalk. It felt as though I stood out in crowds. I worked up the courage to see my doctor when I was fifteen. I thought I would get some kind of magical cure but was told that it was just a phase I was going through and that it would sort itself out. I believed the doctor.

A couple of years later I started feeling a lot of self-loathing. I had extremely low moods, and I slept fourteen hours a day. I lost all contact with friends and was very alone. This was when I started contemplating what it would be like if I wasn't here anymore. I felt that I would not be losing anything, because there was nothing good in my life. I went to see the doctor again, explained everything, and this time was put on an antidepressant. It wasn't any use, though, so the doctor switched medication several times.

During that year I started looking for ways I could kill myself. I spent a lot of time on the Internet looking for methods, trying to find out success rates and fail rates for the different methods. I became obsessed with the thought of suicide. If I was waiting for a train, I looked at the rails and thought, "What if I jumped now?" I was at the point when it could happen at any second. All that would need to happen would be a click and then I'd jump. This went on for two years, and by the time I was nineteen I was nearly ready. That's when I took up smoking cigarettes. It was a way of harming myself, because I knew that each cigarette would do some damage to my system. It was also a way of trying to make myself not think about suicide so much.

I had a friend in the United States with whom I had been talking for a year. He said, "Why don't you come visit me?" I had nothing to lose. So I flew out to America and we had a great two weeks. I got to do a lot. But when I came back, I became very low. I had had a fantastic time, but came back to nothing. It felt as if I had everything stripped from me.

I started doing CBT–Cognitive Behavior Therapy–but it didn't work. When I went to a session, they gave me things to do so that I would have an action plan for the week. As soon as I left the session, though, I couldn't do any of it. One of the tasks was to get onto a bus and travel someplace. I was so cut off from everything that I couldn't do that. Then I stopped taking my antidepressant meds because I was constantly drowsy and tired all the time. I didn't tell my family or my doctor that I stopped, so I kept getting more meds. I built up a large stock of them.

> *"There wasn't enough in my life to keep me here. I had had enough.*

By November of that year, I decided that the time was right for me to go. I thought, "I'll give myself one last enjoyment, get as much out of it as I can." One of my favorite artists was playing a gig in early December. I decided I would kill myself the following day.

I went to the gig and afterwards ended up sleeping on the floor of someone's room whom I had met that night at the show. When I opened the curtains in the morning, I realized that that was the first time I had seen sunlight in two weeks. At home I always had my curtains closed. I went to bed at seven in the morning and woke up around nine at night. So when I opened the curtains that morning I was blinded by the sunlight, not having seen it for so long. I distinctly remember that, because that day was the worst I had ever been.

I went home, bought a large bottle of whiskey, and waited until the rest of my family went to bed. That was around one in the morning. I opened all the packs of meds I had saved up and took five at a time, downing them with the whiskey. My plan was to get into bed. But I must have passed out at the desk I was sitting at and fallen onto it. My mum heard me and came to my room. The rest of the pills were on my desk, so she knew what I had done. She phoned the ambulance service.

When I woke up in the hospital, I was angry at myself because I hadn't succeeded. And I was upset because of all the stuff I would have to explain to everyone. While I was in the hospital, I was diagnosed with major depressive disorder, plus generalized anxiety and social anxiety disorder. I was there for eight days, some of it in the psych ward. After I got out, the crisis team came and visited me at home to see how I was getting on.

That is one of the things that kept me alive. I felt that I was making friends, because the people on the crisis team asked me how I was feeling. I had a way to express my thoughts. I also started seeing a counselor for the first time. In the past I had only done the cognitive behavior therapy. I found the counselor to be a lot of help. I could unload all of my feelings and get everything out of my head.

The big thing that is keeping me alive now is the relationship I have with my girlfriend. She and I have been together for almost a year. When we first met, I came clean and told her about my disorders and suicide attempt. She was okay with that, which gave me a boost. Usually, suicide is viewed as a bad act, and you feel a lot of guilt for having tried it. But being in this relationship is a constant reminder that I am worth something. I am trying to stay strong for her as well.

Also, I have started to make my own music. I can put my feelings into lyrics, and I go to music gigs, where I have made some friends. When I'm feeling bad, I can go and stay with my girlfriend or other friends for a time. I'm not just cooped up in my dark room. I now have things worth living for.

A major depression resulting from living in the dark, having no friends, and constantly being anxious can be extremely difficult to fight off. But Aaron did, by accepting the sincere interest of the hospital crisis team, savoring a relationship, and creating music. Though earlier he thought that life had nothing for him, he later was glad to find that it did.

11 BREAKUP OF A SIGNIFICANT RELATIONSHIP

If you have invested intense emotional energy in someone over a long period of time, you will be hurt if that person breaks off the relationship. And if you have a history of depression or other stresses, you may entertain thoughts of suicide. The following stories show how two people dealt with breakups, first by wanting to die and then by remaking their lives.

THERESA: "I DESERVED TO DIE"

When Theresa's boyfriend threatened to kill her because she had cheated on him, she felt that she deserved the threat. Her account of what it was like to tell others about her suicide attempt follows her story. Theresa lives in England and was twenty-one when we talked.

When I was seven or eight, my mum and dad separated, and when I was twelve, my dad died. My mum and I had a bad relationship. We used to argue, and I felt like a black sheep, because all my friends had stable families. I pretended that everything was okay, but I ended up cutting myself, which was a sign that I was depressed. I couldn't talk about it, so I just pushed on with life.

When I was eighteen, we had to pick where we were going to university. I was a bit lost about life and didn't know where I wanted to go. I turned to my boyfriend, who was sitting next to me in a class, and asked, "Which university are you thinking of going to?" He put his hand over his computer screen. I said, "What are you doing?" He said, "I don't want you to go to the university I am going to, because it is my future. You should go to the one you want to go to."

That hit me hard because it meant that we were going to split up, physically at least. I pretended I was okay with it, but I wasn't. I ended up cheating on him, and after a while I figured I had to tell him, because one of our friends knew about it. So I did. He got very angry and called me names and constantly put me down when he rang me up. I thought, "He's got a right to

110

be upset," but after two months of his doing this, it got to me. When he found out that I'd actually cheated on him twice, he flipped out. He called me and threatened to kill me.

He wanted to meet up with me. We hadn't seen each other for those two months. His sister said to me, "It isn't a good idea to see him." I think she thought he was going to punch me or something. But because he had threatened to kill me, I felt that somehow I deserved it and that it was the right thing to do. That was a warped way of thinking, but it seemed to make sense to me at the time. I thought, "If he's not going to do it, I will do it to myself. I can't handle him being angry at me anymore."

I took an overdose of painkillers that you can get from any shop. I walked around to different shops, because you can't just go into one and say, "Can I have a hundred pops?" They will think you want to harm yourself. So I had to go to lots of shops. I took tons and tons of those pain killers.

While I was walking, I thought, "You should write a note so that everyone knows it was definitely suicide." I needed to get a pen and paper, so I headed toward my mum's house. (I had been living on my own at this point.) I thought she would be out, because it was the time of evening when she was always at the pub. But on the way, by pure coincidence, I bumped into her going to the pub. When I saw her, I felt an odd mixture. I was determined to end my life, but I also wanted her to look after me. It's probably a child thing, wanting your mum to help you out. Wanting to die and also wanting your mum to help you–that's a bit of a paradox.

She asked, "Are you drunk?" I told her I wasn't. But I was acting weird. She took me back to her house and was really nice to me. I passed out on the sofa. She found packets of pills in my jacket pocket, so she woke me up and asked, "What were you doing?" It was kind of obvious, so she called an ambulance. I stayed in a mental hospital for almost two months.

At the hospital, they put me on antidepressants and anxiety medication and antipsychotics. I don't think I was really psychotic. Maybe I was. I don't know. My head was in a mess. My official diagnosis was severe depression and psychotic episodes.

I have a family history of mental illness. When my mum was a teenager she was in the hospital for a bit, because she attempted suicide. And her grandma apparently had mental problems. I was about thirteen when I learned that my mum tried to kill herself. I don't like knowing about it, because it's oddly like what happened to me. My mum feels guilty about my knowing. She feels that somehow she's impressed it upon me, and she lets it get her down. I tell her that it wasn't her fault, it wasn't the reason I tried to kill myself.

I am happy now. But I have to keep on top of my mental health. When I sleep well, I feel somewhat better. I exercise, too. If I go more than two or three days without exercising, I feel like rubbish. And I eat well, too. When I was depressed, I wasn't eating anything with nutrition, just loads of sugar or a piece of toast the whole day. I make sure I see people. People cheer me up. And my mum's good. My grandma's been amazing. They keep me alive now.

When things get hard, I think of things to release tension. I am still trying to stop cutting myself, because it's not good for the long run. I'm trying to replace it with anxiety management. Also, I recently have been doing quite a lot of meditation and yoga, trying to keep myself calm. If you're feeling suicidal, you're so worried about the future and so despairing about the past that you forget about living in the moment. Yoga and meditation help me live in the present, because a lot of yoga is about not worrying about unnecessary things. Meditation is good for anxiety as well. And it helps me sleep.

If someone is fragile when a significant breakup occurs, they may not have emotional resources to survive the breakup. This was the case with Theresa. Her strategy for staying alive after her suicide attempt involved the very activities that are recommended for everyone, suicidal or not—eat well, exercise, and get enough sleep. To these Theresa added yoga and cognitive behavioral therapy. Yoga helped her live in the present instead of being consumed with guilt for the past and worry about the future. Cognitive behavioral therapy helped her change the negative thoughts and actions that had become habitual without her being aware of the damage they were doing to her.

Telling Others

It may be difficult for people who have not been suicidal or depressed to know what to say to someone who is. But it is even more difficult for someone who has attempted suicide to tell others. Will those others give you an odd look, say something inappropriate, or even react judgmentally? You can, of course, keep quiet about it most of the time, but sometimes you can't, especially if you have been a cutter and the scars are visible.

Also, as William (whose story is on page 129) remarked, "When you try to kill yourself, it defines you, especially if you live in the same place for a long time. And it leaves a stigma on you." It is hard to tell people what you have done if you know they will always think of you as the one person they know who tried to kill themselves. "I still feel shameful around others. After I got out of the hospital, I apologized to people I knew," William said. In what follows, Theresa describes what it is like to tell other people about her suicide attempt.

A lot of people choose not to say they have attempted suicide. I understand why. But I feel I have to tell people the truth, because I feel a bit weird when someone says, "Oh, I'm so sorry you had stomach problems," or whatever I made up. I don't like false sympathy.

I have a good friend who asked me why I had been in the hospital. So I told him the truth. I said that I had taken an overdose and had tried to kill myself. There was complete silence, very complete silence. I understood why he was silent, because what I had said was heavy. After a while I said, "It's okay that you don't know what to say. It's fine." He stayed silent for a long time, and then we started talking about something else. His silence was supportive, though. I didn't feel that he was angry at me or had other negative feelings toward me.

I told my flatmates in university, and they gave me some funny looks. I tried to reassure them that I wasn't planning on doing it again, because I did not want them to worry about me. They looked very uncomfortable with it. I don't remember what they said.

I had a new job once, and the person there asked, "Do you have any illnesses we need to know about?" I lied and told her I had had glandular fever (infectious mononucleosis), and she said, "Oh, I'm sorry." She kept talking about it—"Did you try this? Did you do that?" I felt really guilty. But I won't ever tell anyone in a work situation about my suicide attempt, because I have no idea who's going to understand and who isn't. Some people judge you for having attempted suicide, and they might not hire you.

Another friend has been on antidepressant medication, so he understands the mindset I am in. I told him what I had done, and he gave me a big hug. He said, "I feel sad that you felt that way," which was nice. We were walking, and after he hugged me, we kept walking.

I also feel bad about my scars, because even though I'm trying hard to stop harming myself, I still am covered with them from years ago. If you cut yourself deep, it will raise up and stick out. If you burn yourself, it makes a scar, but it's not so severe. I have to explain the scars to people or hide them under sweaters in the summer, which is pretty uncomfortable. If I go swimming I always get stares. Usually, though, I go swimming on my own. Once I went on holiday with friends to Croatia, and while they were hanging around on the beach, I went away from them because I had no idea whether they would understand the scars.

I have gone around in a T-shirt sometimes when it is hot. If I catch someone looking at me, the expression on their face gets me down, because I feel they are judging me or thinking I'm a freak. That is annoying, because I want to wear whatever I want to, short sleeves, long sleeves, according to the weather, without having to think about what others think of me.

I have started using a special gel that's supposed to reduce the scars, and they do look smoother. I have also been using a skin camouflage cream. From far away, my skin looks good. I use it when I want to go swimming in public. It makes me feel more confident.

It took courage for Theresa to tell her friends that she tried to kill herself. Although she didn't always get encouraging responses, she could live with herself better when she told the truth. At the same time, she was sensitive to her context, for she realized that some people would react negatively if they knew what she had done. She learned that it takes discernment to know which is the right context.

MARK: LOSING EVERYONE

Mark was in his first year at an evangelical Christian seminary when his girl-friend broke up with him and he lost most of his friends. His account of struggling with his Christian faith appears after this story. He was twenty-three when we talked.

Six months ago, right after second semester started in my first year at seminary, my girlfriend and I broke up. That resulted in the loss of most of my friends. After I graduated from college, my friends dispersed and I got connected to the people at my girlfriend's church. Her friends became my friends. For the first time in my life, I felt that I was right where God wanted me to be. It was as if God had said, "This is the place I have been leading you to."

But after the breakup, I didn't feel comfortable going to her church. It is very small and tight knit. So I lost contact with my friends there. I fell into a place of isolation and didn't know what to do with myself. Two weeks after the breakup, I went on a trip to Israel that was sponsored by the seminary I was attending. It was a very powerful experience. But I found it difficult to be all there. My mind kept going back to the losses I had just experienced.

At one point, those of us on the trip were standing on Mount Precipice right outside Nazareth. It is thought to be the place where the people of Nazareth wanted to throw Jesus to his death after he had declared himself to be the fulfillment of a passage in the Old Testament book of Isaiah. It was amazing to be there. However, the first thought I had when I stood on that cliff was, "What's stopping me from jumping?" It was frustrating to feel that way, because I wanted to be fully there. But I had a growing sense of hope-lessness. I wasn't sure what I would be going back to after the trip was over. The people who had made me feel that my life was significant and reward-ing would not be there.

When I got back to the seminary, I found that I had very little desire to keep going. I didn't know what church to go to or where to seek out connection again, and I felt isolated even when I was surrounded by my fellow students. I wanted to feel connected to people when I was with them. But I didn't feel that, and that made me feel even more alone. So I pulled back from others even more. It got to the point where I was actually the loneliest when I was with people.

Near the end of the semester, I saw a psychiatrist, who diagnosed me with MDD–Major Depressive Disorder. I got on antidepressants. I also started seeing a therapist once a week. But as the semester ended and summer break began, I felt myself getting worse rather than better. Just after the semester ended, I had discovered self-mutilation. It is hard for me to talk about that, because cutting is such a bizarre thing. I never thought, "You know what I can do? I am going to cut open my arteries and that will help me feel better." That is insane. Yet I fell into it. I was never conscious of deciding to cut. It just happened. Still, I was very much present while I was cutting. I think I was trying to distract myself from the emotional pain I was experiencing, just for a moment. But it didn't work. It just created more pain.

That, though, is why I think I kept doing it. I was very angry without knowing it. I was angry at the world. I was angry at God. I was angry at my girlfriend and my friends. I took all that anger and turned it toward myself. I made long, deep gashes on my left arm. I didn't tell anyone about my cutting, because I didn't know what to say. At the time, I didn't understand why I was doing it. It was a strange compulsive thing, like an addiction that kept coming back.

During the first few weeks after the semester ended, I was wrestling so much with anxiety that I wanted to be done with everything. I tried to suffocate myself with a bed sheet while I was in bed. I wrapped it around my face and neck and started strangling myself. But after a point I gave up, because it didn't seem that it would work unless I kept going at it for a long time.

Several weeks later, I spent a couple of days at a friend's house, an old roommate from college, and his wife. They knew I was depressed, but they didn't know about the cutting or the suicide attempt. I enjoyed spending time with them, but I still felt empty and lonely. As I was driving home from that visit, I thought to myself, "How has it come to this, that it hurts to be with one of my best friends and his wife–people whom I care about dearly?"

That night I went on a frenzy with pills–my antidepressant pills and whatever else I could get my hands on at my parents' house, where I was living. To top it all off, I downed some vodka. I don't know where I got that, because my parents don't drink and I only drink beer occasionally with friends. My psychiatrist told me later that if I had used any other antide-pressant pills than the ones I had, I would have died, because the ones I had combine well with other medications.

I did not go to the hospital to get my stomach pumped, because it emptied on its own. I lived in the bathroom for hours. That was the sickest I have ever been in my life. I wanted so badly to die and be done with everything, but my body said, "No! Let's get rid of this poison." I did not attempt suicide again, though I did keep falling deeper into despair and emptiness and melancholy. I think I stayed alive not so much because I wanted to live as that I felt I was such a failure I couldn't even die. Life seemed like some absurd joke.

Before the breakup with my girlfriend, it felt as though God had been leading me. I was sailing along. Then life took a hard right and I dashed into rocks. My girlfriend abandoned me, my friends abandoned me, and God pulled back. I knew in my head that these weren't what they seemed to be, but experientially the truth seemed far off. My parents, psychiatrist, and therapist all highly recommended that I go to a clinic that specializes in counseling for people who are struggling with anxiety and depression. So I did, for three weeks in their day program.

Being at the clinic was an intensive counseling experience, along with group therapy, eight hours a day. It opened my eyes to the horrible ways I was treating myself. I had been having a lot of self-talk, behind-the-scenes conversations in my head that had brought me down. It also showed me all the anger I had—at the world, at God, at people, at myself. At life, really. And the people at the clinic gave me a lot of resources to work through my anger and grief, and I learned how to face loss. The clinic is Christian, so we prayed together, did devotions, and tied faith into every program we did. I felt encouraged by that, because I felt so starved of Christian fellowship.

I won't say that being there cured me, because I am still struggling with depression. Part of what keeps me going now is that I believe I survived the suicide attempts for a reason. I have no idea what that reason is, but God does. Sometimes, though, that is very difficult for me to believe. Another part of what keeps me going is uncertainty. Life seems completely ambiguous to me right now. In one way that is bad, because I am terrified at not knowing what to do next. In another way the uncertainty is good, because good things could come from my experience with depression. I don't know what those things might be, though.

> *"Depression is not something you can just take away. You need to fight back at it."*

I am trying to hang on for dear life. I'm holding on with what strength I have left, and hoping to God that the strength is renewed every day. God hasn't failed me yet and promises never to do so.

After the breakup with his girlfriend and the loss of his friends, Mark needed to find inner resources to keep going, which he did only after he had tried to kill himself. These resources involved his faith, because having faith had been central to his life before he fell into depression. They also involved revelations about himself–his anger and self-hate–along with practical ways he could deal with grief.

Struggling with Faith

Religious faith may contribute even more to a suicidal person's trauma. Faith is supposed to help one be emotionally healthy and stable. And suicide is commonly held by various religions to be wrong. A person of faith, consequently, may feel guilt or shame when they want to kill themselves. At the same time, religious faith may be an important element in one's recovery from depression. In what follows, Mark reflects on the connections between his faith and his suicidal feelings.

One of the greatest losses I felt during the time I was depressed was access to God. It seemed as though God's voice went completely silent after the breakup with my girlfriend and the loss of all my friends. I hear God's voice very strongly through other people, so when I lost everyone, I lost God. I also hear God's voice when I'm praying or while reading scripture or meditating. But I did not hear from God for months and months. God felt very far away.

It became a lot harder to keep reading my Bible. Actually, it was painful to read it. I didn't feel that it was reaching me. It, too, seemed far off. I let a lot of lies get into me–"I'm worthless. I'm never going to get out of this. This is what life is going to be like. God must have abandoned me." I also asked God, "Why are you punishing me?" I became really angry at God.

Reading some of the Psalms in the Bible was helpful, because the Psalmists said things like, "God, how long are you going to abandon me?" It was comforting when I realized that God wanted me to stay with him even in my most incensed, furious times. That, though, didn't make it much easier for me actually to stay with God.

I also thought of Job. He argued with his friends for nearly forty chapters before God said anything. And God never answered Job's questions about why he was suffering. God just said, "Hey, I'm here and I'm in charge and I'm with you." That was enough for Job.

I didn't lose faith in God, but it was something I had to keep working at during the dark time. Keeping faith almost felt like a job, when earlier it had been a part of who I was. Actually, when I was depressed everything felt like a job—getting out of bed, eating. But they were all ways of caring for myself. Trying to keep walking with God was a way of taking care of myself.

When Mark lost his friends and became depressed, he entered into a love-hate relationship toward his faith in God. He continued to believe in God even though he became angry at God. He kept reading the Bible even though it was painful to do so. Despite his deep ambivalence, he regarded keeping his faith as a way of taking care of himself.

12   WANTING TO DIE, WANTING TO LIVE

On New Year's Day, 2007, a twenty-three-year-old man jumped from Thor's Overlook at the south rim of the Grand Canyon. After sliding for 600 feet down a sixty-to-seventy degree slope, he stopped just short of a vertical drop. After being rescued some hours later, he told the park rangers that though he had leapt over the edge of the canyon with the full intent of killing himself, he instantly changed his mind and tried everything he could to slow his slide.[1]

In 2000, nineteen-year-old Kevin Hines jumped from the Golden Gate Bridge in San Francisco. Not many survive that jump, as the middle of the bridge is 230 feet high. Hitting the water from that height, or even half that height, is almost like hitting concrete. Nearly everyone dies. Kevin survived. "The very second I let go, I knew I had made a big mistake," he said.[2]

It is impossible to know how many successful suicides have involved a change of mind at the last second. What does seem true is that many, perhaps most, people who consider committing suicide experience ambivalence. Ambivalence is defined as a "simultaneous and contradictory attitude or feeling (as attraction and repulsion) toward an object, person, or action" or a "continual fluctuation (as between one thing and its opposite)."[3] Ambivalence does not often cause anguish in daily life. But when a suicidal person experiences ambivalence, it may do so.

Anne must have experienced this ambivalence when she called friends while she was taking pills (see her story on page 145), and Dese'Rae, too, when she called her partner while cutting and drinking (see her story on page 140). When Theresa accidentally met her mother after having taken an overdose of pills, the desire for her mother to take care of her sprung up even though she continued to want to die (her story is above on page 110). In what follows, Logan tells of a suicide attempt in which he both wanted to die and wanted to live.

---

1. Michael P. Ghiglieri and Thomas M. Myers. *Over the edge: Death in Grand Canyon* (Flagstaff, AZ: Puma Press, 2012), 435–438.
2. Kevin Hines. *Cracked, not broken: Surviving and thriving after a suicide attempt* (Lanham, MD: Roman & Littlefield, 2013)
3. http://www.merriam-webster.com/dictionary/ambivalence

LOGAN: AMBIVALENCE

Logan was twenty-four when he wrote to me.

I had a pretty difficult time in high school with depression and anxiety. When I got to college, the stress overwhelmed me. I was diagnosed with major depression and social anxiety disorder. Because I was an Emergency Medical Technician and a nursing assistant in an intensive care unit, I had seen the results of several attempted suicides. So I had a good idea of what would and wouldn't work. During my sophomore year in college, I became steadily more bored and more depressed until I decided I could not take it anymore.

After several days of contemplating the meaning of my life, I walked about a mile to a local bridge, and walked out to the middle it, where the drop to the ground below was about 200 feet. I thought about what I wanted to do. I decided that, in keeping with my history of self-mutilation as a coping mechanism, I didn't want to jump off a height that would guarantee my death. Instead, I walked back to the beginning of the bridge and jumped off a part that was about fifteen to twenty above the ground. The idea was that, at fifteen to twenty feet, the fall would seriously harm me, and could possibly kill me, but wouldn't be high enough to guarantee my death—sort of a Russian Roulette thing, I guess.

I had no idea what I was in for. I hit the ground and was immediately overcome by an excruciating pain in my back and hips. I quickly realized that I was in serious trouble. It was winter, in the middle of the night, and it was cold. In the fall, both my glasses and cell phone had flown off into the dark. I have no idea how my cell phone flew out of my pocket, but it did. I discovered that I was not able to stand easily and could not call for help. For the first time, I honestly thought I was going to die, and to my relief, I did not want to die. I cannot express how liberated I felt to want to live again. Eventually, I struggled to my feet, climbed over a fence, and walked back to my dorm. My injuries were pretty substantial—a fracture to my L1 vertebrae, a fracture in my pelvis, and a fracture in my wrist that required surgery to fix.

I have gone through years of therapy and psychiatric medications since then and have come to terms with my depression and anxiety. Now I am working as a nurse in a city hospital. I am much happier now, and though I would never try to kill myself again, I credit my attempt with turning my life around and giving me back my will to live.

Logan's ambivalence was so pronounced that his suicide attempt was explicitly designed not to kill himself, though there was a small risk that it would. The effect of the attempt was to restore his will to live.

Most of us the majority of the time seem to keep living in default mode—we drift along without actually choosing to keep living, without relishing and savoring our lives. Logan's attempt did more than restore this default mode. He engaged in a good deal of effort to overcome his previous depression and anxiety and found that he could be happy in his chosen vocation.

13 LACK OF SUPPORT

Although not being helped or supported is different from being actively harmed, it can have the same result—a sense of abandonment or estrangement. If other aggravating factors are present, it can lead to giving up on life.

WILLIAM: ESTRANGED FROM FAMILY

William's life deteriorated when, at forty, the medications he had been taking for twenty years were abruptly changed. He was forty-seven when we talked.

I had psychiatric problems when I was eighteen. I was in a manic state and had hallucinations. I heard voices. I thought the CIA was after me and that everyone wanted to kill me. Nothing was real, except when I hit a police car. I had a gun at my head, but was let go and taken to another town, then arrested again for walking in the middle of the road. It was all terrifying.

At first I was diagnosed with schizophrenia. Then it was changed it to bipolar disorder, because the hallucinations stopped. After three or four hospitalizations, I was fine. I just had to take small amounts of medicine. I was a normal, functioning, working person and only saw a psychiatrist every six months. I never needed to see a counselor.

When I was thirty-seven, as I was working at my job as a roofer, I slipped and fell thirty-five feet. My whole side was crushed. After a failed surgery, I had chronic pain, plus a twisted back. Still, I was handling everything okay. I kept seeing the psychiatrist every six months, and I had no problems except for the pain in my back and side.

Three years later I had to switch doctors. I told the new doctor what medicines I had been taking, and he said, "I'm not giving you any of those medications." I had been taking high doses of different drugs for nearly twenty years. The doctor didn't offer to wean me off those drugs, so I had to stop them, cold turkey. I tried to get my old medications from other doctors, but they just looked at me as if I were a drug addict even though I had all my records. I wasn't, though. I never abused the drugs. I just wanted my regular medication.

After I stopped the medications I had been taking, I couldn't sleep. I became incontinent. I had seizures. I had been a very jovial, laughing person who turned everything into humor. But I couldn't do that anymore because I was falling deeper and deeper into illness. In the two years after going off my old medication, the only sleep I got was when I passed out from exhaustion.

I finally realized I was eligible for Veterans' Administration care, because I had been in the air force. I didn't stay in the air force long, because I broke my ankle in basic training and I went past the time allowed for it to heal. When I went to the VA, they gave me a small dose of a tranquilizer, but it wasn't enough to pull me out of the hole I was in. I asked the doctor there, "Please, can you give me something to sleep? Anything?" But he just looked at me as if I wanted drugs. I don't know why. It was very confusing to me.

During this time I was getting nothing but negativity from my parents. I had become estranged from them when I was eighteen because they thought I was on illegal drugs when I came down with mental illness. I couldn't convince them otherwise. They never changed their minds—my father still believes it and my mother went to her grave believing it. The hospital did a drug test on me, and it showed I was clean.

My wife and her family, instead of helping me, attacked me. My wife's father became very abusive, and my wife, who was very close to her father, sided with him. She was always mad at me. I had thought she understood. I was a little snappy with everyone, but I don't think I went overboard. I was always the most easygoing one in the family.

Also, my wife had come down with multiple sclerosis some years earlier. That was very traumatic to me. She got better, but she still had attacks, and I was taking care of her. I kept asking myself, "Why wouldn't she care for me, and why does her family turn on me?" because I always helped them. I kept her brother-in-law from driving when he was drunk. I picked up her sisters hours away. But they forgot about me, all because I was having problems.

I was at a point of exhaustion, terrible exhaustion, with everything that was going on—the chronic pain from the fall, which was intensified because of the other problems, waking up in the night on the floor because of my insomnia, my wife not understanding me, being attacked by her family, the loss of my medications. I needed someone to help me, but I didn't know where to turn.

I was so tired that I could barely function. And I was being given tons of steroids for my chronic pain, which was not good for a person who has the illness I have. No one understood what was going on with me. I just wanted to talk it out with someone. But I didn't have anyone.

> *"I was screaming for help, I thought that the people who loved me, and who I loved, would help."*

One night I was so exhausted I could not think straight. This was two years after I had to stop the two effective medications I had been taking. I called my wife downstairs to talk. She was very mean to me. She said, "I don't think you even like me." And she walked away. So I grabbed all my prescription medication, got into the car, and drove until I found a hotel. I had nowhere else to go, because my parents would not accept me back. And I had no friends.

At the hotel I took a bunch of morphine pills and some tranquilizer pills, nothing that had not been prescribed for me. I was really scared, because I'm a religious person. I believe in God, and I believe in heaven and hell. I believe that killing yourself is an unforgivable sin. That tells me I was not thinking straight when I took those pills. It was not a cry for help. It was real. I never thought I was going to wake up when I took the pills.

Someone found me, I don't know how. I didn't drink any alcohol, but I threw up on the floor. I was airlifted by a helicopter to the VA psychiatric hospital. I almost checked out, which I could have done, but I decided to stick with the treatment and talk to the doctors. They understood what was happening to me and where I was coming from. They pulled me out of the hole, even though I felt as if I was caged in.

My wife came to the hospital. She told the doctors things that were just hokey. I don't know whether she was confused or whether she was lying. After I got out of the hospital, my wife's family told me off. I had to apologize to all of them. I have a close friend who is a priest, and he said to me, "You were sick. That was not your fault." That gave me peace of mind. Now I see a counselor because I need someone to talk to. It is a lonely world when you have no one to talk to but yourself. Loneliness is the worst companion in the world.

One of my battles now is dealing with the chronic insomnia I have. When I can't sleep, I just sit in front of the computer or in front of the television. I watch sunrise after sunrise. But I'm learning to deal with not getting enough sleep through counseling and medication.

My wife was my high school sweetheart, but she is very distant from me now. I still can't make peace with my father. I know, though, that if I ever get to the point like I was that night, I can check myself into a hospital. There are people out there who will help you. And I'm not afraid to go get it.

Also, I've seen the aftermath of suicide, what it does to the families of the persons who killed themselves. That's another reason I won't try to kill myself again. Even if my wife doesn't care for me, I still couldn't do that to her or her family. I've seen too much grief and sorrow because of suicide. I've seen how it has torn families apart. The whole family blames itself for the suicide. I have a daughter, and I shudder to think what she would have felt if I had been successful in my attempt.

My faith in God is the main reason for never attempting suicide again. I was confirmed in the Roman Catholic Church, and I believe that if I ever actually kill myself, I would go straight to Hades. Plus, I have more zeal to live now. I believe I have to do good on this earth.

When William failed to get support at a moment he needed it the most, he ran. He decided to return, though, after he was taken to the hospital and found that the doctors understood him. Even though he still felt estranged from his father, his wife, and her family, he stayed alive because he did not want to hurt them. And he found a new passion for living.

MARISSA: FEELING ABANDONED

Marissa begins her story with her most recent, most significant suicide attempt, and, she declared, the one that will be her last. It occurred just before her twenty-first birthday. Before the attempt, she felt abandoned and alone, but the attempt made her realize that she was not alone. She was twenty-two when we talked.

My boyfriend and I had a huge fight, and he ended up getting hauled off to jail, not because of something he did to me, but because someone called the cops and they picked him up for a DUI that he missed the court date for. Everything was awkward when he got back from jail. He always talked about getting a job, but he never made any significant effort to get one. I ran myself ragged because I was supporting two adults at minimum wage.

My boyfriend was a deadbeat, but I rationalized that away. I tried to make it seem that it was my fault for the way he was. Guilt has always been a comfortable emotion for me. I don't know why. I felt that I was holding him back. I didn't want to be a negative part of his life anymore.

One evening we were hanging out in our apartment, getting dinner ready, and we wanted to get messed up that night–have a few beers, smoke some weed. At that moment I felt, "Okay, nothing is going to change with this guy. I love him too much to get rid of him. There's only one way out of this, and that is for me not to be around anymore."

I wasn't sure how to go about it, because at that moment I didn't have anything to cut myself with. That was my earlier mode. This time I went for the overdose method. You go to sleep and don't wake up. But there is always the risk of it not working, or throwing up, or being found.

After dinner we sat down to watch a movie. My boyfriend's guard was down. He was just sitting there, chilling out. To him nothing was wrong, the world was great, his girlfriend was with him. I was totally causal, too—I'm glad you're back, let's smoke some weed.

I had psychiatric meds in the medicine cabinet, a slew of everything I had been on over the years. I excused myself to use the bathroom and went to the medicine cabinet. At first I didn't think I had the proper medications, so I looked at a couple of different ones and tried to remember the combination of ingredients that would be lethal. I put a bunch of what I thought were the right ones into my pocket.

The evening went on. I figured that when I took the pills I would pass out, maybe, even, he would pick me up to put me into bed, and that would be it. I was getting more and more nervous, though. In the back of my mind, I was scared of what I was about to do. But I wouldn't let myself recognize that.

I wasn't thinking like a human. A human strives for survival, and I was not thinking about survival. I was thinking about what I could do in the time before I died. Eventually I figured I would tell him that I was taking my nightly meds, and I would just die.

At one point in the movie he had his arm around me. He wasn't even looking at me, so I figured, "Okay. This is it." I popped the pills in, chased them with a beer, and shut my eyes. He saw me take the pills and said, "Are you sure you should be taking those pills? And chasing them with alcohol?" I said, "Don't worry, I've done it before." Then I said, "I'm going to shut my eyes for a second."

I shut my eyes and waited. Ten minutes later I opened them. The pills did not have the proper ingredients to kill me, but they did have the proper ingredients to send me into some kind of psychotic rage. I got up and looked around. Something was different, something was off.

I got angry because I didn't want to be there. I didn't want to wake up. I didn't want to see my boyfriend. So I picked a fight with him. I told him what I didn't like about our relationship. Eventually we both started going nuts. He didn't know what was going on and didn't know why I was saying what I did. I didn't want to tell him that I had just tried to kill myself.

I blacked out off and on that whole night. All I remember is snippets of me screaming at him, throwing things. I ran around to all the rooms. I almost blew out a window. I found a razor blade, slashed myself up real good, and eventually blacked out entirely.

I woke up the next morning and there was blood everywhere, on the bathroom floor, on my sheets, on my clothes. I asked my boyfriend, "What happened?" He said, "I was hoping you could tell me." I was afraid he was going to leave me. I was afraid I was never going to see him again. That day I went through a big change. After so many previous attempts to kill myself, I realized that I was powerless over my own life. I realized I had no right to have total control over my own being. That was the day that I truly learned to believe in God.

> *"All desire of ending my life left."*

I went through a lot of religious turmoil when I was younger. I got involved in witchcraft at one point. I tried God a few times. He never really worked out. About eighteen I turned to Christianity, but it was empty. It was like, "I'm sick of being alone, and they tell me God will always be there. So I'll accept him." But it didn't work. The day after I took the pills, though, I felt a closeness to God that I had not felt before. It was almost as if God was right there to snatch me away from suicide. I realized that there had to be some force with me to save me from what I had tried to do to myself.

I prayed for the first time in months that day. The first thing that came to my mind was apologizing to God. I felt as if I had insulted God for trying to take my life, as if I was slapping him in the face. So I asked for forgiveness. At first I felt unforgivable. Forgiving myself is one thing that has always been extremely hard.

The attempt made me think a lot more about every little thing I did. I used to be very careless. I did a lot of really stupid things. I got high and I partied hard–popped morphine pills and took swigs of vodka. But I don't do stuff like that anymore. I think it's because I realize how fragile life is. And I want to make up to God for the times I spat in his face. I want to make up for my rudeness to God.

The evening I took those pills was probably the time I felt most alone in my life. But the next day was the polar opposite. And since that day I haven't felt alone in the same way. That's very strange for me. Growing up I've had very severe abandonment issues.

A lot of people thought my abandonment issues came from being adopted as a young baby. But that's not the case. I was adopted into a very fortunate family. My parents, my mom and dad, are the best parents I could ever ask for. My abandonment issues stem from my peers. When you're a kid, you listen to your friends. No matter how much my parents told me I was the greatest thing on earth, it was always my fault whenever I got into a fight with my friends, and I had to apologize. I grew up being taught that I was worthless by the people around me.

One time I was playing at the house of a little girl I grew up with. We were coloring. I was using the green marker, but she wanted to use it. I said, "Can you hold on? I'm almost done." She said, "Marissa, go home." That was just a little thing, and as an adult I shouldn't let it bother me. Still, it was things like that that turned me into a person who thought that everything was my fault and I always had to make up for something bad I did. I still feel that way. I still feel that I have to earn people's friendship and earn their respect. Eventually that girl got tired of me and didn't want to be my friend anymore.

At school, I was a complete outcast, getting beat up all the time, shoved into the lockers. I never really had a solid group of friends, because they saw the way other people treated me. As soon as they realized my flaws, they let me go. So my abandonment issues stem from the fear of never having anyone to really care about me.

My parents would die for me, though. I didn't realize that about them until after several suicide attempts and doing drugs and cutting myself. I knew my parents would miss me if I killed myself. I knew my boyfriend would feel bad. But I thought that other people would say, "Oh, that's too bad. I guess we always knew that would happen one day." I felt that my death would just blow over. So I didn't feel that I would make that much of a negative impact on anyone if I were gone.

Sometimes I play a movie reel in my head–the paramedic walking out of the emergency room, my parents sitting in the waiting room, "I'm sorry, Mr. and Mrs. B. , there's nothing we could do. She took a lethal combination. The toxins killed her before she even got to the hospital." The looks on their faces keep me awake at night now. That never happened before. Now it kills me to think of it, because they tried so hard for years to keep me alive. Now their caring affects me much more.

I started cutting myself when I was twelve or thirteen. Originally it wasn't a mode of killing myself. It was punishing myself–if I did something stupid, or if I felt that I hurt someone, I would punish myself for it.

> *"I'm alive now because my parents would be broken and devastated forever if I were to kill myself."*

I covered my arm with scars, and not just my arms—my shoulders, stomach, legs, even on my back. I don't know how I did it on my back. My face and my neck are the only places I don't have scars. Maybe there are 150 to 200 on my arms. It was an obsessive thing.

I've seen a lot of death. I've lost people to suicide. I've lost people to drugs. When someone died or walked out of my life, I'd carve their name into my skin. So it was as if I never really lost them. I'd always have something of them with me. You can almost see "Eddie" on my arm. One day I went over to see if he wanted to hang out, and I found him hanging in his garage.

I first attempted to kill myself when I was sixteen. I had written my friend a letter in school that day. I said, "I may or may not be in school tomorrow. If I'm not, don't worry." She knew there was something wrong with me. So she took the letter to the school shrink.

I was at home that night, sitting with a razor blade. At the time I didn't know how to cut myself to make it work. I thought that if you made enough cuts, you would just bleed out. So I went at it. All over the place. I started to get lightheaded and lay down on the bed. I thought, "So this is it. This is awesome." I felt almost triumphant. Of course, nothing happened. I was lying there, blood all over my sheets, my arms covered. It was thick. It was gross. It looked like a horror movie.

At seven o'clock my mom called me on the phone. I didn't answer. I was fifteen minutes into trying to kill myself and was starting to get annoyed because it wasn't working. So I took a bunch of pills. After I took the pills I sat down on the bed and blacked out. I woke up in my mom's car and said, "Where are we going?" She said, "We're going to the hospital." She was terrified.

I was hospitalized for three weeks, but that didn't make a difference. When I got out, I went back to high school but was kicked out several weeks later. They said I had a rage problem, and they didn't want to deal with me. Then I was sent off to a wilderness program in Arizona for two months, which was a detox thing. I spent Christmas Day at the bottom of the Grand Canyon. At the end of the two months I wasn't ready to come home because cutting wasn't my only problem. So I went to a therapeutic boarding school in Utah, then came home and went to a therapeutic day school, and finally went to a public high school, which I graduated from.

I tried killing myself two other times after graduating from high school and before going to college. One time I tried to hang myself in my bedroom and I tore the ceiling fan out of the ceiling. I had to explain to my dad why the ceiling fan was on the bedroom floor. I told him I was trying to clean it and it just fell out. He took me to therapy the next day.

The person I was dating at the time was horrible. I knew that if I married him, it was going to ruin the rest of my life. But I didn't have the courage to break up with him. Eventually I became an empty shell. I wasn't allowed to have feelings of my own. I wasn't allowed to have friends of my own. My life didn't belong to me. I didn't even have control over my own body. So I did not feel that I was killing myself with those two suicide attempts. I felt as if I was stealing from my boyfriend. I was robbing him of his little love slave.

Now things don't affect me as negatively as they used to, because I realize how short life is. I don't want to waste time being depressed anymore. I feel as if most of my life has been wasted doing that. Being sad takes up too much time and energy, and so does being upset and feeling lonely.

I'm not carrying the burden of depression anymore, not because of medications I was prescribed, not because of therapy I went through, but because of the change I went through myself. None of those things created as much of a change in me as that last suicide attempt.

I don't have much hope for the future, but I'm going to face it anyway. I recently got clean from heroin. I have a lot of hope for that. It got to the point where it wasn't fun anymore. I take each day as it comes, and I try to forget about the day before. If I wake up today holding a grudge from yesterday, I could die being angry at someone who doesn't deserve it.

This morning was one of those days when I didn't want to get out of bed. I looked out the window and felt that the sunshine was mocking me. It took everything I had just to sit up. I used to take those days and lump them into, "Life sucks, I can't deal with this." But tomorrow I could want to wake up and run out and roll around in the sunshine. You never know how you're going to feel in the morning, and it's not fair to say that tomorrow's going to suck.

I found my biological family on my twenty-first birthday. I went down to the adoption center, opened my file, and found my birth mother and two younger sisters and a brother. That felt awesome. The biggest dream in my entire life came true. There were two letters in my file. The first one was apparently written when I was sitting in a crib across the room from my mother. One of the letters said that she hoped one day I would come knock on her door. If I had succeeded in killing myself, that never would have happened.

I don't believe I'm alive for myself. My birth mother gave me life. She tried to take care of me for ten months. But she was too malnourished to breast feed me. My diapers were rags, and I was getting a bleeding diaper rash. I was sleeping in a box on the floor. I was getting horribly sick. She knew I was going to die if she didn't give me up. She was fifteen then. If I had succeeded in killing myself, I would not have been able to call her on my twenty-first birthday.

Many people who do not succeed at killing themselves are angry that they are still alive, or dismayed, or feel that they are an even bigger failure than they already feel themselves to be. Marissa's attempt, however, changed her. She began accepting that her parents cared for her, she forgave herself, she got off drugs, she didn't let negative events disturb her as much, and she found her biological mother. No longer did she feel abandoned, and the desire to end her life left.

14 SHAME AND ADDICTION

Shame is a crippling emotion. It can make one feel inferior. It can incapacitate one. And it can make one try to get rid of it in unhealthy ways or by killing oneself, both of which Joseph tried.

JOSEPH: USING DRUGS AND ALCOHOL TO ESCAPE SHAME

From his early childhood Joseph felt disconnected from others. He also felt shame, though he didn't recognize what it was until decades later. He used alcohol and drugs to evade these feelings, but became addicted to them. At one point he traded his addiction to alcohol and drugs for an addiction to religion. That didn't last long, though. We talked when he was participating in Alcoholics Anonymous. He was forty-seven then.

I am the youngest son of six boys. Two of my brothers died before I was born, and my mother was depressed and emotionally unavailable. My father was a workaholic. Although he lived in the house, he was gone a lot. He was emotionally closed, too. So early on I felt a disconnect, not part of the family, as if I was just an appendage to it. The brother who was right above me teased me that I had been adopted. To me that was validation of my fear that somehow I was different and not part of things. When I was four or five years old, I was sitting on a bench with my mother late one night, very distressed, telling her I wanted to be adopted into another family.

My brother bullied me a lot physically, and my mother didn't do anything about it. The way she dealt with our stuff was to get emotional and cry. I felt a lot of shame when I did things that upset her. It felt as if I was "less than."

Even though I was sad and felt disconnected, I remember fun things in childhood. But my innocence left when I was nine or ten. I discovered pornography, because my brother had a two-foot stack of *Playboys* in his closet. The first time I had a drink of alcohol was when I was ten years old. I got drunk and blacked out.

In the seventh or eighth grade, I had a big project due. I had borrowed a friend's answers, and I was going to cheat. Somehow I got overwhelmed. I grabbed a shotgun and headed out of the house to shoot myself. My brother saw me walking out of the house and said, "What are you doing?" I dropped the gun and ran up into my tree house. The next thing I remember was my mother screaming, "Where's my baby? Where's my baby?"

The next morning my father called me—my parents were divorced by this time—and he asked, "What's wrong with you? Are you all right?" I said, "Yes, I'm okay." That was it. No therapy. No punishment. No change. Nothing. My father never came over, never said another word other than that "What's wrong with you?" So I felt a lot of disconnected ambivalence from him.

I was drinking pretty regularly on weekends in the seventh and eighth grades. That became my social lubricant, the way I could show up in a crowd. If I was in a crowd of people without a drink, I felt all alone. But when I had a drink or a drug in me, I became a different person. I was always the one who drank five extra drinks, looking for the next thing to make me happy.

I went to a boarding school after my freshman year in high school because I thought that would make me happy. I got there, and sure enough, it didn't. I got drunk and was arrested. The first month I was at boarding school they sent me home for three days. Again, my father got on the phone and asked, "What's wrong with you? Do you want to be there?" My answer, as it always had been, was that everything was fine. So they just sent me back.

In my junior year I was feeling really sad, not part of the community at school. The night before spring break, as I was getting ready to go on a ski trip with friends, I got very depressed over a girl who was paying attention to another guy. I started to walk out into a nearby lake as if I was going to kill myself. I was alone, but a guy who was sitting on the shore of the lake said, "Hey, man. What's wrong?" So I started crying and told him how lonely I was. He said, "I'll go with you to the counselor at school." I said, "Okay."

The thing about that guy was that he was a super jock—great guy, super smart, Mr. Big Man on Campus. I took a lot of shame from that, because he was who I wanted to be. And I could never accept that I wasn't that. I felt even more shame that he was the one who wanted to help me.

I never went to the counselor with that guy because when I woke up the next day I said, "Oh, I'm okay." When I got into a bad place at that time in my life, I wanted to get away from it as quickly as I could. So either I medicated with a drug or alcohol, or I ignored it and acted as if I was okay.

My mother died from cancer at the end of my senior year of high school. I missed the whole process of her dying, because I was away at boarding school. There was no goodbye. I visited her in the hospital a month before she died when I was home from boarding school. My mother said to me, "You don't want to be here, do you?" The shame I felt from that was immense, because I really didn't want to be with her. I had wanted to go out with my friends.

In college I had a pervasive feeling that I was different. I had a lot of sadness, and suicidal ideation started kicking in. I got interested in near-death experiences and read books on it. There were multiple nights when I drove my car toward bridge abutments at a hundred miles an hour and veered at the last minute, crying all the while. Then I woke up the next day and went about life. I never told anyone what I was doing.

I dropped out of college at the end of September in my sophomore year. I called my family and said, "I'm doing drugs, I'm doing alcohol, I'm miserable." They said, "Just get home." I moved into a house with a bunch of guys who did drugs and were going nowhere. I started doing cocaine, ecstasy, acid, marijuana. You name it, I was doing it. Drinking, too. And I was still very suicidal. By March of that year, when I was twenty-one, the depression and the overwhelming feeling of aloneness got to me. I said, "I'm done."

> *"I learned early on to keep secrets. If I kept the secret of the chaos that was going on inside of me, then somehow I would be okay. I never learned that secrets keep you sick. What I learned was 'Keep it all inside.'"*

My buddies had bought a big load of acid for the weekend. I was sitting on a couch in the house about ten o'clock at night, drinking and feeling overwhelming despair and oppressiveness toward myself. I popped twenty-nine hits of acid, all at once. One hit of acid rearranges your brain pretty good for about six hours. During the next twelve hours I thought, "This is going to kill me. I'm going to die." So I wrote suicide notes up and down my arms as if I was saying goodbye to the world.

About eight or nine in the morning I began to think, "Wow, something's not working here." I walked out onto the porch just as an African-American woman was walking past. She smiled at me and said, "Good morning." I said, "Good morning" back. That was probably the most pure love connection I ever had in my life until then. I felt an overwhelming sense of con-

nection to her in spite of having been raised in the South with a very preju-
diced, racist view.

I immediately got depressed again. So I crawled up into the attic and
started to paint myself. I had in my head that if you painted your whole body
it would suffocate you. I had gotten that from a James Bond movie,
Goldfinger, in which a girl is painted gold.

I had torn up my room and had torn up some of the house, so when my
roommate came home from work, he called out for me. I called back to him,
and when he got to the attic I told him what had happened. He immediately called the ambulance. At the hospital, they shackled me to the bed. There
was a big handcuff around my ankle and a chain around the bed railing.

My father didn't come to the hospital. This was normal to me, so I don't
remember being angry. That came later. Maybe there was a hint of sadness,
but his not coming to visit me was just the way it was with him and me. I
ended up in the psychiatric hospital, doing alcohol and drug treatment. I got
into the program and was the star patient because I wanted everything to be
okay. But I had no clue who I was. I didn't know my anger, my sadness, or
my anxiety. I wasn't in touch with reality. I just played the game.

While I was there, a guy I knew came to the hospital and did the Campus
Crusade for Christ "Four Spiritual Laws" with me. For an addict who was so
messed up mentally, that sounded like the best thing since sliced bread. And
so I was "saved." I became a hard-core evangelical Christian. I was out evan-
gelizing, doing Bible studies, and going to prayer groups. I went back to college, got good grades, then went to a prominent university in the west, where
I was president of Campus Crusade for Christ. But I had no clue what it all
meant. I think what happened was that I went from one addiction to another–from alcohol and drugs to religion.

In my senior year I began to have doubts about Christianity. I intellec-
tualized everything. The Campus Crusade people couldn't satisfy me with
their apologetics. My response, in my typical black and white, all or nothing,
way of thinking, was that I chucked the Christianity because nobody could
give me the answers I wanted.

In a period of about a month I went from being president of Campus
Crusade to telling them that I didn't believe any of it. My friends told me that
I was going to hell. The suicidal ideation came back with a vengeance. I
became disconnected from people emotionally. I knew I didn't want to
return to the alcohol and drugs, so losing my religious medicator just left me
with all of my raw emotions.

I spent hours in the university library researching how to kill myself so
that it wouldn't hurt too badly. That's when I got the Sudafed idea. I took
three or four boxes of them in my dorm room one night. But I got sick and

threw them all up. That was like having my stomach pumped. I ended up being sick in my dorm room for two days. I was dehydrated, so my room-mate took me to the hospital, where they gave me an IV. Nobody ever knew I had tried to kill myself. About a month later I tried to hang myself in my closet, but I couldn't do it. I didn't tell anyone about this, either. I was twenty-four at the time.

I kept a lot of secrets–self-loathing, hating myself, suicidal ideation, overwhelming loneliness. Suicidal thinking became a comfortable place where I could escape from myself. My head was running all the time. I was a master at presenting a good front, a false self.

"Normal" people who are sad and depressed learn when they are kids, "Hey, I can tell somebody about this. It's not shame that's attached to it. It's just being human, it's being real." Somehow I missed that message. The message I got was, "Man, that just confirms I'm 'less than.' If I don't speak it, I can control it in my head. If I speak it to somebody, that makes it more real."

I graduated from the university with honors in the spring and went to law school in the fall. I had not had a drink since the suicide attempt three years earlier. In law school, I was still feeling lonely, sad, and depressed. I had dumped all the religious people, and all my friends were drinking. I said, "I'm going to have a drink." Friday night I promised myself I was going to drink only one or two beers. But when I took one drink, I was gone: "Give me another, give me another, give me another." I did that with every drink.

> *"To be human is to be broken and imperfect. That wasn't okay for me."*

Back at law school after Christmas break, I saw a movie in which someone killed a person by draining all their blood out of their body with a needle in their arm. I tried that. I took the needle from a football pump and filed it down to a sharp point. I went to the hardware store and bought tubing, which I put onto the end of the needle. It looked like a little medical device. Then I stuck the needle into the vein in my arm right where they take blood from you. I had bought a cooler, which I put beside my bed. I lay on my bed and put the tube down into the cooler. Blood started seeping into it. I thought if I could do that long enough I would go to sleep and die. It didn't work because the needle clogged up.

They talk about alcoholism as being a progressive disease. That's what my suicide history was. When the drinking quit working, I did drugs. When the drugs didn't work, I turned to suicide. All of it was to mask my pain. I was not okay feeling pain. I did not want to be a patient. I did not want to feel sick. But I never learned how to connect with people and be human.

After the blood attempt, I reached out for help. I spent nine months in inpatient therapy. I don't know what brought it about, but I made peace with some form of life and got okay enough with being me. And I went back to the faith thing. That carried me through for seventeen years. I was a church-goer, a Bible study leader, a member of a discipleship group. I went to a cool Metro Jesus church where they wear blue jeans, a hip version of Jesus. I got married, had four kids, and did well in business.

I never felt comfortable in the faith skin, though. About three years ago I stepped away from evangelical Christianity, because I still could not answer any of the intellectual questions I had. All I got were simplistic answers to complex questions. I've lived most of my life mired in complexity. People of a simple faith who have never gone through complexity, I am not attracted to. I am most attracted to people who have been broken by complexity and found a "second simplicity" on the other side of it.

The religious experience over seventeen years kept my addictions in check, whether it was pornography or lust or food addiction or isolation or taking pain pills. But it was just a shame-based thing. When I lost my faith identity again, I had nothing to keep me in check. I started drinking cold medicine, taking pain pills, and engaging in my food and sex addictions. And I was co-dependent as all get out—I judged my insides by everybody else's outsides.

Now I am going to Alcoholics Anonymous. I go just about every day. Picking up a white chip was a huge event for me, because I quit telling myself the lie that I was sober just because I wasn't drinking alcohol. I was taking my wife's pain pills and taking muscle relaxers and chasing them with cold medicine. So I was still very active in my addictions.

The first three steps at Alcoholics Anonymous have been really hard for me, because I've got a lot of religious baggage over terminology. When they talk about God and God's will—that triggers something in me. I don't like to be controlled. I don't like to be dependent.

I just did the third step with my sponsor last night. Turning my will and my life over to God as I understood him is really hard for me. Twenty-two years ago when I was in my dorm room and getting all the Sudafed ready, I yelled to God to show up and relieve my pain, and God didn't show up. I F-bombed God for a good twenty minutes. I remember it vividly—I was sitting on my bed and looking up at the wall in front of my bed, just F-ening, because I was so angry. My earthly dad—he didn't show up. God, religious God, father—he didn't show up either. So my God was a no-show, and I was pissed about that.

They keep telling me at AA, "God, as you understand him. You don't have to have a big concept of God." That's the only way I can stay in that AA room right now. I know there's something outside of myself that's going on with that community of people. I know it is a power greater than myself. I don't know who or what it is, but I'm willing to show up and be teachable.

In AA we talk about the definition of humility as being teachable. One of the curses of the addict and the alcoholic is that we think we're God. In the twelve steps, part of those first three steps is that there is a God, and you ain't it. For an intellectual like me, that's a hard thing to accept. My intellectualism is what I did for my ego. In AA that doesn't get you very far. As a matter of fact, it takes you backwards.

The first step in AA is, "We admit we are powerless over alcohol and our lives have become unmanageable." The second step is that we come to believe that a power greater than ourselves can restore us to sanity. The third step is to make a decision to turn our will and our lives to the care of God as we understood him.

You wake up in the morning and work the first three steps every day. It goes back to the evangelical Christianity I got caught up in where the gospel was a one-time event. It was mind-blowing to me to read writers in the Christian world talk about the gospel as something you get up and live and experience every day. I'm not saying you get "saved" every day. But you show up and you have to turn yourself over every day. The first step in AA is, "I can't." The second step is, "He can." The third step is to let him. This sounds like the whole salvation gospel experience to me. And I've got triggers and baggage from that.

What keeps me alive now is hope. I have a very strong feeling for what is good and virtuous. James Fowler, in his book on the stages of faith, described the third stage as driven by convention, in which people attach themselves to institutions and systems, and they operate their lives within that. The fourth stage is a questioning, angst, stage, and in the fifth stage you begin to make peace with the questions. I'm in the fourth stage. I have hope that I can make peace with the questions and that I can re-engage God from my heart instead of my head. I have hope that I can make peace with being human. Plus I have four kids and a wonderful wife, a business and friends, a great community. I'm an executive coach, and I help people navigate change. I've never felt gratitude like I have in the last three months. I pick up my red chip at AA tomorrow.

We have a little gimmick in AA–poker chips. When you want to symbolize that you're not drinking or that you have a desire not to drink, you pick up a white chip. Then you go ninety days with continuous sobriety and you pick up a red chip. You go six months and you get a blue chip. It's a gimmick that says, "I'm committed and I'm staying sober."

Life is chaos most of the time. It's a lot of questions we can't answer. But you make peace with that. I'm looking. I'm just looking in different places from where I looked in the past.

I can give a coherent narrative about the big why's and how's of life, but that doesn't get me anywhere if I can't live it into my life. No matter how much I can master that narrative, at the end of the day, I'm just a broken human looking for peace, meaning, love, and acceptance–from God, from others, and mostly from myself.

Joseph's story displays the intense, lifelong struggles that many suicidal people experience. These struggles are often cycles of victory and defeat. They are driven by a need for "meaning, love, and acceptance," to use Joseph's apt words. When a suicidal person finds these needs satisfied in a good way, their life becomes much different from what it once was.

15   A DYSFUNCTIONAL RELATIONSHIP

When a love relationship goes bad, really bad, and when one feels helpless to change things, one may feel very discouraged. If there seems to be no way to escape the relationship, and there are other provocations, the thought of killing oneself may arise.

DESE'RAE: FEELING TRAPPED

Dese'Rae requested that her real name be used. Her suicide attempt came after the relationship with her partner went sour. She is now a photographer in New York City, where she does suicide awareness work through her Web site livethroughthis.org. She was twenty-nine when we talked.

I attempted suicide when I was twenty-three, though I started being suicidal two years earlier. I was in a relationship that became so dysfunctional I could not see any way out except to kill myself.

The relationship began with a whirlwind love affair in my home state of Florida. After we had been together for only a month and a half, my partner moved to Tennessee, and I moved there, too, to live with her. I didn't know anyone when I moved there, so I had to start a whole new life, and she was the center of it. I became completely dependent on her.

After a while the relationship became emotionally abusive and I became suicidal. There was a lot of name-calling. When we got into arguments, my partner said, "Why don't you just go kill yourself?" Our arguments got so bad that I locked myself into the bathroom or whatever room she wasn't in. Sometimes she banged on the door and screamed at me. I felt trapped.

We shared everything, so I didn't have a car. But I bought one so that I could escape the arguments if I needed to. About a year before my attempt, my best friend came to visit me from Texas. This was after I had been living with my partner for two years. Right after my friend left, my partner threatened to harm me physically. I left the house and called my friend. I didn't know what to do, but for whatever reason, I chose not to leave the relationship then.

After the threat, my partner started pushing me and destroying my things. She hit me in places that weren't visible to other people–below the

140

neck or anyplace that was covered by my clothes. I finally said to myself, "This can't be happening. I'm going to have to leave if we can't figure out how not to have physical fights." I started defending myself. To me that was terrifying. I don't think I've ever forgiven myself for laying hands on her, even in distress.

At some point the fights stopped for a while. But seven months before my suicide attempt, I started one. It was on Halloween. Everything contributed to it: the relationship, cutting myself–I had been cutting for nine years–being stressed out from going to school full-time, working thirty hours a week to pay my own way, and generally feeling isolated from the world. Also, I was far away from my family, which felt scary.

My partner and I got into a terrible argument, and I decided I didn't want to do life anymore. So I bought a bottle of vodka with the intention of getting drunk and driving off the edge of one of the big ditches in the hills surrounding the area we lived in. I had already begun drinking when my partner came home and told me I was ruining her life. Her presence kept me from going through with the attempt.

Four months before my attempt, I was informed that I had gotten into a Ph.D. program back in my hometown in Florida, and I made plans to move back there. Around that time the physical abuse started to happen again. One time we had an argument in our bedroom, and she punched me in the face. That knocked me out. She is very small in comparison to me. I am five feet seven and weigh 190 pounds, so there was a lot of force behind her punch. To this day it surprises me that she could lay me out like that. But she did. I had to go to work with a black eye.

My partner and I worked at the same restaurant–we lived together, we worked together, we took the same classes when we could. The day after she punched me I was making a salad at the restaurant. My partner was standing to my left and one of our coworkers was to my right. He saw my black eye and made a joke about it. "Rough sex?" he said, implying that he knew its origin. I was mortified.

The month before my attempt I found out that my partner had cheated on me. We had talked about the structure of our relationship and had agreed on an open relationship years before. When I was interested in someone else, or had sexual relations with someone, I was open with her. But she always threw it back into my face. When I found out that she had slept with someone and was continuing a relationship with that person, I felt that she was going behind my back. I was so upset that we broke up for a time.

When we got back together, we agreed that she was going to be allowed to do whatever she wanted to and I couldn't say anything about it. I loved her so much that I wanted to try to put up with that. But it didn't last. It was terrible. I couldn't handle it. I couldn't deal with the fact that she had gone behind my back after two years of reaming me for being interested in other people when I was open with her about it. The lying was what I couldn't take.

There were still physical fights, and I kept making the ultimatum that if they didn't stop she couldn't move to Florida with me while I was studying for a Ph.D. At the same time, I didn't know what to do. I loved this person. I couldn't imagine living without her.

One day we got into a huge argument at work. We were having lunch together. It wasn't a screaming match, but it was very tense. The argument got bad, so I picked up my keys and said, "I'm going home now." She came home soon after and we got into another argument. It was loud and scary. She told me she was going to go out with the woman she cheated on me with and I was not welcome to go with them. I thought, "I can't do this anymore. I cannot live through this. I can't deal with life." That was my breaking point. I wanted to hurt myself.

I tried everything to take my mind off things. I watched TV. *Harry Potter and the Goblet of Fire* was on. I listened to my favorite music. Nothing worked. So I decided to get drunk and take the pain killers I had from the week before when I had hurt my back. I was going to slit my wrists. There was nothing that could make me want to live any longer.

I started drinking and taking the pills. I made cuts all over my body—my arms, my biceps, my stomach—but just surface wounds, not deep enough to bleed much. I called my partner and begged her to come home, but she wouldn't. I was in hysterics. I kept drinking so that I would get drunk enough to lose control of myself. When you're a cutter and are in control of yourself, you just make surface wounds. There had been a couple of times, though, when I had lost control. I still have visible scars from the deep cuts I made those times. I was hoping for that this time.

At some point in my calls to her, she hung up on me and called the police. Then she called me back and stayed on the phone with me until the paramedics and the police banged on my door. I don't remember much of what happened next other than that the police kept asking me my name. I was in hysterics and couldn't tell it to them. I did have the wherewithal to call my mom while they were there, and I put her on the phone with them. She gave them the information they needed, and then they handed me the phone. She told me to use my education to get myself out of the situation. She said, "If you don't go to the hospital willingly, it will go on your record that you were involuntarily committed, and how are you ever going to get a job in the field you want to work in then?" She said to lie to get out of it.

At the hospital they gave me a psych evaluation. They took my blood to see what was in my system. They gave me a tetanus shot. I told them I was terrified of needles, so when they took my blood they laid the vials of blood on my stomach. They never checked my body and didn't see all the cuts I had. I calmed myself down enough so as to convince the person who did the psych evaluation that I was not suicidal, and they let me out of the hospital in three hours.

My mom had called the only friend I had in Tennessee who I hadn't been isolated from. She was having a party, but she left it to come get me, and I stayed with her that night. She didn't want to take me home in the morning, but I said, "I want to go home. I have to go home."

When I got there, my partner was sleeping on the couch. When I woke her, she said, "I was looking for you. I called all the hospitals." She made herself into a martyr, as if I was the one who had done a horrible thing. She did not account for where she was all night. I said, "My friend took care of me."

I worked the rest of the week. I told my boss I was leaving. She knew something was going on with me and my partner because she could see what was happening between us. My best friend sent me enough money to get to her house in Texas. A week and a half later I got into my car and did not get out of it until I was in Texas. I drove sixteen hours straight, because it felt to me as if it was a matter of life or death. I had to get out of the situation I was in if I wanted to live. That night in the hospital I had made myself a promise that I was never going to hurt myself again.

I have handled my mental health pretty well during the last six years. There have been a couple of times when I hurt myself. Once was when my dad died four years ago, and once was earlier this year. I had gotten myself into another relationship after three and a half years of being single. That first relationship had messed me up badly, and I wanted to be okay enough with myself that I wouldn't be dependent on anyone. I wanted to know that if I got into a relationship again, the abuse wouldn't happen. I spent a lot of time with myself.

I ended up marrying the new person two and a half years after we met, and six months later she started cheating on me. I didn't handle that well, and one night I cut myself. Another night I considered suicide. Luckily I had a support system this time, and I made full use of it. The person I married wasn't abusive, but she was emotionally neglectful. She didn't isolate me from my support system, as my previous partner had done. I knew I had that. I had spent five years working on myself, trying to find better coping mechanisms and spending time on my mental health.

What keeps me alive now is my support system and the experiences I have had since my suicide attempt. I moved back to Florida and started work on a Ph.D. I decided, though, that I hated it and that the bureaucracy and the politics in it were not for me. So I threw all of my stuff into my car and moved to New York City. I had no plans. But then I found my passion in photography. I found a grown-up job. I made new friends and made a life for myself independent of a romantic interest. I met my heroes, interviewed them, and photographed them. When things have gotten rocky, I have realized that I would not have had these experiences if I had died.

The experience of attempting suicide and wanting to die made me appreciate life more. Going through a divorce tested that. While I was married, I was getting a sense of what I thought my future would be like, and I was laying a foundation for creating a family. Then a bomb went off again, and my foundation was shaken. Still, things have been getting better. I'm living a life now that is mine, that I have control of, and that I love. I have lots of people who care about me. I'm doing work that is fulfilling. I can't ask for anything better than that.

Dese'Rae's phrase, "working on myself," is right on target. After her suicide attempt, she did just that for five years. That gave her the resilience to withstand new trauma that came her way so that she would not be tempted to try to kill herself again. In addition, she discovered that she loved photography, which she now uses for her suicide awareness Web site.

16 SUICIDE OF A PARENT

The suicide of a parent can trigger a child to attempt suicide as well, though the attempt may occur years later, as it did for Cara (whose story is on page 33) and Harmony (whose story is on page 3). With Anne, it occurred some months afterwards.

ANNE: SEARCHING FOR HERSELF

Anne's father killed himself when she was forty-five, which led to her own suicide attempt. She did not understand then all that brought about her attempt, but during the subsequent sixteen years, she investigated the main motifs of her life, one of which she realized was self-betrayal for entering a marriage she did not want. In her early sixties, when we talked, she was making fresh discoveries about what she could live for.

The idea of suicide came to me after my father took his life. My mother had died twenty months before that, and three months after she died my father got treated for prostate cancer. He wouldn't accept help from anyone, so he was very alone. Then dementia set in and depression. He had just been denied his driver's license after taking the test three times. He must have come home very despondent. He was in his pajamas, the autopsy said, and he shot himself twice, in the heart and in the lower abdomen. That was what he had been taught to do in the air force if he was ever caught by the enemy and had to kill himself. He flew planes in World War II.

When I heard that my father had killed himself, I called my physician and said, "I cannot go to the funeral home and stand up all that time. I just can't." The doctor sent a prescription to the pharmacy. I picked up the pills and starting taking them. By the time we arrived at my father's house in another state, I had overdosed on the pills. I was very drowsy. I can picture myself in bed and someone saying, "No, Mom. No, Mom. Don't do that."

At the funeral the next day, my father was given a twenty-one gun salute. I got through the funeral, but I kept taking the pills. This was in February, on a cold day, with icicles hanging from the branches of trees.

At the celebration for the fourth of July that year, I listened to the fireworks going off from the boats out on the lake my husband and I lived next to. The sound of the fireworks brought back the memory of the gun salute at my father's funeral and evoked what I imagined was the sound of my father's gun when he shot himself. I replayed those sounds in my mind, over and over, as the fireworks were going off. Finally, I told myself, "I can't take it anymore. I can't take it anymore." My husband was at school in another state, so I was alone. I put on one of my favorite dresses and one of my favorite strands of pearls. I lined up all the pills I had and decided that this was going to be it. I didn't write a note.

I started taking the pills, three and four at a time. For some reason, I called a friend while I was taking them. She kept me on the line for a long time, trying to keep me awake. When I got off the phone she tried to call my therapist, but couldn't get hold of him. I kept taking the pills, and called another friend, who kept me awake for a while. At some point I lost consciousness, so I don't remember my daughter coming home and finding me, though I do remember getting into the ambulance and being strapped down. When we got to the hospital, I could walk, but like a drunken sailor stumbling along the wall.

My husband had been called, and when he arrived at the hospital, he refused to admit me. He took me home and the next day took me to my therapist, then went back to his school. Several days later, filled with drugs, I drove to my husband's graduation ceremony.

A year later I thought about killing myself again. I called a friend, who was an Episcopal priest, and said, "Will you come get me and take me to the hospital?" She did, and I admitted myself. The psychiatrist there said, "You have no business being here. You go home and love your husband and forget about all this." So I went home. Then the question was, "How do I survive? How do I find life after wanting to kill myself?"

These events occurred sixteen years ago. Only recently have I been able to discover what drove me to want to kill myself. It started when my mother made me marry my husband. I told her before the wedding that I could not go through with it, but she said, "You will not embarrass me. You will go through with this wedding. Go back to your bedroom." When I went down the aisle, I thought I was going to vomit. I lied during the ceremony.

After I had been married for a decade, my mother asked me whether I had ever really loved my husband. I was entrenched in motherhood and felt that my children were gifts to me in my marriage, so I defended myself. I did not allow myself to believe that I was really only pretending to love.

When I was told that my mother was dying, I went to her but did not arrive in time to see her alive. I reacted angrily to that, but I was not aware

> ## "*I was very good at faking it.*"

then of why I was angry. Now, sixteen years later, I have come to realize that a large element of that anger was that I had lost my chance to get even with my mother. I had wanted to tell her just how devastating her forceful manipulation of my life had been upon me. I wanted to tell her that the life force of my soul had been covered over, masked, by what she had made me do.

My true self had become a refugee in a hiding place–where, I do not know. I felt as if I were a "walking dead person," grieving my own death. I felt I had betrayed myself and abandoned myself. I did not have the power to follow the star of my own heart. The anger from all this had imprisoned me.

Another part of the whole picture is that part of me has a suspicion that I was sexually abused when I was three and when I was ten. I have never confirmed it, but I have horrific images. In one of them I see the abuser leaving me, walking toward the door and not looking back, my whole body whirling in deep emotions. In another I see someone coming into my room with a knife or a gun. These images make me feel that something has happened, but I don't know what it is or who did it. I have been in therapy numerous times for it.

After my father came home from the war he became a chicken farmer. When I was young I fed the baby chicks and helped my father grade eggs. In fifth grade I helped him build a house next to the lake we lived near. I always felt safe with my father. I thought of him as the one person who loved me. He did not verbally or emotionally abuse me, as my mother did from early on. In a child's eyes, silence is kinder than hurtful words, and I interpreted that as love. He was a quiet man who loved the earth and who was always kind and gentle to animals.

My father's taking his life in such a violent way seemed the antithesis of how I knew him. My situation was like that of the small daughter in *Hope Floats,* the movie, when she screams to her mother, "But my daddy loves me! He loves me!" and in truth he has left the family for another woman. My father's shooting himself with a gun was simply unfathomable. I never even knew he owned a gun.

Still another part of the picture is that I was not getting any attention from my husband or children. There was no intimacy in our marriage–there was no talking and no sharing. My husband had not made contact with me for five weeks when he was at school in the other state. Plus, we had just left a community that we had been in for eleven years, a community that seemed like home. I had no support. I felt very alone. And I was in desperate pain because of that.

So when I heard about my father's death, I was positioned to react to it with irrational intensity and profound depression. The lack of resolution in the relationship with my mother was still raw in me, and I felt that there was nothing in my marriage.

Eight years later I divorced my husband. That was hard to do because I had raised a family with him. But I felt I had to in order to regain the integrity I lost when I submitted to my mother's demand that I marry him. We had been married thirty-one years and had dated seven years before that.

The past eight years, after the divorce, have been a time of unraveling. I have often been lost, often inwardly foggy, but I have been groping for my own soul. I'm not sure what keeps me alive now. I do know that there's a hunger deep inside of me to know that I am loved. That's a constant search for me. I haven't left any stone unturned in that quest. I want to believe that I have inherent worth.

Maybe what keeps me alive is that I have been able to hold onto some of my own self since divorcing. I am no longer living to stay in a marriage that isn't working or living only for my children. I am learning to listen to my own heart. That's what I keep hearing again and again–"Listen to your own heart."

I was driving home from the market yesterday thinking about why I stay alive now, and an answer surfaced like an unexpected, soft breeze. I want to live a life that honors my own person. My history for years was tainted with self-betrayal, coerced circumstances, and conditioned responses. Everything I did came from a false self. I was a pretender, a woman hinged to another's life, never her own. I betrayed myself by appeasing my mother.

Amazingly, when I finally realized that I wanted to get even with my mother for what she had done to me, I experienced freedom from the anger I had at her. Now I am acknowledging my pain, not running from it as I had done my whole life. I have come to see that I must love myself.

> *"I have been running from myself for decades. Blessedly, mysteriously, I am returning to myself."*

The Sunday morning after the Fourth of July celebration sixteen years ago, I went to church. As I sat down in one of the back rows, three-year old Grace, whom I had met at a local bookstore where I worked, slowly appeared, almost climbing over the pew six or seven rows in front of me. She had a big smile on her face, and her chubby fingers made the peace sign. For a long time after seeing Grace, it felt as if she had offered me the message that I should love the child within me. She was offering me the peace of accepting myself as I am, not as someone else wanted me to be—a gift I could receive and know that I was simply and unreservedly okay.

That message faded in the coming years. In those sixteen years, and for decades earlier, I felt that I had to be something other than what I was to be loved and accepted. I felt shame and "less than," unacceptable and unlovable. But her message has come back to life in the past several months, and I have at last been able to accept the gift she offered.

It feels to me now that my creator has been waiting a long time for me to accept this gift of grace, waiting a long time for me to recognize that I had been living a false life. It feels as if I have been given a new life, one that is fresh and unencumbered. I have received the gift of being nurtured, like the nurturing a newborn child is given. Now, with the grace of being loved, the power my false self had over me for so many years has been nullified. I don't feel that I have to be someone else in order to be loved. The anxiety of trying to figure out what life is all about, which for a long time has been an albatross for me, has been washed away.

In the decade and a half since trying to kill herself, Anne wrestled with a number of weighty issues, including betrayal by her father, self-betrayal, a demanding mother, and an empty marriage. She felt that for a long time she had pretended to herself that she was something she was not. When she finally felt that she was loved, she could accept herself as she was and stop pretending. When this happened, she felt that she had been given a new and fresh life.

17 MEDICAL CONDITIONS

A high percentage of suicide attempts involve a mental disorder, such as the ones that many of the previous stories have mentioned. The stories in this section involve medical conditions, as reported by the persons themselves. It needs to be said, though, that these conditions are not the only provocation of suicidal feelings. In nearly every suicide or attempted suicide, there are a number of aggravations, including a range of environmental stresses, along with medical and mental factors.

KYLE: BRAIN INJURY

When Kyle was in the military, an injury to his head damaged his capacity to feel certain emotions. Later, he went through a number of traumatic events until he could stand no more. Kyle lives in England and was fifty-one when we talked.

I am an ex-military man. Back in the 1980s there were lots of problems in Northern Ireland. I was part of a peacekeeping mission that got between the two factions there, the Protestants and the Catholics. I got caught in a bomb blast, and a piece of shrapnel stuck in my forehead. The medics took the shrapnel out, but an infection developed in my head. About a month later, I collapsed at barracks and became very ill. Abscesses had formed all the way to my brain. I had to go to the hospital to have my face drained. They told me that if I did not have it drained I would probably be dead within three days. The procedure was horrible and the stuff that came out was absolutely horrendous. But it got rid of the problem.

The day I walked out of the hospital, I knew I wasn't right. I didn't feel the same. I had lost all the good emotions–feeling happy, being able to feel loved, feeling connected when I put my arms around someone. I became violent and drank a lot.

One night when I was about thirty, my wife, whom I had married several years earlier, had gone out with some friends. It was a red hot summer night, and about half past ten, I went out to the garage. I was mad about motorcycles at the time, and for some strange reason, I don't know why, I started the bike I had in the garage and just sat on it with the door closed. I had been feeling strange all day, feeling nothing, not caring about anything. And I had been drinking heavily. The next thing I remember was waking up on the floor with my wife standing over me. The garage door was wide open, and the room was full of blue fog. The bike had overheated and stopped.

I became very withdrawn after that, moody, argumentative, and violent toward objects in the house. One day I had a row with someone over a cell phone. I put the phone on the ground and smashed it with a hammer. On a Saturday when my wife had gone to work, I lay in bed all day and stared at the ceiling.

My wife begged and pleaded with me to see a doctor. I went to my GP, my general practitioner, who told me to go to the hospital. So I did and saw a doctor there. I told her how I felt. She said, "We're going to have to send you for some tests." So I said, "Right, okay." I had an EEG. Wires were connected all over my head, checking for electrical activity in the brain. They discovered that the front temporal lobe, on the right side of my forehead, had scar tissue in it. That's the part of the brain that handles moods and behaviors.

They put me on medications. But the mood swings were horrendous. I was going up and down like a yoyo, within hours, sometimes within minutes. In the end, we found a medication that worked. I was pretty good for a number of years, until about forty. Then the mood swings started again.

I became snappy at work. I threw tools up and down the workshop. I fought a lot. Once someone said something about my life and I jumped up and down on him and had to be dragged off. When I was out for a drink and somebody looked at me the wrong way, that was it. It didn't matter how big they were. Bang! I hit them. I'm not like that. I'm a mild, easy-going person. So I thought, "There's something definitely wrong here again."

In the meantime, things at home deteriorated. I wasn't sleeping well. My wife and I were trying for a family, but she developed endometriosis and had to have a hysterectomy. I got over that, but my wife had to have hormone-replacement patches, which affected her so badly that she was having black-outs. They turned into epileptic fits.

The doctor put her on medication, but she got worse. The doctor said, "We need to get your wife into the hospital." So I took her to a specialist in a different city. My wife said to me, "I will be in for three days. It's a long way for you to come. Don't worry about me. I'll see you in three days' time." I said, "I will come down every night and make sure you're okay." "No," she said, "don't bother. I'll be fine." I went down to pick her up three days later.

I said, "How are you doing? Has everything gone well?" She said, "Yes, everything's going fine. They changed my medication." "Great. I'm really happy." On the way back, we stopped at a KFC because that was her favorite food. When we got back home, I said, "I'll go make you a cup of tea." I went into the garage where I had hidden a big bouquet of flowers for her. She came into the garage while I was there and said, "I have something I want to tell you." "Yes?" I said. She went on, "I'm leaving you. I've decided I want to be on my own."

What do you say? What do you do? This lovely woman I had put all my time and effort into decided that she didn't want me anymore. Her mum came and picked her up that night. I tried to carry on as best I could, but I was feeling worse and worse. I'm a cat lover. I mean, I love animals. I had an absolutely beautiful cat called Marmalade. I came down one morning and she was dead. She had died in her sleep.

That was the final straw. I completely lost it. I took Marmalade to the vet, where they did a funeral service for her and gave me the ashes in a box. I broke down in tears and fell into the arms of the young vet there. Then I put the box into the car with me and went for a drive. I don't remember much about that day, but I do remember stopping at a roadside café and having a cup of coffee. A lovely waitress came over and I burst into tears as we were chatting. She said to me, "Whatever it is, nothing's that bad." I said, "You would not believe how I am."

On the way out, I bought a bottle of water. I drove back home and went into the medicine cabinet, where I'd been storing up sleeping tablets. I had gotten about a thousand stored. I drove to my parents' house. I wanted to say goodbye to them, because they were close to me. My dad's my best friend. My mum's my mum. Never got it any different. I loved them to bits. They were out.

I drove up into the nearby hills. There's a beautiful place up there where you can see for miles and miles. As young teenagers, I and my friends used to drive there on Friday nights. We drank some beer, smoked some marijuana, and sat and watched the lights from the city. When I got there, I sat for about an hour or two. Then I started swallowing the pills by the handful. I must have done about 150, 200, tablets. I became violently sick, leaned out the door, and threw up. I closed the door and started taking the pills again.

This medication works so fast that within ten or fifteen minutes of taking it, you can feel the effects. I was half in and half out of consciousness. I had to throw up again. I didn't want to get it all over the interior of the car, not that it would have mattered to me, but somebody would have to clean it up. So I opened the door again to throw up. Then I passed out. I woke up in an ambulance. One of the local park rangers had found me. The area where I had parked was the only spot that you can get a mobile phone signal. The ranger rang up the ambulance service. He had a very bad signal, but he got through to them.

At the hospital, I woke up again with a tube down my throat and a funnel at the end of the tube. The nurses were busy pouring charcoal into me. I fought the tube. I fought the doctors and nurses. It took about eight of them to hold me down.

Later, a doctor came to see me. He was very understanding, but gave me the riot act and told me that they had better things to do, which, I had to admit, I agreed with. He said, "I'm going to give you an option—either you go into the psychiatric wing voluntarily or I'll sanction you. I would advise you to go in voluntarily because if I sanction you, you will find it very difficult to get a job should you lose yours." I said, "I'll go in." There is a very bad sting when something rings of suicide, especially here in England.

I also agreed to have my parents come and see me. So they came up. That was anguish for me and them. It was in my mum's face—I had to watch her cry. And my dad, he was not able to understand, and he tried to hold back anger and hurt. We sat and talked quite rationally for a good two hours. That brought me around. Later my wife turned up with her parents. We ended up having a massive screaming match.

The counselor who was assigned to me was extremely talented. As soon as I saw her, I knew I was going to be okay. She and I clicked. I could talk to her about anything. The first thing she taught me was that it is all right for a man to cry. Up until that point, I hadn't shed tears over anything.

She introduced me to a lovely young Polish doctor. He and I got to talking about Poland and house vets. It was then that I realized that if I concentrated on something I enjoyed, such as history, it helped immensely. So I focused on World War II at the expense of everything else. I ended up staying at the psychiatric ward for three months.

After I got out, I went to my former workplace just to see the lads. As I walked in, two particularly nasty characters saw me and burst out laughing. They said, "Oh, wait up. It's Suicide Sid." I crumbled. I turned around, walked straight out again, and went to pieces.

That's when I decided it was time to take control of my life. I bought a house about twenty miles from where my ex-wife and I used to live. I joined a group that does living history and went to shows on weekends in the summer. During the past six years, I've met some of the most wonderful people you could ever imagine. That keeps me going. Without them, I don't know whether I could survive.

Sometimes I get angry with myself and don't take my medications for a couple of days. I feel awful when I do that. The only way I can describe it is that it must be like narcotic addicts when they go cold turkey, except that for me it is emotional, not physical. It is a dreadful feeling.

I have a wonderful support network—my parents, wonderful doctors, and a lovely counselor. And I'm a fighter now. I don't let anything faze me like I used to. Best of all, I am starting to feel emotions—not often, but sometimes, which is a triumph for me.

A key factor in whether someone stays alive after having tried to kill themselves is whether they take control of the situation they are in. It is not always easy to do this. When Kyle finally did, he remade himself. He moved, participated in an enjoyable activity with good people, and embraced the care of his doctor, counselor, and parents. As a result, he was able to combat difficulties more easily.

EDWARD: EMOTIONAL DISABILITY

When Edward was thirteen, he was diagnosed with Asperger's syndrome (which the American Psychiatric Association regards as being on the high functioning end of the autism spectrum). It is thought by a number of researchers and clinicians that people with Asperger's syndrome have a higher suicide rate than those who do not. There is little statistical evidence for this fact, because suicide reports do not regularly or accurately label the victims' medical or psychiatric classifications. Still, it is known that people with Asperger's syndrome get depressed more easily because others do not always accept them. Edward was twenty-six when we talked.

My first suicide attempt occurred when I was a senior in high school. I was dating a girl, and it was my first relationship with a woman. I had previous relationships for two or three weeks at a time, but this one was different. We were together for four months, and then she broke it off. What got to me wasn't that so much, but the fact that I started getting e-mails from her e-mail address saying that my best friend had slept with her and that she was pregnant. It turned out later to be false, but at the time I felt betrayed by her. She and I had never gotten involved sexually.

The thing about the Asperger's syndrome I have is that things upset me a lot faster, and I blow them way out of proportion, much more than a normal person would. It's an emotional disability. For example, in a movie called *Marley and Me,* the two main characters have a Lab—a Labrador dog. It dies in the end. Because I have a Lab, the movie affected me much more than it affected other people. I cried for a week after watching it.

So after the breakup and those e-mails I felt very alone and very much betrayed. I got some string, not very thick but not real thin, either, tied it around my neck with a sliding knot, and attached the other end to the bar in my closet at home. I sat down and the string broke.

My mother came into my room just then. We went to a psychologist, and then I went to a psychiatric hospital for a weekend. That was enough to bring me back to reality, and I finished up the school year. This was ten years ago.

My second attempt occurred three or four weeks ago. This one involved a gun with a bullet loaded into the chamber and the safety off. I was probably about two minutes away from pointing the gun at my head when I stopped.

The story around this episode involves my fiancée, or at least the person who was my fiancée at the time. We met online through a dating site. We were together for about eight months when we discovered that she was pregnant. At first I thought, "I'm not ready for this." She and I talked about our options, including terminating the pregnancy and adoption. In the end we decided to keep our child.

About three weeks ago, I was babysitting our daughter because my fiancée had to go to work. She started crying beyond belief, with a high-pitched frequency that was ear piercing. She did this for almost two hours. I finally lost it. I spanked her, but that made the crying worse and my frustration worse as well. I picked her up and screamed, "You need to stop!" Then I gave her a gentle toss into a pile of clothes. I didn't throw her. And it was a big pile because it was two or three weeks worth of clothes. So she landed safely.

I called my fiancée and told her what happened. She took our daughter to the hospital. Where we live there are mandatory reporting laws, which means that medical professionals have to report certain things to law enforcement. One of these is child abuse or suspected child abuse. So when my fiancée told the hospital people what happened, that triggered CPS– Child Protective Services–to get involved.

When that happened, I cried. My job as a parent was to protect my child, and I had failed. I cried all night. The following morning my fiancée wrote saying that Child Protective Services considered me mentally unstable because of the Asperger's syndrome and that I could never be around our daughter again.

When I read that, I was shattered. I took the pistol I keep for home defense, loaded the chamber, went up into the woods, and sat and cried. I texted my fiancée and told her I was sorry. I texted a suicide note to her. I thought, "I'm going to do this. I'm going to do this." All of a sudden, my fiancée's face and my daughter's face came into my mind, clear as day. I took my finger off the trigger.

One thing that keeps me going now is the hope that my fiancée and I can work things out. Actually, I'm not sure she is my fiancée anymore. Still, she says she would like to try getting back together. I am hoping that in six or seven months, when CPS investigates again, things will be better. The other thing that keeps me going is my older brother. He committed suicide seven months ago. I can't do that to my mother. And I can't do it to my friends.

Images can be powerful motivators—one picture can change a person's mind about an issue. It can also change one's heart. This happened to Edward as he was about to pull the trigger. It was almost as if his fiancée and daughter were present. He could not hurt them by killing himself. Nor, later, could he hurt his mother or his friends.

OLIVIA: WINTER GLOOM

In what follows, Olivia describes what it was like to discover that her depression was due to a treatable physical condition. She was fifty-seven when we talked.

I was driving a blue Volkswagon beetle on a two-lane highway, and a truck was coming toward me in the other lane. I thought, "I can drive this little car into that truck and everything will be over." I swerved into the other lane. But in that split second I thought, "If I live through this, I'm not up to what the rehabilitation will be. I don't want to deal with the kind of shape I will be in if this doesn't kill me." I swerved back.

This happened when I was in high school and living at home in a small town. Although I was doing reasonably well in school, if you had asked me why I was so depressed, I would have told you I was too fat and not smart enough and not pretty enough and not good enough at anything. I didn't have any hope that any of that would change. My near encounter with the truck was in January or February, months in which I never did well.

After I got out of college, I sat down with my roommate one day over lunch and said, "I think I have to kill myself because I can't think of any other way out. Nothing is good enough." She suggested that I go for counseling, and if I didn't like it, I could kill myself later. I laugh now when I think of that—"Just try counseling, and if you don't like it, you can still kill yourself afterwards!"

I went to counseling, and that's when I began to learn about brain chemistry and seasonal affective disorder. Over the next number of years, I learned about the effect on the brain of lack of light. I stopped thinking of myself as defective and began thinking, "If you have diabetes or kidney disease, there are things you can do to take care of the organ. I have a brain that needs some care."

Realizing that has been very freeing and empowering. One of the things that was scary about my depression was that I felt so out of control and so helpless to change it. Discovering that it could be treated has given me hope and a sense of control over my life.

Olivia felt liberated when she learned that there was a specific physical source of her winter melancholy. Treating that, along with counseling, transformed her.

18 IN HOSPICE AND DYING ANYWAY

People in hospice know that they are dying. If they are in extreme physical or emotional pain, they may want to bring on death even sooner.

MARGARITA: "WHY SHOULD I KEEP LIVING?"

Margarita was in hospice when she tried to kill herself. "Why should I keep living if I am going to die anyway?" she wondered. Later, she walked through forest preserves and made miniature clay creations. She was in her late forties when we talked.

I was put on hospice after the fourth doctor I saw said, "You need to think about going on hospice. There's nothing I can do for you anymore." I had a neuromuscular disease and a tumor on my pancreas and had been going to the hospital almost once a week. I was forty-six.

A couple of months into hospice I was sitting on my bed with my daughter, Annabelle. She was in charge of getting me my medications every two hours. There were a lot, and Trevor, my husband, didn't want anything to do with it. Annabelle and I were chatting, kind of giggling a little. Trevor walked into the bedroom and stood and stared at me. He didn't say much, as he wasn't a good communicator, but he kept standing there as if something was on his mind. He finally blurted out, "I want a divorce."

I had no idea it was coming. We had been through some rough stuff in our marriage, and I figured that if he really wanted to be done with me, he could just wait. When you're put on hospice, you have less than three months to live. They told me that I probably wouldn't live for more than two weeks. I thought my dying would let him off the hook in an honorable way so that he wouldn't have to say that he divorced a dying woman. Our twenty-fourth anniversary had been a month earlier.

I immediately fell into hysterics. I cried. He cried. Annabelle cried. But then Annabelle got angry and the two yelled at each other. She said, "If you're that upset, pray about it." He said, "I did pray about it." She said, "No, God would never tell you to divorce Mom, especially when she's dying." It was just a week earlier that Annabelle had said, "I'm the only one of my friends whose parents are not divorced, and I'm so proud of that." He left the room, but he didn't leave the house. He still slept in our bed, but in his own corner. He didn't want to give up the house or anything in the house. He just wanted me gone or dead.

The nurses had called my two kids several times to say that I wasn't going to make it through the night, and they rushed to me. But I'd still be alive. I thought, "Why I am still lingering here? I'm a burden to my kids and my husband. And I don't have any friends." People fell away over the years as I was getting sicker.

I had stopped working a number of years before because I had become disabled. I wasn't strong enough to sit in a chair, so I couldn't e-mail. I could not talk on the phone because my voice was too quiet. And it was hard when people did see me, so it was easier for them just to stay away.

All I had were the hospice people and Annabelle. She had quit college to stay home and take care of me, because the hospice people had turned my husband into the state for spousal abuse and neglect. I had bed sores from not being turned. I was starving, because I couldn't get out of bed, and I did not have access to water or food. And when I did get out of bed, I fell. That's how I broke my front teeth. You can see red nail marks running down the wall where I tried not to fall and a head mark on the wall where once I did fall. I dislocated my hip from falling. I had two black eyes. The hospice people saw all this, and it didn't look good for my husband. He was afraid he was going to jail. I think that was the reason he wanted a divorce.

I had dropped down to eighty-eight pounds at this point. I'm five feet eight inches. I wasn't eating anymore. I remember crying and trying to pray and write down my feelings, but I was so drugged I couldn't even hold a pen. I wanted to be remembered, but I didn't want my kids to remember me this way.

I was supposed to be dying very quickly. And I felt there was absolutely no reason for me to be here anymore. I was actually doing something wrong by not dying. I thought I was flunking hospice and doing hospice a disservice by not dying. I was hoping to hurry up and die, get it over with. My kids were ready for me to die, because they were being prepared by the hospice people. They never said that they were disappointed or that they were upset, but I felt I was a burden to them.

> **"I wanted to end it for everyone."**

Before I went on hospice, I was given a prescription for morphine. But I never opened the bottle because I didn't need morphine at the time. There was a bathroom attached to my bedroom, and the pills were in the cabinet under the bathroom sink. I never thought about not having them. What risk is there of a dying person dying?

I found the bottle–there were a hundred pills, which were supposed to last a month. These were little white pills, teeny, tiny white pills. They were prescribed one to two pills every two to four hours, which is a high dose.

I started taking them. I got a little glass of water from the bathroom, a little dixie cup. It took me three handfuls to get them all down. I wasn't seeing well because I was so medicated, and I was having seizures almost constantly, every fifteen minutes. I took the pills a couple of days after my husband asked for a divorce.

I went into a coma. I remember crying, taking the pills, lying down, and crying some more. I had been crying for days, nonstop, hysterical sobs. The pills knocked me out. I don't know how long it was–days, maybe, a week. They assumed it was the natural progression of my death. No one ever knew about the pills. I have never told anyone until now.

My husband said he saw some of the pills on the floor, and he wondered if I had swallowed them. But he didn't ask me. He just said that in passing. He said he flushed the ones he found on the floor down the toilet and threw away the bottle. I think he was scared that he was going to be accused of forcing me to take them.

When I woke up, my favorite nurse was standing over the bed, saying, "Do you remember me?" It took me a few minutes to figure out who she was. She was crying. She said, "I can't believe you are still alive. You were in a coma and we called your children and they have been planning your funeral, and then you woke up. So they went back home." She never knew that my coma was because I swallowed the pills.

I was still so drugged that I couldn't think clearly. I was hallucinating. I was confused. I was mad that I had not died and gotten off everyone's shoulders. And I was sad because I knew that I was still dying. Yet there was this new feeling that I had not had before–"I wonder if I'm supposed to stay alive."

I was nineteen when I first tried to kill myself. I had been married at fifteen, had a baby at eighteen, and got divorced at nineteen. I had no place to live, I didn't have any job or skills. I had no parents around, no family, and I was living in my car. I met my second husband then, the one who asked for a divorce when I was in hospice. He didn't want children–he was a very controlling person. I had nowhere to live, and I felt I had to give up my child to have a place to live. So I gave him to his father, my first husband. When it hit me later that I had given my son away for a place to live, I hated myself. I could not forgive myself for the horrible thing I had done.

Things with my second husband were also horrible, and divorce was not an option for me. I had become a Christian then, and I thought it was absolutely not okay to be divorced again. I thought I was stuck.

For a while, I was able to keep busy enough not to think about my situation and about what I had done to my son. My husband was dealing coke, so I was taking it. That was an easy way to escape. I also got hold of some narcotic pills from a doctor. Several times I took half a bottle and hoped not to wake up. But I always did.

My husband didn't know that I had tried to kill myself, but he knew that I was very depressed. I had been talking about wanting to kill myself, so he took me to the psych ward at a hospital. I was there for a week, but that didn't help. I just got a little break from an abusive relationship.

While I was there, I called my dad. My brother, who is four years younger than I am, answered the phone. I told him I was suicidal and was in the hospital. He put my dad on the phone, and my dad said, "What are you doing?" and "Don't call me, ever again." Then he hung up. He and I reconciled before he died of ALS about ten years later. He told me he was sorry for everything he had done. I said I had forgiven him long before and that I loved him. He cried. He said he would dance with me when I got to heaven.

After I woke up from the coma while in hospice, and as I became more awake and aware of the process of dying, people came to talk to me, because they knew I was so close to dying. They poured their hearts out, and I validated what they were feeling because I was in a place most people don't get to talk about–a place of dying soon, of not knowing whether I was going to be alive the next day. Sometimes I didn't even know whether I was going to make it through the next hour, because I had heart failure. My kidneys failed. My organs were shutting down, and I had a heart attack while a nurse was with me at home.

The nurse was in a dilemma, because hospice is not about prolonging your life. They're not supposed to help you live, but to make you comfortable while you are dying. Her dilemma was, "Do I give her medication to ease the pain for her heart? Do we revive her if she has a heart attack?" She couldn't decide. I was the very definition of death. Nothing was left. I was gasping for breath. I couldn't speak. I wasn't able to eat.

Yet everybody saw something in me. They weren't quite sure what it was. When I was in the hospital, nurses came in at night and said, "Your light's not on, but when I walked along the hallway I saw a light in your room and I was drawn in here." They could feel something. When we talked, we'd get onto subjects that they'd never told anyone about. I cried with them, shared their pain and sorrow, and gave them something to hope for. I have no idea how they got hope from me. They were supposed to be helping me, yet they always said, "You helped me more than I helped you."

My husband finally moved out after several weeks. My counselor had said, "It's not healthy for him to be in the same house, especially if you're dying." I was afraid of him. His presence was oppressive, and he was screaming and yelling at Annabelle all the time and hiding food.

The hospice people kept upping the medication I was taking because the pain kept getting worse. They had gotten a green light from the doctor, who had said I wasn't going to survive. I was pretty heavily medicated for the rest of the time I was in hospice. They couldn't legally give me any more without Kevorkian-type killing me.

I got off hospice after a year. I wasn't really better. I just never got any worse. It shocked me when they said one day, "We have to release you. The doctor won't sign you back up on hospice." So I was left without a doctor. I was on high doses of narcotics, and I couldn't function. I had been in bed for a year. My muscles had wasted away. I hadn't been able to eat well. And I had nobody.

In going off hospice, I had to go off medication, and in doing that I had a whole ton of seizures. I ended up in the hospital again. Two doctors who happened to be on call said there was something in me they knew they had to fight for. They wanted me to live. When they heard my story, one of them cried. I wasn't speaking properly, I wasn't connecting words properly, because I had so many seizures. But those two doctors saw something worth trying to save. When I saw how hard they were fighting to save me, it gave me the desire to fight. I wanted to live. I wanted to stay alive.

I finally found a doctor to take care of me. He had taken care of me years before but had released me when I got really sick, because we were personal friends and he had said it was too difficult to treat me. He was afraid I would die under his care. But he took me back after I went off hospice. He previously had cancer, and I felt that he could understand me better now because he had suffered. I had no hope of getting better. He said, "That's my job, to get you hope. Let's find hope for you."

I was released from hospice two years ago in June, and by October I found what I needed. I had a bubbliness, a giddiness, a joy, that radiated from me. People could see it. My circumstances weren't a whole lot different. My house was being foreclosed, my divorce was still going through, I had no money to speak of. But I was happy, and I was fighting to be alive.

I am still sick enough that I can't get out of bed several days a week. I get sad about that sometimes, and I feel sorry for myself and cry. But most of the time I appreciate the littlest things—a breeze, the scent of flowers, the birds singing, sitting in the sun and feeling it touch my skin. I like to watch things, and I like to hear stories. I love to laugh. It's exhausting, but I love it.

I'm glad I can be here for my kids. I thought they didn't need me, and yet I find that as adults they need me almost as much as when they were kids. They're glad I'm alive. And I'm glad I'm alive. I'm still not quite sure what

> *"I love to see people have joy."*

I can do with my life, but I see a lot of possibilities. I like knowing that there's joy to be had in the worst of circumstances. That keeps me going and helps me reach out to other people.

When I thought I was going to die, I spent some time planning my funeral. I had songs picked out I wanted played, and because I am an artist, my son had taken one of my paintings and was going to have it fused onto a blanket and have that put into my casket with me.

I was convinced that there wouldn't be enough people to have much of a funeral, maybe a little, tiny get together. No big to-do, just the way I lived my life–quiet and small. I figured it would be only my son and daughter and daughter-in-law, maybe the hospice people, too. I didn't want them to be sad, I didn't want them to cry. I wanted them to say nice things, good things they remembered.

If I could talk to the woman I was when I was completely hopeless and alone and being encouraged by the hospice staff to let go to the process of dying, when I felt that I had to end it all so as to ease the burden on my children, I would tell her to hang on. I would have spoken to her heart quietly but constantly to say that soon things would be different in ways that she could not grasp or imagine.

She could never have dreamed of falling in love, of being surrounded by kind, loving people who would do whatever she needed to feel cared about and worthy of taking up space even though she was not as able-bodied as they were. But most importantly, she never, ever could have imagined that she would experience unconditional love, acceptance, peace, and human kindness on a daily basis. If Margarita from back then knew what was coming right around the corner, she would not have tried to kill herself.

Margarita's story is a fitting end to this book of stories, for it epitomizes the new start that can take place when one steps away from suicide. Because of her troublesome experiences, Margarita can identify with others who are in distress. She can give unconditional love. She can delight in the song of a bird and the gentle whoosh of a passing breeze. She can give kindness to those she encounters.

None of this came easy for Margarita. She fought and battled and combatted. In the end, she won. She found that she could experience joy despite the pain she still endured.

19

FROM DESPAIR TO HOPE: TWELVE NEW VOICES

In this chapter, you will meet a dozen new people. They gave short answers to a number of questions I posed, including "What did you feel when you were struggling with despair and hopelessness?" "What did you feel when you realized you were still alive?" and "What do you like most about living?" The people range in age from twenty-one to fifty-seven. Six of them live in the United States, three live in England, and one each lives in Canada, Ireland, Poland, and Scotland.

Struggling with Despair and Hopelessness

Every day over many months I felt absolute helplessness. I felt lost, and I cried uncontrollably. I felt complete isolation, with nobody to turn to that I trusted with my symptoms and feelings. I had a sense of deep and bottomless loneliness. I had palpitations and breathlessness, and I wanted to run away from everything. I wanted everyone to leave me alone. I stopped opening mail and answering the phone and speaking to people. I had feelings of failing myself and others.

I experienced extreme physical symptoms I had not encountered before–huge headaches, nausea, dizziness, loss of sight, deafness, loss of motor control, extreme sensitivity to light and noise, loss of memory, disrupted sense of smell. It felt as if I was having brain spasms or contractions, like someone had their hand inside my head and was squeezing.

I had terrible feelings of guilt for being unable to cope and for burdening others who would have to deal with me as I disintegrated. I lost self-respect and care for myself. I stopped looking after my appearance and cleanliness.

Now I find it hard to believe that I actually withdrew from everything to the point where I lived in my car for several months, even though I had property to live in at the time. I still marvel at the bizarre nature of that and wonder what it was all about. – Ethan

It was almost as though I felt nothing at all. There was a lot of numbness and an element of not caring–an apathy that in some ways was strangely liberating. At the same time, everything I did became incredibly difficult. Even talking and conversations became draining. For various reasons, I couldn't tell anyone how I was. It was a great strain to keep up the appearance of normality. – Corey

In high school my grades crashed so low that I felt like a failure. I had a slight case of being overweight, and I had been bullied since early childhood in a small private school. I also struggled with attention deficit disorder and non-verbal learning disability, and I had been on antidepressants since the age of six. I had a few friends, but I didn't talk to them about my suicidal thoughts. The antidepressants I was on were actually making my depression worse, but my mom, who was a psychiatric nurse, didn't understand at the time how that was possible. She just saw that my concentration was better when I was on the meds, so I was encouraged, even pressured, by my family to take the medicine. That felt as if I had a broken arm that somebody kept pounding against a wall, claiming that it was all okay, it shouldn't be causing me any pain, and it would set the bone. Suicide kept looking like a better and better option. – Rachel

I was isolated and didn't want company. Yet at the same time I was crying out for help. I was completely lost and not thinking properly, almost pushing others away and trying to carry the weight alone. – Alistair

Four years ago, when I was sixteen and one of the biggest harms of my life happened, I needed someone immediately. But there was no one I could turn to. I cried. I imagined being found and saved by someone. I imagined a lot of good solutions, but they never happened. I had an imaginary friend, but she stayed in the imaginary world. Imagination could not save me, but it was all I had. I didn't want to stop existing; I just wanted to stop feeling so lost. Unfortunately, there was no way to stop feeling lost except to stop living.

Everything could have been so different if only someone had been concerned about me. But no one was. Completely no one. If it is true that "No one is an island," then I'm probably not a human in others' eyes. It felt as if I wasn't, since I was living and dying like some homeless dog. – Cecylia

I felt isolated, though this was not reflected in my social life. Here in Ireland it's a sign of weakness to express your emotions and true feelings, though that's just teenage life, I guess, the alpha male syndrome. Through writing and music, I acquired a way to release my feelings. – Torrey

I felt sad, depressed, worthless, and unloved. I felt I didn't deserve life and I shouldn't be around. I told myself how ugly I was and that I was the cause of everything bad in the world. I was very hard on myself all the time. I felt exhausted, sick of the world and myself and the way things were.
– Sarah

For some time I had felt neglected by my two brothers. They had their own lives, and I didn't see them much. My two grown children had their own lives, too, and I didn't see them much, either. My wife and I were heading toward divorce. I was out of work and no one wanted to employ me.   No one wanted to hear my depression story. I thought, "Who needs me? Who cares?" Suicide seemed like a good way to get out of my problems.
– Alexander

I hated myself so much that I didn't want to live. – Allyson

While Deciding to Commit Suicide

I felt calm, a sense of direction at last, a way to make the pain go away.
– Ethan

People have asked me what the suicide decision moment was like. I think they expect a great philosophical, "To be or not to be," Hamlet moment. But it wasn't like that for me. There wasn't a light bulb moment of, "I know this is what I will do." I had had a gradual decline mentally. I felt myself to be a horrible person, a worthless piece of crap, so deciding to kill myself was pretty much the next step. – Corey

When I was twenty-seven, I climbed Arthur's Seat—a large old volcano near the heart of Edinburgh in Scotland. Since graduating from university five years earlier, I had been unable to make the transition from student to adult. Depression had a grip on me and was systematically taking any pleasure I had gotten out of life. I felt that I had been dying inside for years.

Before climbing to the top, I sat at the foot of the hill, clutching a cognitive behavior therapy textbook. I saw the book as my "instructions on how to live." I mocked myself for that—why did I need a book to stay alive? I wondered how things had come to be so bad. I had no addictions, didn't drink, had no criminal record. Why was I in such pain? I felt as though I was faced with an unanswerable riddle. My survival depended on solving it. – Alistair

I felt deeply sorry for myself. This world never gave me a chance to have a real life. I was sure that if I had this chance, I would definitely do big things. – Cecylia

I was seventeen. My girlfriend at the time and I went to a friend's house for a party. We got into a huge fight, which ended up with my overdosing on a lot of pills. I left the party and headed toward a bridge, where, I decided, I would jump and end it all. I was completely intoxicated and tanked up on pills. I had only one thought–to destroy myself, completely, for good. – Torrey

I felt a lot of confusion. I debated with myself, sometimes going ahead with the attempt and sometimes talking myself out of it. – Sarah

My wife and I had started filling out paperwork to get divorced, but we had not finished yet. It was time to get it done. We had no real issues to contend with, and we just wanted to move on. The court hearing was on the second Wednesday in January. The judge said, "Any objections?" "No!" He stamped the document, and that was it. Goodbye.

I was numb and felt myself going downhill that day and the next. I had been feeling more and more depressed during the previous weeks. When I called the psychiatrist I had been seeing earlier for an appointment, I was told that I could not be seen for another four weeks. Two weeks before the court hearing I had restarted taking antidepressant medication I had left over from previous prescriptions. That gave me more energy so that I could take action. So on the Friday morning after the court hearing I thought, "I may as well kill myself. I'm divorced. All is dead. I have nothing to live for." It seemed like a good idea. I thought, "Just do it already. What are you, a chicken or something?" – Alexander

It took me a long time to decide how to kill myself. I was prepared to do it only if I was one-hundred-percent certain that it would work. The technique I chose was that I would be sleeping initially, so that there would be no pain during the process, just ultimate sleeping forever. Everything would be peaceful, my pain would end, and I would stop damaging people. – Tyler

After Deciding

I felt certainty that a decision had been made, with no further room for doubt. I felt a sense of withdrawing from the world and leaving it behind. I did not feel the need to explain the decision to anyone, nor did I want anyone's okay with it. – Ethan

Once I decided I wanted to die, the despair and the hopelessness and all the negative feelings became secondary. I had a dull, numbing acceptance of what I was going to do. – Corey

I was very at peace with the decision and was waiting to die. – Rachel

I was in a state of confusion and anxiety. I was absorbed within my own thoughts and feelings. – Torrey

I had been going to the hospital every day and doing therapy and trying to get all the emotional stuff out of me, plus taking the medicine when I was supposed to. I had done everything I could think of for as long as I could remember. But everything had gotten worse. I felt that I was going to lose my mind.

Once I decided to kill myself, I felt so much better. I had dignity, because I was going to do something for myself. I felt as though I was a human being again instead of a wild, rabid animal. There was a lot of comfort in that, because I was in such extreme distress that I had not realized I did not feel like a human being. It was as if I had joined the human race again and come home. That created an overpowering feeling that I had come across the right solution. There was an enormous sense of peace in that. – Bryanne

My life was pretty meaningless, so there wasn't much difference after deciding that I was going to kill myself. It was just a plan that I was going to carry out. I wasn't anxious about whether my method would work–I was one-hundred-percent certain that it would and that I would not wake up again. – Tyler

During the Attempt

I stopped thinking about tomorrow and believed it wouldn't come. My death was going to happen. However, my attempt was interrupted by something so unusual that it stopped me from continuing with it. – Ethan

Once I decided I wanted to die, the despair and the hopelessness and all the negative feelings became secondary. I had a dull, numbing acceptance of what I was going to do. – Corey

I was angry and frustrated, but I also had a sense of finality. I had to deal with nausea and stomach cramps the whole time, but I curled up in bed and tried to make myself as comfortable as possible. After six to eight hours, my boyfriend called, and he encouraged me to get help. – Rachel

I felt helpless. I was at the mercy of an unstable mind. It was as if I was being "remote controlled," like a car being steered by something else. It was the feeling of having no choice in your own hands. I had resigned myself to what felt like some kind of destiny. I was completely convinced that there was no way out and that I would jump to my death from the sheer drop off on the volcano hill.

As I climbed the hill—Arthur's Seat in Edinburgh—I cried tears from a place deep within me. I looked hard into the smiling face of someone descending the hill. I longed to be saved.

Something happened, though. It's hard to say what exactly. Perhaps my heart won over my head. I don't know. Maybe I never will. I returned to my friend's apartment I was staying at. That night I and two of my best friends rented a movie. It was a dark comedy and involved suicide plots. I said nothing. – Alistair

With every drop of blood I was becoming more and more calm—no anger, no sadness, and no pain. Nothing. When I realized I had survived, my emotions stayed the same. I had this lack of feeling for the next few months. I felt nothing, and I felt like nothing. So in a way I did die on that day.   – Cecylia

For most of my attempts I felt anxious, though for some of them I was totally relaxed and absolutely ready to die. – Sarah

I was in the locked ward of a state psychiatric hospital. I bought a soda (which I was surprised at being able to do, even twenty-five years ago), drank a little of it, and poured the rest out in the bathroom. Then I went to my room and cracked the can back and forth, back and forth, until I could tear it in half. I pulled off a piece of aluminum that I could hold between my fingers and started cutting myself.

I cut my left wrist, then my right. They were bleeding everywhere. But I realized after a while that they were not bleeding fast enough. It wasn't going to work. I thought, "Now I'm stuck. I have to go out and show the nurses that I cut myself, and they are going to think, 'Another patient flipped out.' I will have to get the cuts stitched up. And it's going to be a big drama. I'm just going to sit here and cry." I was angry. But there was nothing else I could do.

I got up, walked out of my room, and said, "I cut my wrists." They said, "Yes, you did." They put me on a stretcher and took me to the doctor's office and started to stitch me up. But I hit bottom again, because I realized I was trapped now. I pled with them to kill me. I was in complete despair. – Bryanne

Still Alive

The interruption to my attempt made me change my mind, and I decided to try to fight, although I didn't know what I was fighting for or how to do it. – Ethan

I had been out of contact with my family for a couple of weeks. Normally we are very close, so they figured something was wrong. My dad eventually came and broke my door down. That was a crushing moment. My best chance of killing myself was gone. And I couldn't lie anymore. I knew I had to tell my dad what I was doing. When I did, it wounded him deeply. – Corey

I was embarrassed. I not only had let myself down, but everyone close to me. – Torrey

I felt pathetic. – Sarah

I felt confusion and surprise—who were these guys with the ambulance? At the same time, I was very, very, very happy. – Alexander

When I woke up and realized I was hooked up to an oxygen tank, I was in total shock that I wasn't dead. That was further confirmation that I couldn't do anything. I couldn't even kill myself, which made me even more convinced that I was completely useless. – Tyler

What Keeps You Alive Now?

Every day I remind myself that things are worse for a lot others. That sustains me. I also make a point of getting out of my house as often as possible, engaging with others, and trying to get energy from them.

I try to look people in the eye and smile, and I occasionally greet others with a hug or an embrace. Before my attempt, I had completely stopped doing what clearly were lovely things to do.

I am still incredibly sad about so much in life and what happened to me. I lost much of myself as a person. I lost a partner, who could not take what was happening. I lost my job, my savings, my property, and there are a broad range of businesses still after me for debts I owe them. In some ways, however, all that seems trivial when I think about what I almost did. – Ethan

I know myself better now, so that I can put the brakes on when I get into a dark place. I look at people and think, "If I had killed myself, I would never have known this person." And now I can think about what I am going to do tomorrow and be excited about it. I'm excited about life. – Corey

What I love best in life, and what keeps me alive now, is surprises–the good kind, like when you unexpectedly run into a friend you haven't seen for a long time or when you first hear about a movie you know you're going to want to see. In the next few months alone, I'm looking forward to seeing *Life of Pi, Les Miserables,* and *The Hobbit: An Unexpected Journey.* At twenty-nine I still struggle with suicidal feelings sometimes, but these good surprises are the main thing that keeps me alive. – Rachel

Doing Buddhist meditation has helped hugely. It relaxes me enormous-ly. It gives me space from my thoughts and keeps me from being caught up in things too much. I get into a state of deep peace. It is almost as if I have found a sanctuary within myself that nothing outside me can affect. These are states I had never experienced before and didn't think were possible. – Alistair

Only my imagination keeps me alive. I have an imaginary friend who keeps saving me. But there's nothing to like in my real life. I feel as if I am a living dead person. The days go by, the peaceful, unchanging days, but days that feel empty. – Cecylia

What keeps me alive now is music, passion, food, flowers, birds at dusk, the sun at dawn, frost on the hills, the glaze of the trees, wet autumn morn-ings, the sky at night, the aura so green from the hills in Ireland, the sound of traffic, the buzz of people, the smell of my coffee, the chilies from my gar-den, all the fruit and vegetables that grow and blossom, eggs and bacon, a fresh pint of Guinness, the smile of a woman, gentle kindness, opening doors for strangers, the sounds of Jimi Hendrix, the sweet hum of Neil Young, the air in misty evenings, light sleet that glows the roads, stop motion animation, tenor alto choirs, the fiddle with harp, the sound of my Vespa scooter, the bark of a dog, capturing a photo forever in a day, short poems, folklore tales, the smell of marijuana in the late night garden, sitting beside a fire, complete utter desire–everything keeps me alive! – Torrey

One summer I met a guy on a Web site called Compassion Pit. We felt very trusting toward one another right away, so I set up a Skype account so that we could keep in touch. He has talked me out of suicide multiple times. I am glad I haven't succeeded, because then I would never have met him. That's a scary thought to me. He's my best friend in the world, and we're only about a year apart. I talk to him as often as possible. That's the only thing keeping me going. – Sarah

I am taking my medications consistently now. They help keep my brain in balance so that I can see the natural beauty of the world. Despair is a dysfunctional state. A nihilist might disagree, but I believe the world is a wonderful place. There are bad things going on in it, but certainly not enough to kill myself! Also, I'm working now and in a wonderful relationship with a woman. Both are very sustaining. – Alexander

As soon as I had my son, I said to myself that suicide was not an option for me anymore. From then on it was not about me. To have a parent kill themselves would do irreparable harm. –Bryanne

I married eighteen years ago, when I was thirty, and five years ago we had a child. When you have a child, you can't think about anything except looking after it, so that has stopped me from killing myself.

Also, work is distracting me. I have a new job and am meeting new people. During the past twenty years, I have had twenty different jobs, which has kept me from having suicidal thoughts. It is the same for technology. I have spent hundreds of pounds on gadgets, notebooks, computers, and other technology. Right now I'm giving therapy one last chance. If it doesn't work out, I don't have much hope for the future. – Tyler

I tried to suffocate myself once, but just as I was about to gray out, I had a burst of energy and freed myself, because I knew my dad would be devastated if I died. And I almost slit my throat a few times, but didn't only because I thought of my dad. I now feel that no matter how much I suffer, no matter how much I hate myself, and no matter how much I want life to end, I will live for those who love me. I could never hurt them with my death. – Harvey

What Do You Like Most About Living?

I like the joy of interacting with people, hearing appreciative comments from them about me as a person, and wondering whether I will ever be able to jump onto the bandwagon of life again. It has been a number of years since my suicide attempt, and I still have not been brave enough to meet up with a new partner. I was so shattered by my whole experience that I feel I have little to give. I remain hopeful that that will change. – Ethan

I like not knowing what's going to happen. I like friendships and human contact and talking to people. I like helping people who are depressed, who are in a similar position to what I was in. I like to pass on a positive message to them without being too preachy. I like giving them empathy. – Corey

I like my new perspective on life. It is no longer about striving, but about savoring–enjoying small pleasures and not taking myself too seriously or allowing the modern world to place pressures upon me. After feeling quite close to death, I feel appreciation for people, the world I live in, what I see. Little things that annoyed me in the past or seemed important no longer are. – Alistair

I like networking and learning new things day by day. These are my inspiration. – Torrey

I like talking to my Internet friend, discussing philosophy and other topics that most people don't find interesting. I also like to research various topics. Other than that, I still hate myself. Sometimes, though, I tell myself I have no reason to think life sucks. I just don't know how to be happy or to be less depressed or pessimistic. So I trudge forward with the hope that I can move to England one day. – Sarah

I am a massage therapist and am happiest when I'm working and interacting with a client. I like to see them improve in ways they didn't know they could. I am also happiest when I'm doing Christian practices, whether it's reading the rule of Benedict, being in the Benedictine community where I am an oblate, doing Bible study, or doing prayer practices. These are definitely the times when I'm most alive. – Olivia

In this section, we see clearly and starkly how suicidal people felt at each of the stages through which they passed. The similarities in their reports mirror the similarities in the stories–depression, meaninglessness, hopelessness, and isolation in the first stages, and delight at having found something to live for in the last stages. The differences in their reports, however, are much more numerous than the similarities. When Ethan was struggling with despair and hopelessness, he felt deep guilt for being unable to cope. Sarah felt worthless and unloved. After Rachel decided to kill herself, she was at peace with herself. Bryanne felt that she was a human being again because she was doing something for herself. When Torrey found that he was still alive after trying to kill himself, he was embarrassed because he had let himself and his close friends down. Alexander felt confusion and surprise at first but then felt supremely happy.

The largest variety is evident in what kept each person alive. For Ethan it was looking people in the eye and smiling, sometimes embracing them. For Rachel it was surprises, and for Cecylia it was an imaginary friend. Alistair and Olivia found meaning in religious practices, one Buddhist and the other Christian. Torrey delighted in an array of everyday activities, while Alexander took his medication regularly, which enabled him to see the world as a wonderful place. Suicide was not an option for Bryanne or Tyler, because each had a child. Sarah's conversations with an Internet friend kept her going.

These responses to my questions show that we must listen to each person tell their own unique story. Though suicidal people display common patterns, each person exemplifies these patterns in distinctive ways.

These responses also raise questions for us who read them. We might wonder how we would have acted with the conditions and in the situations the people in this book found themselves in. We might also wonder whether we have found something to live for that motivates us as strongly as what now motivates these once suicidal people.

20

"WHEN I WAS SUICIDAL": TWENTY-ONE RESPONSES

When I first encountered a suicidal person, I had no idea what to say. I was apprehensive in case I said something that would not help or that would make things worse. The stakes were high, I felt, unlike everyday conversations, in which I need not be guarded or fearful.

Who better to know what to say to a suicidal person than those who themselves have been suicidal? In this section, a number of those who appear elsewhere in this book tell what they would have liked for someone to have said to them when they were contemplating suicide.

Instead of shame and judgment for having feelings and needs, which is what I would likely have received from my mother, I would like to have heard, "I'm not going to beat you up for what you're feeling or for how you got where you are. I just want to help guide you out of it. I'm here to help and love you."

At the time, though, I would never have given anyone the chance to comfort me, because I was so afraid of being hurt. Even though I wanted to open up and have someone help me, it felt dangerous to do that. I was afraid of being judged and shamed. Years later, when I met someone who was accepting and vulnerable himself, I finally was able to receive comfort. By his body language, he conveyed to me, "Harmony, it's okay. I will help you and love you. I don't want to lose you." I finally realized that I needed to emulate what he did in order to heal. – Harmony

There's nothing anybody could have said. When I was in that frame of mind, people could have told me anything and it would not have made a difference. My mind would have had some way to justify what I was trying to do, and I would have dismissed what they said. When I was that low in depression and overwhelmed with mental anguish, nothing anyone would have said would have mattered.

I guess the only thing that may have made a difference would have been for someone to reassure me how much I was loved and how much I was needed. That would have been helpful, because to know that I am impacting people affects me. That snaps me out of depression from time to time.

Also, if someone had told me how much they would miss me if I succeeded in killing myself, that might have interrupted my suicide plans. Knowing what I would be leaving behind would have helped save me. – Garrett

I would have liked for someone to come to me and hug me and tell me to be calm. I would have liked to hear someone say, "I'm here with you, don't be afraid, you are not alone. I understand what you're going through and how painful it is. I promise that we'll get out of this together." – Orlando

It would have helped greatly if someone had done more than simply listen. I know that the message to us is, "Talk to someone," but even when I dared to talk to a few people, it didn't help the way I thought it would. I found sympathy, but I didn't find change. And at that point, I needed things to change. I needed someone to step up and fight for me. – Cara

Someone could have joined me in my innermost feelings and thoughts without judgment or comment. Someone could have sat next to me while I sat in silence staring into the forest all day. Someone could have looked for clues to all the inner pain I had and held me close and let me cry on their shoulder. Someone could have said that it was okay for me to forgive myself and then helped me understand how. – Nolan

I was incredibly lonely. I needed people to spend time with me, show they cared about me regularly—call me, come over, invite me out. I felt completely repulsive, unlovable, disgusting. Having people say that they cared about me would have been great; having people show that love in their actions would have been even better, because I had been lied to a lot in my life and trust was a major issue. Also, it would have been a huge help if someone had been able to intervene in my abusive family situation, although that would have been terrifying.

I was afraid of people knowing too much about me, afraid that if they knew what I was really like, deep down, they would reject me, afraid that if they found out I was anorexic and suicidal, they would send me away to be locked up in some facility. I was terrified that if they found out I was still in an abusive situation they would report it and I would be responsible for destroying my family.

These fears kept me from reaching out to people, accepting help when it was offered. I needed someone who could spend time with me, show me they loved me, and be patient with my trust issues, be patient with my fear. I wasn't able to talk about any of that openly at first. I needed people who were patient enough to keep on trying to talk with me for as long as it took. – Penny

"I love you just the way you are." That sounds simple, but no one said it to me. As a child what I got from my parents was, "You can't come out of your room. Is there something wrong with you? You're the only one who can't smile or be social. You think about yourself too much. You spend too much time in your head." It was a lot of negative reinforcement. My parents weren't trying to be cruel. That was just what they knew and what they understood. It would never have occurred to them that I was unhappy and fearful.

When I was spiraling slowly downward in my twenties, if someone had said, "There's nothing wrong with you. You're fine the way you are. I love you just as you are at this moment," that may have made me stop and think about my suicide plan. – Louise

If someone would have listened to me and not tried to tell me what to do, I probably would have been a lot better off. – Pixie

I like animals a lot. I have a lot of pets. There have been a couple of times when my animals have convinced me not to go through with suicide. If someone had brought one of my pets to me when I was suicidal and I had looked at its face, I might have thought, "What is this little creature going to do without me?"

And if someone had given me a hug, or touched me, that might have brought me back to life. But if someone had said, "Oh, you're smart and you're beautiful. You have all these good things," I would not have believed them, especially if I had a plan and was really wanting to kill myself. And I would not have wanted anyone to do a guilt trip on me, because I was already feeling that I didn't deserve to live, and making me feel guilty would just have made things worse. – Eva

What I wished for, to the point of violence at times, was to be listened to, without interjection, until I was done saying what I had to say. I did not want judgment or worry or threats of hospitalizations. I did not want to be told that people knew how I felt, because that was a lie and a condescension, and it broke my heart every time someone said it to me. I wanted to be listened to, and to get all the thoughts that were trapped inside my head out into the air, so that maybe they would leave me alone. I never got the chance to see whether that would have worked, but I think it would at least have helped. – Catherine

I don't know how far they would have gotten with it, but it might have made a difference if one of my co-workers had pulled me aside by the shirt collar and said, "What's going on with you? You're way off. Your head is totally not here. You doing drugs?" "No, I'm clean." "What's the story?" If that person could have led me to break down emotionally, to let things out, that could have devolved into, "Hey, you know what, let's go see if we can't find you some help." – Bryan

I would have liked for someone to sit and listen without saying anything. I would have liked to feel that I could unload everything in my head onto someone. They would just let me speak. I didn't have that at the time I was suicidal. I do now, though. I have people who listen. So usually I feel quite good. There are days when I still feel alone in my own thoughts. But for the most part, I feel more settled now, as if I actually have a life. – Aaron

I wish I had known it was possible I could feel better someday. This thought seemed so impossible when I was suicidal that I am not sure I could have listened properly if someone had said that to me.

It seemed as if I had only two choices, to get better or to give up. Getting better wasn't happening and felt impossible. I also felt that I didn't deserve to get better because I was feeling a lot of guilt and low self worth. I would have liked for someone to have explained to me why it is never the right choice to give up. This is something I can see only in hindsight, mainly because I have felt the effects that people who have ended their lives have had on their friends and family.

It has taken me a long time, with a lot of effort, but now I can deal with bad things that come my way–losses, depression, psychosis. I feel I can deal with anything because I know I will never feel as bad as I did then. If only someone would have told me that! Perhaps it is a knowledge that suicidal people have to find themselves. – Theresa

What I wanted was for someone simply to be present, to dwell in my depression with me. I think of Job in the Bible. When his friends showed up, they sat with him for a week in silence, complete silence. For days and days they didn't say a thing until he finally started crying out.

Everyone wanted to help me, but no one was very knowledgeable about depression. They tried to help with words, but depression is not something that can be reasoned with. Everything you loved and everything you were passionate about is now dead inside you. It's a place where you need people to be comforting even if they don't use any words. I think that would have been the most helpful thing for me.

When I was depressed I found that my fellow students at the Christian seminary I was at to be the least supportive and the most judgmental. They were the most difficult people to talk to. That was strange, because they were pastors-in-training or people who were already pastors and who were getting more education. They said to me, "You must not be praying enough or reading the Bible enough." Or they said, "Where is your faith? Don't you believe God will get you through this?"

Because I am a Christian, I think there is a spiritual side to depression. But I also think there is a physical side. You don't go up to someone with autism and say, "Why are you like that? You have to pray more."

It is strange that there is such a stigma against depression and bi-polar disorder and other mental illnesses in churches. Churches should be the first place where people can seek comfort and help. But they can be one of the worst places to go. I found, in the evangelical Christian world, at least, that it was very discouraging to talk about my depression, because I was almost condemned for being depressed. – Mark

I would like to have been told that I was loved. I wish my kids and extended family had been more caring in my time of need. I wish I had been told I was not a hassle or a pain, and not told that I was worthless. I wish nice memories had been brought to life. I wish that the attempt had not defined me, as it does now even though I have repeatedly pleaded that I will not try to kill myself again. I would like to have been reminded that suicide is a permanent solution to a temporary problem. – William

I don't know what I would have liked for someone to say to me when I was suicidal. That was such a dark, shut down place that I couldn't see or hear anything remotely positive or encouraging. Perhaps it isn't what someone could have said, but what someone could have done. Sometimes I just wanted someone to sit with me and not talk. That would, in some way, have been a simple reminder that someone cares and that I was still connected to the human experience. – Joseph

I would have wanted someone to hold me. That is all. No enthusiastic petting, deep kissing, or sexual expression, but a much more profound and tender presence. A simple and sincere holding. This desire has been with me since birth. It is a deep hunger, simply to be held as myself, for who I am. But I have never had anyone offer this holding experience.

Because I am female, I would have wanted a male to do the holding. Once a nun held me in her arms as we lay on her bed before we ventured into a desert for a spiritual retreat, because I was terrified of being alone in the desert. She later told me she was imagining herself as Jesus holding me.

When I was suicidal I did not have anyone I could ask to hold me. And I do not have anyone now. So now I ask God and Jesus and Angels to hold me, especially at night before I go to sleep. I find that if I really believe, I can actually sense being held.

With this holding, it feels that someone cares for me as I am. Maybe this is what David was talking about in one of the Psalms in the Bible when he said, "Be still and know that I am God." That being still feels like being held. – Anne

Normally, a small upset won't bother me when I am in a rational frame of mind. It's not a big deal. But when I was in an irrational frame of mind, little things preyed on my mind. I worried and fretted and couldn't sleep too well.

If I could have found someone I trusted enough who would have said, "Let's sit down and talk," I could have let everything out. If someone had put their arms around me and held me, I would have let go of my worries. Even now, when a girlfriend holds me, it feels wonderful. That is human warmth. For me to be able to feel that is a wonderful thing. – Kyle

I would have liked for someone to say, "I may not understand what you're going through, but I can see that this is not how I've known you. I know this is serious and I will try to help you if you let me know how," or "I will give you the help that I am able to, and I will not judge you as you go through this," or "Help me to understand what you're going through, describe it to me, talk about it," or "I can talk to you anytime, and when I say anytime, I absolutely mean that." I was silent much of the time. I neither asked for, nor received help. It was quite frankly torture, by myself to myself. – Ethan

I would have liked for someone to listen without replying, to make no attempt whatsoever to help, not even to try to bring reason to my head. I would like to have been hugged, to be held, perhaps complimented, even insincerely. I would have liked for someone to give me some time, because I felt pretty invisible and worthless. – Alistair

It would have helped me if someone had said, "Nothing lasts forever. You're going to come out of this stage. Just don't do anything to hurt yourself." That may have given me a little hope that things were going to get better. Also, if someone had said that what I was going through fit a pattern of what suicidal people generally go through, I might have understood what was happening to me. If someone had said, "The way you're feeling is life threatening. Your life is in danger because of your depression and despair," I would have realized that I wasn't just a loser. I wasn't just giving up. What was happening to me was more like a disease. Knowing that would have straightened out my perspective on myself. When you're depressed, your perspective is pretty narrow. – Bryanne

Like the previous section on the movement from despair to hope, the answers in this section contain both patterns and variety. The variety shows, again, that when we talk to someone who is suicidal, we must look for their distinctive needs. The most notable patterns are being loved and being listened to—"I would have liked to have been loved, no strings attached, and I would have liked to have been listened to without being judged." These patterns tell us that everyone can play an active role in saving lives—by learning to love well and by learning to listen well. The following section lists some specific ways these can be done.

21 HOW TO DEAL WITH SOMEONE WHO IS SUICIDAL

It can be startling to find out that an acquaintance is thinking of committing suicide. One's first reaction may be panic or fear of saying the wrong thing. These are natural reactions, for it is, after all, another's life one suddenly fears for.

The very first thing one should do is encourage the suicidal person to see a therapist or physician, volunteering to go with the person if necessary or even calling 911 if there is imminent danger of an attempt. Therapists and physicians have access to medical care and professional skills that a suicidal person may badly need. The suggestions that follow are not meant to be substitutes for professional help, but additions to it.

- Be an active listener. Ask process questions, such as "How did that make you feel?" or "What happened next?" Listen patiently to the answers. Make eye contact or otherwise show that you are listening. When a person is listened to, they feel cared about and understood.
- Text, e-mail, call, or visit. Be present.
- Ask the person to promise that they will call you before killing themselves.
- Do not say things that the suicidal person will interpret as being judgmental—they already know that they are not doing well.
- Ask how the person is doing at a time and in a place in which they can give you an honest answer.
- Don't panic. Stay calm.
- Take seriously a person's talk of suicide. Do not dismiss it as a passing phase or as just a way of getting attention.
- Look for indicators of suicidal thoughts: past attempts, recent losses, depression, mental illness, giving away possessions, chronic pain, expressions of hopelessness, substance abuse.
- If someone expresses negative thoughts or emotions, say, "It sounds as if you may be depressed," and if they tell you about their depression, ask, "It sounds as if you might be thinking of killing yourself." The worst that can happen if you ask someone whether they are thinking

182

of killing themselves is that you will be embarrassed. (I have been embarrassed only once even though I have asked a number of times.)
- Ask whether a suicidal person has a plan to kill themselves. If they do, the risk of suicide is higher.
- Ask, "What are your options?" This may be the single most powerful question you can ask, as it prompts the person to try to figure out what they can do about their trauma.
- Encourage the person to call one of the national suicide hotlines: 1-800-273-TALK (8255) or 1-800-SUICIDE (1-800-784-2433)
- Do not just do nothing.

RESOURCES

Suicide Crisis Hotlines

- 1-800-273-TALK (8255) National Suicide Prevention Lifeline
- 1-800-SUICIDE (1-800-784-2433) National Crisis Help Line

Web Sites

- www.suicide.org – Suicide prevention, awareness, and support
- www.metanoia.org/suicide/ – For those thinking about suicide, hosted by Mental Health Information at Psych Central
- www.twloha.com – To Write Love on Her Arms: presents hope for people struggling with addiction, depression, self injury, and thoughts of suicide
- http://attemptsurvivors.wordpress.com/ – A blog for suicide attempt survivors and others with suicidal feelings, sponsored by the American Association of Suicidology and edited by Cara Anna, whose story is on page 33.

Organizations

- American Foundation for Suicide Prevention, 120 Wall Street, 29th Floor, New York, NY 10005; (888) 333-AFSP (2377); www.afsp.org
- American Association of Suicidology, 5221 Wisconsin Avenue, NW, Washington, DC 20015; (202) 237-2280; www.suicidology.org
- National Institute for Mental Health www.nimh.nih.gov/health /publications/suicide-in-the-us-statistics-and-prevention/index.shtml
- Centers for Disease Control www.cdc.gov/violenceprevention/pdf /suicide-datasheet-a.PDF

Books

- Richard A. Heckler. *Waking up alive: The descent, the suicide attempt and the return to life.* New York: Putnam (1994).
- Kevin Hines. *Cracked, not broken: Surviving and thriving after a suicide attempt.* Lanham, MD: Rowman & Littlefield (2013).
- Kay Redfield Jamison. *Night falls fast: Understanding suicide.* New York: Random House (1999).
- Linda Gray Sexton. *Half in love (surviving the legacy of suicide): A memoir.* Berkeley, CA: Counterpoint (2011).

Volunteering

- Kristin Brooks Hope Center – www.hopeline.com
- National Suicide Prevention Lifeline – http://www.suicideprevention-lifeline.org/

CHARLES C THOMAS · PUBLISHER, LTD.

THE SOCIOLOGY OF DEVIANCE (2nd Ed.)
By Robert J. Franzese
2015, 398 pp. (7 x 10), 21 il., 6 tables.
$64.95 (paper), $64.95 (ebook)

THE PROFESSIONAL HELPER (2nd Ed.)
By Willie V. Bryan
2015, 354 pp. (7 x 10)
$53.95 (paper), $53.95 (ebook)

PUBLIC SAFETY SUICIDE
By Mary Van Haute & John M. Violanti
2015, 136 pp. (7 x 10)
$24.95 (paper), $24.95 (ebook)

**DEALING WITH THE MENTALLY ILL
PERSON ON THE STREET**
By Daniel M. Rudofossi
2015, 252 pp. (7 x 10)
$51.95 (paper), $51.95 (ebook)

**HELPING SKILLS FOR HUMAN SERVICE
WORKERS (3rd Ed.)**
By Kenneth France & Kim Weikel
2014, 384 pp. (7 x 10), 6 il.
$59.95 (paper), $59.95 (ebook)

**BEHAVIORAL GUIDE TO PERSONALITY
DISORDERS (DSM-5)**
By Douglas H. Ruben
2015, 272 pp. (7 x 10), 31 il., 1 table.
$42.95 (paper), $42.95 (ebook)

SERIAL KILLERS
By William M. Harmening
2014, 280 pp. (7 x 10), 28 il.
$39.95 (paper), $39.95 (ebook)

THEORIES OF SUICIDE
By John F. Gunn, III & David Lester
2014, 352 pp. (7 x 10), 1 il., 2 tables.
$52.95 (paper), $52.95 (ebook)

SUICIDE IN MEN
By David Lester, John F. Gunn, III & Paul Quinnett
2014, 394 pp. (7 x 10), 3 il., 19 tables.
$59.95 (paper), $59.95 (ebook)

CRISIS INTERVENTION (6th Ed.)
By Kenneth France
2014, 338 pp. (7 x 10), 3 il.
$54.95 (paper), $54.95 (ebook)

**CRISIS INTERVENTION IN CRIMINAL
JUSTICE/SOCIAL SERVICE (5th Ed.)**
By James E. Hendricks & Cindy S. Hendricks
2014, 472 pp. (7 x 10), 5 tables.
$59.95 (paper), $59.95 (ebook)

DYING FOR THE JOB
By John M. Violanti
2014, 212 pp. (7 x 10), 7 il., 3 tables.
$36.95 (paper), $36.95 (ebook)

HOSTAGE/CRISIS NEGOTIATIONS
By Thomas Strentz
2013, 198 pp. (7 x 10), 18 il.
$32.95 (paper), $32.95 (ebook)

**DEVOTIONS AND PRAYERS FOR POLICE
OFFICERS (2nd Ed.)**
By Steven J. Voris
2011, 226 pp. (7 x 10), 1 il.
$29.95 (paper), $29.95 (ebook)

ART, ANGST, AND TRAUMA
By Doris Banowsky Arrington
2007, 278 pp. (7 x 10), 123 il.
$48.95 (paper), $48.95 (ebook)

POLICE SUICIDE (2nd Ed.)
By John M. Violanti
2007, 196 pp. (7 x 10), 7 il., 2 tables.
$35.95 (paper), $35.95 (ebook)

**SUICIDE IN PROFESSIONAL AND
AMATEUR ATHLETES**
By David Lester & John F. Gunn, III
2013, 262 pp. (7 x 10), 13 tables.
$38.95 (paper), $38.95 (ebook)

**UNDERSTANDING AND PREVENTING
COLLEGE STUDENT SUICIDE**
By Dorian A. Lamis & David Lester
2011, 360 pp. (7 x 10), 21 il., 11 tables.
$49.95 (paper), $49.95 (ebook)

Find us on
Facebook
FACEBOOK.COM/CCTPUBLISHER

TO ORDER: 1-800-258-8980 • books@ccthomas.com • www.ccthomas.com